to

DISNEYLAND® RESORT PARIS

2006–2007

simon & susan veness

foulsham

LONDON • NEW YORK • TORONTO • SYDNEY

foulsham

The Publishing House, Bennetts Close, Cippenham, Berkshire, SL1 5AP, England

Foulsham books can be found in all good bookshops and direct from
www.foulsham.com

ISBN 13: 978-0-572-03179-4
ISBN 10: 0-572-03179-3

> *Dedication*
> *To Anthony and Mark – the best little research team a father could wish for.*

Look out for the latest editions in this series:
A Brit's Guide to Orlando and Walt Disney World, Simon and Susan Veness
Choosing A Cruise, Simon Veness
A Brit's Guide to New York, Karen Marchbank with Amanda Statham
A Brit's Guide to Las Vegas and the West, Karen Marchbank

Printed in China through Colorcraft Ltd., Hong Kong

Contents

7. Walt Disney Studios Park

(or, Lights, Cameras, Action!). Queuing, tactics and a full tour of the movie-making world in the Front Lot, Animation Courtyard, Production Courtyard and the Backlot, including Rock 'n' Roller Coaster starring Aerosmith, Moteurs... Action! Stunt Show Spectacular, Studio Tram Tour and Streetmosphere. Plus, what the future holds!

8. Beyond the Theme Parks

(or, Let's Shop Till We Drop and Other Fun Pursuits). Exploring the restaurants and bars, entertainment and shopping opportunities in *Disney Village*, including Panoramagique; having a swing at *Golf Disneyland* and Davy Crockett's Adventure; what's in store at Val d'Europe, Sea Life Centre and La Vallée shopping village.

9. The Attractions of Paris

(or, Getting an Eiffel of the City). The highlights of the real must-see and must-do opportunities of Paris, public transport in the city, trips on the Seine and sights further afield including Versailles and Provins.

10. Your Holiday Planner

Examples to help you plan a 3-day or 5-day stay in *Disneyland Resort Paris*, with blank forms for your holiday.

Brit Tips

Got a red-hot Brit Tip to pass on? The latest info on how to beat the queues or the best new restaurant? We want to hear from YOU to keep improving the guide each year. Drop us a line at: Brit's Guides (Disneyland Resort Paris), *W. Foulsham & Co. Ltd, The Publishing House, Bennetts Close, Cippenham, Slough, Berkshire SL1 5AP. Or email us at britsguideplanner@yahoo.com.*

Foreword

Simon says…

Welcome to the third edition of the brightest guidebook on Europe's No. 1 tourist attraction, as compiled by Britain's leading Disney experts (even if we say so ourselves!). And an exciting and adventurous edition it should be, too. For, not only have we changed the format to include colour pictures throughout the book but, for the first time, the Brit's Guide to Disneyland Resort Paris *is now a joint work, since Susan and I became a true partnership in every sense of the word. We have been visiting Disney parks for some 45 years between us, and writing about them for more than 12.*

Since the opening of the Walt Disney Studios Park *in March 2002, which added a dramatic new depth and breadth to the theme park offering, the* Disneyland Resort Paris *has become a much more rounded – and time-consuming! – place to visit. Other developments have been springing up in parallel to Disney's, hence your choice for things to do in this corner of the world is now hugely varied and great fun. It is a world of fantasy and adventure, but it is also complicated, detailed and demanding – especially in the summer – so it is vital you are armed with all the necessary* Brit's Guide *insider information to tackle it. This book aims to be your Good Companion throughout the Disney experience – from the moment you start planning, to your journey there, how to enjoy it all while you're on site, and on to all the extra things to appreciate in the vicinity, notably in the city of Paris itself.*

Susan says…

After years of enjoying Disney's American parks, my first visit to Disneyland Resort Paris *was an eye-opener. Foolishly, I did not think that anything could top the parks I already knew and loved, so I was quite unprepared for the hold this charming resort would have on my heart. It offers a perfect balance between the familiar and the unexpected.*

The Disneyland Park *in particular matches the best of the American parks, then goes one better, with more elaborate theming outside the attractions, added elements within many of the attractions and a sense of excitement around every bend. I never quite knew where the next pathway would lead but I was certain I wanted to explore every one of them. By the end of our stay, I was completely captivated by* Disneyland Resort Paris *and, without hesitation, would call the* Disneyland Park *my favourite of them all, both sides of the Atlantic.*

Therefore, turn the pages and let us be your guides to this magical place. The prospect alone always fills us with great anticipation, so let's not wait another moment – on to Neverland…

1 Introduction
(or, *An Open Invitation to the House of Mouse*)

There is one simple reason why Disney's theme parks are the world's most-visited attractions, be they in America, Japan or, in this case, France. They are simply the best family entertainment that you will find anywhere.

And the guaranteed fun is not restricted to families either. For, while children find the allure of Mickey and Co almost irresistible, there is something for everyone in a Disney park, be they young or old, single, a couple or with the whole family in tow. In fact, we reckon there is more all-round entertainment value here than anywhere else we've seen.

It is a great short-break destination, a perfect location for a week (or even longer, given the additional attractions of the Paris region) and it is easy to reach; it is ideally suited to families (especially those with young children), yet it also attracts honeymooners and other couples; and its appeal is timeless, harking back to a nostalgic yesteryear but remaining contemporary in so many areas.

Pixie dust

A holiday at *Disneyland Resort Paris* is a beguiling prospect, and it is also one that is sure to bring out the child in (nearly) everyone. If you can envisage grown-ups rushing to hug Mickey or Minnie, then you can imagine the effect the Disney 'Pixie dust' has on just about every person who walks through the gates.

Indeed, Roy Disney, nephew of the great Walt himself, opened the Paris park with words his uncle first used for *Disneyland California* in 1955. He said: 'To all who come to this happy place, welcome! This is your land. Here age relives fond memories of the past and here youth may savour the challenge and promise of the future. We hope it will be a source of joy and inspiration to the world.' It certainly shapes up that way.

But enough of this tantalising glimpse of make-believe. Let us paint a picture of the reality and try to provide a basic understanding of how it all works. This can be a complicated business and you must keep your wits about you at all times. When the crowds start to flock into the parks, it is a challenge to keep up with the ebb and flow of it all. When the queue for a ride tops an hour, you need strategy on your side and the essential tool of all Disney-goers – a plan!

In fact, *planning* is an essential component of your holiday. At quieter times of the year, you might just get away with a free-wheeling, make-it-up-as-you-go-along approach if you are on your own or just a couple. But, at even moderately busy periods or with youngsters in tow, there are plenty of pitfalls that await the unwary or the unprepared. This is definitely not like a trip to Alton Towers or Thorpe Park, where a day is usually enough to see everything.

With two fully fledged parks in the Disney experience, there is a significant element of choice. Behind that lies a matter of scale that is hard to convey completely in advance and which includes an attention to detail both breathtaking and a little bewildering. It is easy to get side-tracked by some of the clever scenery, shops and other frippery, so that's why planning is important.

Not for nothing did they change the name to *Disneyland Resort Paris* in 2002, for truly this is a resort experience *par excellence*, and that means a multi-dimensional approach in all things, from the attractions to the hotels, the restaurants and even the shops. There is fun almost everywhere you turn and a host of options at any one time. Therefore, you need to do your homework carefully in advance so that you can be aware of all that lies in store.

Chequered history

The *Disneyland Resort Paris* story began in the mid-1980s when Michael Eisner, then the new Chief Executive Officer of the Walt Disney Company, came to Europe in search of a new outlet for their theme park creativity. Both France and Spain were firmly in the frame, and the former was chosen for a variety of reasons, not least the strong French connection in many Disney films (*Cinderella*, *Sleeping Beauty*, *Hunchback of Notre Dame*) and the wonderful central location offered by the Paris region.

As far back as December 1985, Mr Eisner signed a letter of intent with the then Prime Minister of France, Laurent Fabius, to build a park in Marne-la-Vallée, some 32km (20 miles) east of Paris. That agreement was formalised with Jacques Chirac in March 1987 and what was then about 1,900 hectares (4,700 acres) of beet fields became the planning ground for a great adventure in architecture and engineering, or Imagineering, as the Walt Disney Company likes to call it.

The first earth-moving equipment moved in on 2 August, 1988, and a 4-year construction period began. Despite some challenges from Mother Nature, the Euro Disney Park (as it was then known – it soon changed to Euro Disneyland) opened right on time on 12 April, 1992, to a massive blaze of film and TV star publicity.

Despite the glittering launch, however, a sceptical press, some French hostility (going back to the project's announcement), aimed at the supposed 'Americanisation' of their culture, and some over-optimistic attendance forecasts all contributed to a painful initiation for the new park.

The media focused on anything negative – long lines for meals and longer queues for some rides, high prices, rumours of empty hotels and staff unhappiness – and the combination of problems both real and perceived almost brought the whole place to its knees. The park and its associated development – hotels, shops and restaurants, all grouped around a 'village' core, then called Festival Disney – had gone way over budget, and the lack of the immediate huge profits forecast to pay off the short-term debt, coupled with a Europe-wide recession, meant there was a real threat that it might close after little more than a year – despite 10.8 million visitors in the first 12 months.

A major financial restructuring was necessary in 1994, at which time it became Disneyland Paris, and, from there, the story has been one of recovery, although battles with that initial debt continued. Attendances built up through the late 1990s and more development began to spring up around Marne-la-Vallée, both commercial and residential.

The success of Disney's on-site hotels (six of them, plus the camping ground of *Disney's Davy Crockett Ranch* a short drive away) encouraged a mini proliferation of hotels in the vicinity, while the development extended to a new town centre at neighbouring **Val d'Europe**, a combination of businesses, shopping and housing which adds even more to the picture locally. Here, the immaculate shopping mall competes with the excellent outlet shopping of **La Vallée**, the **Sea Life Centre** and some enticing restaurants.

At the same time, a Disney-run **golf complex**, with three nine-hole courses, was developed just 10 minutes' drive from the resort itself, offering yet another diversion for people wanting to combine their theme park experience with something more down to earth (but equally vital).

The new park

The original plans for the resort included a sister park, along the lines of *Disney-MGM Studios* in *Walt Disney World Resort in Florida*. This was scheduled to open just three years after the first park, but the financial and other headaches of

1994 meant the concept went into storage until 1998. Construction began in earnest shortly afterwards. The eagerly awaited *Walt Disney Studios Park* then opened on 16 March 2002, with another burst of publicity – and another rebranding to *Disneyland Resort Paris*.

> **BRIT TIP:** *Disneyland Resort Paris* is just under 2 hours from Ashford in Kent on the direct Eurostar service and only 2 hours 50 minutes from London Waterloo. For the great convenience the train provides, it's definitely worth considering.

Here, finally, was the true resort expansion as originally envisaged by Eisner and his Imagineers, completing a well-rounded picture of accommodation, shopping, restaurants and theme parks, and providing a multi-day experience, even out of busy periods. Festival Disney, now known more appropriately as *Disney Village*, has grown to encompass nine restaurants, three bars, a multi-screen leisure and cinema complex (including a new IMAX screen theatre), an adjoining dinner show (the exceptionally family-friendly

Disneyland Park entrance in winter

Facts and figures

- The whole site of *Disneyland Resort Paris* covers 1,943 hectares (4,800 acres), or one-fifth the area of Paris
- Groundbreaking took place in August 1988
- 51km (32 miles) of roads were built and 120 million cubic metres (157 million cubic yards) of earth moved
- Around 450,000 trees and shrubs were planted
- It employs 12,500 people every year (on average)
- The *Disneyland Park* covers 57 hectares (140 acres)
- The *Walt Disney Studios Park* stands on 25 hectares (62 acres)
- The seven themed hotels have a total of 5,800 rooms
- There are 68 counter and full-service restaurants throughout the resort
- In all, there are 47 different shops and boutiques
- Some 140 million people have visited since it opened
- Around 40% of visitors are French, 23% British, 8% German, 8% Belgian, 8% Dutch, 8% Spanish and Italian with 5% from other nations

Buffalo Bill's Wild West Show), a big nightclub and a choice of nine shops. There is also the wonderful new Panoramagique tethered balloon ride and a host of other games and activities (see Chapter 8).

With the Marne-la-Vallée railway station at the heart of the whole development, linking the resort with central Paris, Charles de Gaulle airport and, most importantly, London via Eurostar, it is also a wonderfully convenient location, easy for arrival and well organised to allow access either straight to the Theme Parks, to the hotels (using an efficient bus service) or directly to *Disney Village*.

Anyone familiar with the Orlando resort set up – 12,173 hectares (30,080 acres) of four parks, two water parks, 22 hotels and a mini-town area called *Downtown Disney* – will almost certainly be impressed by the ease with which you can move around this resort by comparison. All of it is within reach by a 20-minute walk at most and the scale is big enough to be exciting, yet manageable enough not to be daunting. Indeed, it is a triumph of the designers' art in making this hugely complex development one of very human dimensions, a riot of visual stimulation and yet easy to negotiate. Yes, there is a lot going on here, but it is not difficult to get around and enjoy.

Sleeping Beauty Castle

Disney Village

Offering a positive riot of sights and sounds, both by day and night (when the contrast is quite startling, from the peaceful Lake Disney in early morning to the near-disco proportions of the late-evening hubbub), *Disney Village* acts as a conduit between the parks and hotels. It is an exit for weary park-goers (and you can be pretty tired by park closing, believe us!) and offers a new source of fun for all those who enjoy their nightlife. It is a heady cocktail but it also requires a good deal of forethought, especially if you have the family in tow, to ensure you get the most out of it, whether it be for a meal, some more shopping, the new Panoramagique balloon ride or the amusement of some of the fairground-type games before you head back to the hotel.

Of course, *Disney Village* is not reserved purely for Disney's on-site hotel guests. It does attract a good number of locals (especially on Friday and Saturday) and its large car park makes it easily accessible for guests at the nearby hotels, while the RER service (the main local commuter train line) runs until after midnight for those who have chosen not to drive.

The European touch

Truly, *Disneyland Resort Paris* is a wonderfully impressive set-up and is easily the equal of any of Disney's other parks and resorts around the world. In fact, we believe it is the clever 'Europeanisation' of the traditional Disney style that gives it the extra appeal. There is more than a hint of French flair, Italian chic, Spanish partying, German organisation and Dutch friendliness about the resort, which comes together best in the Village. Yes, there are some drawbacks – especially for non-smokers, as avoiding cigarette smoke can be difficult at times – and the mixture of cultures occasionally causes some awkwardness as well as empathy. The toilets could be kept cleaner in many instances (for some reason, this seems a bit of a blind spot in the *Disneyland Park* and *Disney Village*) and there is occasionally a bit of push and shove (which you don't usually find at the American parks), notably in the scrimmage for character autographs, getting in position to view one of the parades, or trying to board a hotel bus at the end of the evening.

It won't be a restful holiday, unless you go out of season in winter and are blessed by mild, dry weather, and it can make a serious dent in your bank balance. But, all in all, it offers great value and richly rewards those who go with an open mind and the willingness to try those few words of school French you can dredge from memory.

More importantly, it is guaranteed to put a smile on the faces of young and old alike and hopefully reaffirm simple family and friendly values. When Walt built Disneyland in California back in 1955, his most famous statement (now etched on the bronze Walt 'n' Mickey statue in front of the Sleeping Beauty Castle) was: 'I think most of all what I want Disneyland to be is a happy place… where parents and children can have fun together.'

So, don't forget to take time out to reaffirm those values during your visit; watch your children's faces at one of the parades, on the Dumbo ride or in the queue to meet Mickey (or just look at the reaction of other children); and ensure you do things together, however silly they may be! There is artistry all around you, in the rides, the architecture and the Cast Members, but the most meaningful feeling you can invoke is the bond with your loved ones – and nowhere brings that to the fore quite

1

Our Top 10 Family Attractions

1 Pirates of the Caribbean
2 Cinémagique
3 'it's a small world'
4 Wonderful World of Disney Parade
5 Legend of the Lion King
6 Peter Pan's Flight
7 Tarzan Encounter
8 Art of Disney Animation
9 Phantom Manor
10 Animagique

like a Disney park, whether it be for kids of six or 60.

However, perhaps the question most seasoned Disney-goers will want to ask is: if I have already been to *Walt Disney World in Florida*, do I need to go to *Disneyland Resort Paris*? We would say unequivocally yes. Apart from the obvious advantage of this being a closer and more convenient short-visit destination (no 9-hour flights and long queues at Immigration to deal with), we believe the more luxurious theming of the *Disneyland Park*, the updated versions of classic rides like Space Mountain, Haunted Mansion and Big Thunder Mountain, and the all-new thrills of most of the *Walt Disney Studios Park* make it an absolute must to visit here as well as Florida. For some, it is also a handy 'refresher' of Disney magic in between visits to Orlando (and of course it is cheaper to spend a few days in Paris than a week or more in America). Anyone familiar with the vast Florida 'park-opolis' will also appreciate the simple convenience of being able to walk everywhere!

See the city

Another big bonus of the location is the nearby lure of Paris itself, and you certainly do not need to have a car here to benefit (in fact, driving into the city is not advisable). The reliability of the RER service (see Brit Tip) and local buses means you can easily enjoy an evening along the Champs Elysées or the Bastille district and still get the train back to the resort.

A highly recommended night out for couples is the **Lido de Paris** show in the Champs Elysées, while another recent development is the **Cityrama** bus tours of the city, picking up at *Disney's Hotel New York* every day. The latter provides an excellent whistle-stop visit of all the main features of this fabulous city, with the great convenience of staying outside the crowds and hubbub. It is also only about 40 minutes on the RER train into central Paris, which is then easy to negotiate either on foot or by the Métro or bus. It is a truly magnificent city with a wealth of history, architecture, art and amazing monuments, plus a dazzling array of fine restaurants and shops. If you are planning a 4-day Disney visit, you should definitely think about spending at least half a day and an evening in Paris itself, especially as there are plenty of attractions geared to the family audience (see Chapter 9).

Those who bring the car can benefit from exploring further afield

BRIT TIP: Need to find your way around Paris public transport? Options are the Métro (the underground), RER train service (regional rail, part underground), Transilien SNCF (suburban rail – not strictly relevant to *Disneyland Resort Paris*), bus and tram. Visit www.ratp.fr for more info in French and English.

Top Thrill Attractions

1 Rock 'n' Rollercoaster starring Aerosmith
2 Space Mountain: Mission 2
3 Indiana Jones and the Temple of Peril
4 Big Thunder Mountain Railroad
5 Star Tours
6 Armageddon
7 Panoramagique
8 Driving in central Paris!

– and there are some wonderful towns and villages in this region of France, notably the medieval walled town of Provins to the south-east. The road links are good (France also has a system of toll roads which are quite superb) and rarely subjected to the kind of congestion we experience in the UK – apart from in central Paris, of course.

You can also stock up with some wonderful food and wine along the way, as well as in Val d'Europe, where the **Auchan hypermarket** is a highly civilised alternative to the rather tired supermarkets of Calais.

The main focus, however, should be the Theme Parks themselves. The original *Disneyland Park* remains the heart and soul of the Magic, especially for families with children under 10, while the new *Walt Disney Studios Park* has added an element of excitement and thrills for the older age group. The two parks provide a complementary experience, but the time requirements of each are quite different. Don't be fooled into thinking you can spend 2 days here and do it all, even during off-peak times. The older park will require at least 2 days to ensure you have seen and done most of what is on offer, while the Studios usually needs just a full day to absorb properly its variety of entertainments.

BRIT TIP: In keeping with their seasonal approach, the New Year period from January to Easter has become the great Family Value time to visit, with plenty of Kids Go Free (with each adult) deals.

The Orbitron and Space Mountain: Mission 2 rides

© Disney

1

Speaking French

The resort has been a multi-lingual operation since Day One and all Disney employees (or Cast Members, as they are known) should be able to speak at least two languages (many speak four or five). This means you shouldn't have any trouble being understood. However, it is still good practice (and simple good manners) to try to remember a few words of French to get by from time to time. All Cast Members wear a badge with their name and home country, so you can easily spot the occasional Brit working here but, for those who can't remember their basic school French, here is a quick guide to those handy vital words:

ENGLISH	FRENCH
Do you speak English?	Parlez-vous Anglais?
Good morning/Hello	Bonjour
Good evening	Bonsoir
Please	S'il vous plaît
Thank you	Merci
I would like…	Je voudrais…
Do you have…	Avez-vous…
How much is…	Quel est le prix de…
How much?	C'est combien?
A receipt	Un reçu
The bill, please	L'addition, s'il vous plaît
Coffee	Café
White coffee	Café au lait
Where are the toilets?	Où sont les toilettes?
Toll booths	Les péages
Motorway service areas	Aires
Autoroutes (toll roads)	Autoroutes des péages
Hypermarket	Hypermarché

Seasonal fun

Disneyland Resort Paris is unique in the Disney empire of theme parks in providing a huge range of seasonal celebrations. While all their other resorts can lay on a brilliantly themed backdrop for Christmas and Halloween, only here will you find a real in-depth and broadly arranged series of attractions throughout the year, with special winter festivities, the spring Lion King Carnival, a Latin Festival in June, the amazing and quite superb transformation of Frontierland to Halloweenland in October, a series of Bonfire Night specials and the magic of Christmas in full *Disneyland Resort Paris* style.

There is even a special celebration now to mark Chinese New Year.

Disneyland Resort at Christmas

© Disney

Top 10 campaign tips

1   Decide what you want to do and try to plan a rough daily schedule (especially in summer).

2   Work out if you want to Do It All (remember in summer, when opening hours are longest, everything is available but queues are at their longest, too) or have a quieter time in spring or autumn (with shorter hours and more unpredictable weather).

3   Stay in the resort or outside? The former offers unequalled convenience and essential 'Magic', but the latter is cheaper.

4   Choose your mode of transport. Eurostar, car, coach or air – where you live will determine which one is the most convenient (see Chapter 3).

5   Long weekend or holiday? The temptation is to pack it all into a weekend, and the ease of the Eurostar makes this appealing. But the weekends are busier and going for 4–5 days instead allows you more variety (see page 19).

6   Whether you have a day in Paris, an outing to Provins or Versailles, or just a shopping expedition to Val d'Europe, you'll benefit from a Disney break at some stage.

7   Stop and admire the scenery. Often.

8   Enjoy the fact you can have a glass of wine or a beer in the *Disneyland Park*. Alcohol is not served in *Walt Disney World's Magic Kingdom Park* in Florida.

9   Try a little French. The locals are usually more hospitable and forthcoming if you make even a token effort to speak their language.

10 Get everyone in your party to read this book!

Rain and shine

This is still Western Europe and the climate can be depressingly like our own at times – wet, grey and cold. However, much of both parks have been built with rain and wind in mind, which means there is nearly always somewhere you can escape to if the weather turns nasty. Indeed, almost 80 per cent of the *Walt Disney Studios Park* is under cover, so you don't have to worry too much about the vagaries of Mother Nature. Providing you pack a light raincoat, you will be well prepared to carry on enjoying the fun. In fact, spring and autumn can offer some of the best times for visiting *Disneyland Resort Paris* as they rarely come up with any seriously anti-social weather, while the crowds are far more manageable. And, while the delights of Paris in the springtime is a wonderful cliché, that doesn't mean it isn't true – in fact the months of April (after Easter) and May are just about the best time to visit, with a heavenly combination of pleasant weather, convivial atmosphere and generally lower-than-average attendances.

Yes, this is the biggest tourist attraction in Europe – with 12.4 million visitors in 2004 (and a likely increase to almost 13 million in 2005), some 2.5 million from the UK alone – but it can easily be a breeze of a place to visit if you get your tactics right.

And so, with that firmly in mind, it's time to move on to the vital area of Planning…

2 Planning
(or, How to Do Disney and Stay Sane!)

It used to be the case just a few years ago that you could pop across the Channel to Marne-la-Vallée, have a fun day out and be back home again for tea the next day, safe in the knowledge you had 'done' Disney. Not any more.

The addition of the *Walt Disney Studios Park* in March 2002, the expansion of the surrounding area and continuing influx of visitors mean this is now somewhere you need to consider carefully before you set out for that 'perfect' holiday. It is not quite the same as *Walt Disney World Resort in Florida*, where any visit has to be planned with the precision and accuracy of a military campaign, but you must have a good idea of what you are letting yourself in for and it is still advisable to plan around some of the pitfalls that await the unwary.

> BRIT TIP: Can't find the characters? Check out Main Street USA in the *Disneyland Park* in the morning and the Animation Courtyard area of the *Walt Disney Studios Park* throughout the day. Better still, you could book one of the character meals at a restaurant like Café Mickey or the Lucky Nugget Saloon.

First of all, the two parks – the original *Disneyland Park* and the newer *Walt Disney Studios* – are a complete contrast from each other. They are different sizes, with different time requirements, and appeal to different people. They provide a complementary experience for all but the youngest children (the Studios has fewer attractions for under 5s), but, while you will probably need 2 full days to explore all of the *Disneyland Park*, a day is usually sufficient at the *Walt Disney Studios Park*.

The Disneyland Park

The *Disneyland Park* follows the rough formula of the *Magic Kingdom Park*, in Orlando, and *Disneyland California*, in Anaheim, Los Angeles. It is subdivided into five 'lands' around a central hub and features a range of almost 50 attractions in the form of rides, shows, parades and other live entertainment. There is also an impressive cast of accompanying shops and restaurants, all themed to the various lands and offering some useful browsing opportunities. At 57 hectares (140 acres), it requires some serious shoe leather to see it all, and you will be amazed at how time-consuming it can be to get from land to land with the number of diversions you encounter on the way.

This is the park where families tend to concentrate (although there are also several terrific thrill rides, most notably Space Mountain: Mission 2 and Indiana Jones and The Temple of Peril). There is a huge choice for dining and some wonderful character meal opportunities (which kids adore), but you need to pace yourself here as it's easy to get worn to a frazzle – and end up with fractious children – with too much to-ing and fro-ing.

Walt Disney Studios Park

This park is subdivided into four areas and is slightly less than half the size of its sister park. It is therefore easier to negotiate. As the name suggests, it is geared around the magic of the film world, but it is a different proposition to the *Disney-MGM Studios* in Orlando (although two of the rides are similar and another is a transplant from Orlando's *Magic Kingdom Park*). It is much more show-based, hence its attractions are geared around specific times of the day (like the

amazing Stunt Show), and more of it is indoors, which is handy when the weather is too cold, hot or wet! There are fewer things to appeal to younger children here and the dining opportunities are distinctly ordinary, but you will still encounter the all-important Disney characters and some wonderful live entertainment as well.

Beyond the Theme Parks

Once you have visited the parks, the delights of *Disney Village* await you. You can dine, dance, shop, go to the cinema or catch a show in this lively, bustling hub, which is a pure delight at night with the clever lighting effects. The choice of dining is terrific – the elaborate international theming of Planet Hollywood (one of our real favourites), Rainforest Café, the superb Steakhouse and the fun Bavarian-style of King Ludwig's Castle (which replaced the old Rock 'n' Roll America bar/diner in 2003) are the pick of the bunch. Then

Rainforest Café

© Disney

Café Mickey

there is the 1950s' Americana of Annette's Diner, the country and western style of Billy Bob's Saloon, an all-day character-fest at Café Mickey (with excellent food, too), a Sports Bar and a New York Sandwiches deli, not forgetting a large McDonalds.

Live bands are an outstanding feature of Billy Bob's, while Hurricanes disco (free to Disney resort guests) starts bopping around midnight (although it can be quiet Sunday to Thursday out of season).

BRIT TIP: Too crowded for lunch in the Theme Parks? Step outside and enjoy a more relaxed meal in *Disney Village*, with none of the long queues, at restaurants like Planet Hollywood, Café Mickey and Annette's Diner.

Nine fully-fledged boutique stores stay open usually until midnight, and the Central Stage is the venue for more live entertainment from time to time. The Gaumont Cinema is a 12-screen complex showing the latest movies but, unless you speak good French, there is only one English-language presentation – every Monday night. The new large-screen IMAX theatre, which opened in 2004, adds an extra dimension here as they should now be able to provide multi-lingual headphones for all performances (but check before you book). There is also the inevitable video games arcade.

For live entertainment, **Buffalo Bill's Wild West Show** is a *Disney Village* institution, a corny-but-fun dinner show which is usually a huge hit with kids (even grown-up ones!) and offers the chance to shout, cheer and wave your (free) cowboy hat in support of the various acts, who perform in the indoor auditorium during a typical cowboy dinner. Daily in the summer, there is a Wild West parade outside before the first of the two shows (around 6pm).

A new element in 2005 was **Panoramagique**, a breath-taking tethered balloon ride over the Village that soars to some 180m (600ft) and provides an awesome view of the surrounding area. Add in pedal boats, bungee trampolines and other hands-on activities (including

Buffalo Bill's Wild West Show

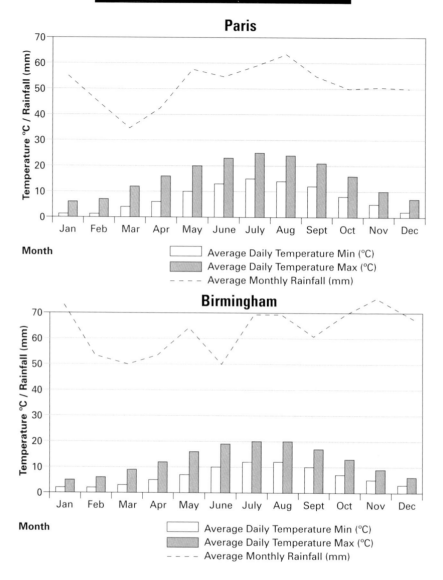

Paris

Temperature °C / Rainfall (mm)

Month

☐ Average Daily Temperature Min (°C)
▨ Average Daily Temperature Max (°C)
– – – Average Monthly Rainfall (mm)

Birmingham

Temperature °C / Rainfall (mm)

Month

☐ Average Daily Temperature Min (°C)
▨ Average Daily Temperature Max (°C)
– – – Average Monthly Rainfall (mm)

cycling and, in winter, ice-skating) and you have a veritable interactive playground that will keep everyone amused for up to half a day. For the full details on *Disney Village*, see Chapter 8.

As if all that were not enough, you will find the additional lure of **Val d'Europe** quite strong (it continues to develop as a major business centre), and there is some excellent shopping (most notably at the adjoining **La Vallée** outlet village). This is just 5 minutes away on the RER train (free buses run between the Disney resorts and La Vallée at various times) and can provide a refreshing break from the world of the Mouse after a few days. Here you will find a huge indoor shopping

Four nights – barely enough

To get an idea of the full resort set-up when it was first in full swing in summer 2002, Simon took his boys (then aged 4 and 6) on a standard 4-night/5-day package with Leger Holidays, the big coach tour operator (see page 59). Staying at *Disney's Hotel Santa Fe*, Simon semi-planned an itinerary for each day and found this was a valuable strategy (especially where meals were concerned), although he also had to keep his plans fairly fluid at times to allow for tired boys! Here, Simon reports on how the trip worked out:

DAY ONE: Arrive at *Disney's Hotel Santa Fe* at 9.30pm after 8½-hour journey, including P&O Ferry crossing. Everyone straight to bed!

DAY TWO: Up at 8am for hotel breakfast and off to the *Disneyland Park* soon after. Full day in the Theme Park, with lunch (pre-booked) at The Lucky Nugget Saloon. Younger son in need of a break after 3pm parade, so back to the hotel for a rest. Dinner at Planet Hollywood at 6.30pm, followed by a slow wander back to the hotel through the *Disney Village* (with much to sidetrack both boys!).

DAY THREE: A late start – not up until 9.30am; hotel breakfast at 10, then off to the *Walt Disney Studios*, just in time to catch the 11am Stunt Show. Take in two more shows before lunch at Backlot Express (self-service), then complete the full range of attractions by 5.30pm. Switch to *Disneyland Park* for dinner at Silver Spur Steakhouse at 6.30pm (pre-booked), then one last ride before catching bus back to hotel.

DAY FOUR: An 8am breakfast (pre-booked) in the *Disneyland Park* at Walt's – An American Restaurant (with various characters). Then spend 2 hours doing many of the rides in Fantasyland. Leave park to take RER one stop to Val d'Europe and visit the Sea Life Centre*. Have lunch and shop, and the boys played in La Vallée play area, before catching the train back. Revisit the Studios for another chance to see the Stunt Show and Animagique before heading back to the other park for our planned late night. Dinner at 8pm watching a show at Videopolis, and both boys happily keep going on various rides until the 10.30 evening parade and fireworks.

DAY FIVE: Quite surprisingly, we make an 8am breakfast and pack our luggage back on to the coach. Visit the petrol station next to the hotel to grab a few snacks for the long journey back to Calais. Coach departs at 10am, non-stop to Calais hypermarket. Home again – very tired but with very happy boys! – by 4.30pm UK time.

*If the boys had been a bit older, we would have considered the full-day Paris sight-seeing tour with Cityrama (see Chapter 9) for our break from the Theme Parks.

mall, some excellent restaurants in an upmarket food court and the exceedingly child-friendly **Sea Life Centre**, a major aquarium run by the chain that owns 13 similar attractions throughout the UK and Europe. It is a great diversion for kids aged 2–12 especially and provides a good 2-hour lure if Mum or Dad want to go shopping!

When to go

Unfortunately, the majority of people who visit do so in full family mode, so they are usually here in the

Wonderful World of Disney Parade

school holidays. Unfortunate because both the cost and the crowds increase during those times, while the summer can also be uncomfortably hot – in excess of 30°C (and two of the resort hotels, *Disney's Hotel Cheyenne* and *Disney's Hotel Santa Fe*, plus the Explorers Hotel, do not have air-conditioning). So you will need to consider your options carefully.

If you are confined to the main school holidays, try to opt for late Easter or late summer. The spring and autumn half-term holidays are also prime opportunities, although, once again, the cost increases at those times. The big pay-off with a summer visit is the bonus of

Easter egg painting

France on holiday

France has 11 public holidays when government departments, banks and shops are usually closed: 1 January, Easter Monday, 1 May, 8 May, Ascension day, Whit Monday, 14 July, 15 August, 1 November, 11 November and 25 December.

French schoolchildren have no less than FIVE holidays a year: a week at the end of October, 2 weeks at Christmas, 2 in February, 2 in spring, and the whole of July and August. Consequently, *Disneyland Resort Paris* and the roads are noticeably busier during these periods. More details on French school holidays at: www.education. gouv.fr/prat/cal.htm

You may also want to negotiate around some of the other main European school holidays, see www.eurydice.org

extended opening hours (usually to 11pm) and a full show and parade schedule. If you can avoid Le Weekend crowds, you still benefit from the pure magic of long nights in the *Disneyland Park* with the evening finale fireworks. As ever, it is a case of swings and roundabouts, and you really need to consider what might work best for you, or what appeals most.

Busy times

If you are able to visit in the non-peak times, you will really feel the benefit. And, by non-peak periods, we also mean weekdays rather than weekends. For, while the local populace didn't embrace Disney at the beginning, the Theme Parks (and *Disney Village*) have developed into a major source of local recreation. So much so that the French attendance on a Saturday and Sunday can be 50% or more. Put simply, this is where much of suburban Paris comes to play at the weekend, and it can be hectic, especially on Saturdays.

Both parks cope pretty well with the thousands who pour in during the first few hours of the day, but the queues do build up quickly at most of the main rides (and just about everywhere in Fantasyland in the *Disneyland Park*). The standard wait time for rides like Peter Pan's Flight and Dumbo can easily top an hour, which means an uncomfortable period in a queue, especially when it's hot. However, Disney has developed a nifty virtual queuing system called **FastPass** (see page 109), which takes a lot of sting out of the waits for many attractions. But even that has its limitations, and so during Easter, summer and Christmas (and any weekend when the weather is fair), you will be spending a lot of time on your feet.

> BRIT TIP: Disney's FastPass system is an invaluable aid to your park visit, but many people overlook it because they don't understand it. It is FREE to use and simply gives you a time to return to the ride and bypass the main queue with only a short wait. It is fully explained in Chapter 5.

If you prefer to avoid school holidays, most of the summer and the weekends, when *should* you go? Well, the spring usually sees Paris at its best, and this tends to rub off on Disneyland, too. Of all Disney's parks around the world, this one is designed and landscaped with distinctly European tastes in mind. There is a much greater emphasis on plants and greenery, providing a naturalistic element to the *Disneyland Park* in particular, which is a joy to behold in the spring and early summer.

That is not to say both parks don't have a good deal of charm all year round (especially at Christmas and New Year, when Disney really lays on the charisma), or that you can't have as much fun on the rides in November as you can in April, but there is something genuinely special about a bright spring day that perfectly sets off the Magic provided by Disney's Imagineers. The Adventureland section of the *Disneyland Park* is particularly noticeable in this way, as it is an area which completely envelops you with its sense of grand design and wonderful creativity.

Visiting off peak

The weather tends to be more consistent in a Paris springtime than back across the Channel, too. Here you can compare the two typical temperature and rainfall charts for Paris and Birmingham on page 18. However, the winters can be equally unpleasant as our own in terms of wet and cold, so there are several factors you must bear in mind if you

Shopping at Constellations

© Disney

opt to visit from November to February. The most obvious is the downturn in business in the winter, with not only the crowds dropping off appreciably, but some of the restaurants and attractions closing too. All Disney's rides, shows and attractions go through a regular process of refurbishment and much of this is carried out in winter, so you may find one or two things shut down at this time. For example, if you enjoyed the Lion King-style dining at Hakuna Matata (in the *Disneyland Park*) during a summer visit, be aware it is frequently one of the counter-service outlets that closes at off-peak times.

BRIT TIP: The excellent German-English website www.dlp.info/Guide/ includes a section on Closed Attractions, which lists rides due for a revamp more than 6 months in advance (go to Tips & Info, then Planning Your Holiday and click on Closed Attractions).

Some entertainment is geared only to peak periods, when the Theme Parks are open longer. A nightly fireworks show, Wishes, and a special evening parade extravaganza in the *Disneyland Park* are real highlights in summer and at Christmas, while the Winnie The Pooh & Friends show is high season only. Bad weather (notably heavy rain) can scupper some of the outdoor entertainment at any time, but this is more likely to happen in the winter. However, the Disney team is adept at creating extra Magic in the form of shows and theming at various times of the year, which makes **Halloween** and **Christmas** especially appealing and provides an extra reason for visiting at these times (see opposite).

The obvious advantage of visiting out of season is the lack of any serious queues. We have been in the Theme Parks at a variety of different times and nothing beats being able to wander around places like Fantasyland and Discoveryland with the choice of any ride without queuing (and without tripping over toddlers or being run over by pushchairs!). The staff have more time for you, too, and the whole atmosphere is less frenetic, which adds to the enjoyment.

The other big bonus is the regular **'Kids Go Free'** season (another unique Disney feature here) whereby, with any Disney hotel package, every child stays free with a full fare-paying adult, including free continental breakfast and park entry. Of course, park hours are shorter at this time of year (usually 10am–8pm at the *Disneyland Park* and 10am–6pm at the *Walt Disney Studios*), but it is that much easier to get around, so you shouldn't feel short-changed at all (while 8pm is often late enough for many children anyway).

A weather eye

Ah, but what about the weather, you might well be asking. *Disneyland Resort Paris* can organise many things, but they have yet to discover how to keep the rain at bay. That means your day in the parks might fall foul of unwelcome precipitation that could literally rain on your parade. But the park designers took the weather firmly into consideration when they were busy Imagineering and you will find more attractions protected from the elements than at any other theme park in the world. It is even possible to walk deep into the *Disneyland Park* mainly under cover (follow the route in Chapter 6).

The provision of arcades down both sides of Main Street USA (the entrance to the main park), some capacious indoor restaurants and very few real 'outdoor' rides (not to mention all the shops, which can provide welcome shelter) means that much of your enjoyment should be unspoilt by the vagaries of the weather. In addition, if you bring a waterproof (or buy one of the cheap plastic ponchos on sale throughout the resort) you will be able to continue enjoying the rides with fewer people around.

Christmas events

You may want to take the resort's seasonal events into consideration when planning your visit. First and foremost is the Christmas programme, which features special shows, parades, fireworks, characters, decorations and other events in the Theme Parks, hotels and *Disney Village* from early November to early January.

Main Street USA in the *Disneyland Park* becomes the focus of all this festive fun as it is transformed into a genuine winter wonderland. There is the daily **Christmas Parade** featuring Father Christmas, Santa Goofy and their reindeer along Main Street USA (plus a host of other Disney characters in seasonal costume),

BRIT TIP: Some of the Disney characters have different names in France, and will occasionally give their autograph in French fashion. Chip 'n' Dale translate into Tic and Tac, Goofy can become Dingo and Winnie The Pooh is Winnie l'Ourson.

along with a guaranteed **snowfall** up to five times a day. Children can also greet (and have their photo taken with) Santa in a special **Meet Father Christmas** tableau (complete with sleigh) to a backdrop of the new crystal **Gallery of Light** illuminating Main Street, a series of sparkling, crowned street lamps representing the Disney Princesses.

Other highlights are **Belle's Christmas Village**, a charming medieval village themed on *Beauty and the Beast*, with a chance to meet favourite characters from Disney's animated classic (and sample some Yuletide fare!), and **Mickey's Winter Wonderland**, a 20-minute song-and-dance ice-skating frolic with Mickey and the gang at the Chaparral Theatre in Frontierland (which is the one Christmas element that usually continues until the beginning of March). The extra new element in 2005 was the **Enchanted Fairytale Ceremony**, a truly magical finale to each festive evening, with Aurora, Snow White, Belle and Cinderella (and their Princes) in a musical extravaganza culminating with an appearance by Tinker Bell, who waves her magic wand to light up the Main Street USA illuminations and bring the Castle to colourful life. A nightly performance of the grand **Disney's Fantillusion** parade rounds out the park's festive events.

At the *Walt Disney Studios Park*, the theme is a glamorous Hollywood Christmas, with a seasonal celebration centred on the entrance courtyard, where **Father Christmas** waits to greet visitors in his (ahem) Cadillac-sleigh. Inside **Disney Studio 1**, the Ciné Folies invite park goers to be the 'stars' of their Christmas-themed movie productions while musicians in *lederhosen* serenade guests with a festive repertoire inspired by *The Sound of Music*. The new travelling show **Merry Christmas Walt**

Disney Studios departs Animation Courtyard every day at 10.30am for Production Courtyard, where Santa Goofy, Minnie Mouse and Daisy Duck leave their limousines for a rousing festive sing-along.

Goofy also conducts regular rehearsals of the **Swing Along Santas** here during the day – with much comic mayhem as the action usually descends into a bout of slapstick. Finally, at the Umbrellas of Cherbourg in the Backlot area, the normal sprinkling of rain turns to snow for the festive season (and beware lurking Disney characters who may just have a few snowballs in hand!).

The highly decorated theme is recurrent through all areas of the resort, with a special **Christmas market** and a chance to sample a host of traditional culinary specialities, including mulled wine. If you have seen how brilliantly Disney prepares its Orlando theme parks for the festive season, we can assure you they take it to new heights in *Disneyland Resort Paris* and, you can take it from us, it is definitely worth braving the wintry elements for the experience.

> BRIT TIP: If you can visit in late November or the first 2 weeks of December, you will benefit from the full Christmas festivities but without the heavy crowds which they attract later in the month.

You can enjoy another great winter touch at *Disney's Hotel New York*, with a clever **ice-skating rink** outside, while all the Disney resorts feature a spectacular **Christmas Tree** in the lobby area with more decorations than you can shake a Mickey wand at. From 21–31 December, *Disney's Newport Bay Club* hotel also features a special musical dinner show, **The Magical World of Tinker Bell** aboard *HMS Newport*, with Mickey, Minnie and Co joining Tink on a journey of song and dance around the globe. To enjoy it, you should book from the UK on 00 33 1 64 74 54 02.

NB: the *Disneyland Park* closes at 8pm on Christmas Eve, but is open until 1am on **New Year's Eve**,

---

Mickey's Winter Wonderland

© Disney

when there are party festivities throughout the park, as well as *Disney Village*.

Party time

Disney knows how to throw a good party, and the first half of the year is usually studded with notable one-off events. In January, there is a special event to mark **Disney's Chinese New Year**, which is followed by the annual **St Patrick's Day** celebration (17 March) and the **Festival Latina** (salsa, samba, beautiful girls and Latin rhythms) every June, all centred on *Disney Village* and the Central Stage (and in the bars, in the case of St Patrick's Day – and, yes, they do serve Guinness!).

In addition, 16 March is the 'birthday' of the *Walt Disney Studios Park*, the key for even more festivities, while 12 April is the annual party for the whole resort. What's more *Disneyland Resort Paris* will celebrate its 15th anniversary in 2007, and we are expecting a significant party to mark it.

Summer season

From mid-July until the end of August, the full range of park entertainment is up and running, the *Disneyland Park* is open until 11pm – and crowds are at their highest. At this time of year, the **Fantillusion** parade is one of the main highlights, followed by the fabulous **Wishes** fireworks, which bring down the curtain each evening. The Studios also features the new **Good Morning Walt Disney Studios** event, a mini-parade with a big character meet 'n' greet.

Halloween

The next great landmark period is Halloween – and Disney makes a big feature of this. While the idea is certainly more American than European, the style with which *Disneyland Resort Paris* has adopted this tradition is quite breathtaking. Not only is there a daily **Halloween Happening** parade but the whole of Frontierland becomes Halloweenland for all of October, with a wonderfully imaginative series of tableaux (and it is amusing rather than scary for young children). The parade follows the same route as the usual daily one, but it is a showcase for the Disney Villains (and is actually more fun!). Kids automatically gravitate towards the Halloween **face-painting** stalls, and two late evening **Halloween Parties** mean that the Theme Park opens from 9pm–2am for more ghostly goings-on (see page 126), plus a late-night party in *Disney Village*.

Finally, the **Bonfire Night specials** run for 3–4 nights each year around 5 November in best Guy Fawkes tradition. This magnificent firework spectacular takes place above Lake Disney, adjacent to *Disney Village*.

How long do you need?

So, once you have worked out WHEN is the right time for you to visit, you need to work out HOW

Halloween Show in Frontierland

© Disney

LONG you would like to go for. First time visitors should opt for the maximum time they can afford, especially at busy periods. The standard packages now offer 2-, 3- and 4-night stays and, as indicated on page 19, the 4-night duration is only barely enough these days, especially if you have young children to consider. If you can afford a week in summer, you will have the ideal amount of time to explore fully and see some of the surrounding area and Paris as well (and not return home frazzled!). However, because the majority book one of the standard packages, we have drawn up an example of how to plan for each length of stay in **Your Holiday Planner** in Chapter 10.

If you're already familiar with the *Disneyland Park* and have yet to see the *Walt Disney Studios Park*, you will probably be comfortable with a 2-night stay, concentrating on the newer park during your full day on site. Couples without children or with older kids who can safely survive the demands of a bit of hectic park-hopping can probably negotiate both parks and, perhaps, Val d'Europe on a 3-night package. But let us stress – you simply will not be able to 'do it all' in one of the peak periods!

Ideally, you should gear your trip towards avoiding the weekends if at all possible. The perfect 4-night visit would run Monday to Thursday, returning on the Friday before the place starts to get seriously busy. However, if you can't go for long enough, or if you have to include a weekend, let us reassure you that you can still have a great time, and there are a number of dodges, tips and short cuts which will give you a head start over the rest of the crowds. These will become obvious in the three chapters on the Theme Parks themselves.

Disneyland Resort Paris Calendar

January: Disney's Chinese New Year festival in *Disney Village*

Jan–March: Kids Go Free season

16 March : Birthday of *Walt Disney Studios Park*

17 March: St Patrick's Day

12 April: Birthday of *Disneyland Resort Paris*

Mid-June: 3-Night Festival Latina

14 July: French National Day fireworks

Mid-July–end August: Summer Season

October: Disney's Halloween Festival

3–5 November: Bonfire Night Specials

December: Christmas Season

Clothing and comfort

The most important part of your holiday wardrobe is footwear – you will spend a lot of time on your feet, even during off-peak periods. The two parks may not be gigantic but that is irrelevant to the amount of time you'll spend walking and standing in queues. This is not the time to break in new sandals or trainers. Comfortable, well-worn shoes or trainers are essential. Otherwise, you need dress only as the climate dictates. T-shirts and shorts are quite acceptable in both parks when it's warm enough, and most restaurants accept informal dress. In summer bring a mac for those sudden showers. Shoes and shirts must be worn at all times, though. Warm, waterproof footwear is best in winter, along with extra-thick (or thermal) socks.

If you feel you will need a change of clothes after a long day or some extra layers for the evening, you can leave them in a bag at the Luggage Check next to Guest Relations in both parks (€2 per bag) when you arrive. Both parks are well equipped with pushchairs (or strollers, if you happen to get an American Cast Member) for a small charge and baby-changing areas can be found in most toilets.

Disney with children

We are often asked what we think is the right age to take children to Disney for the first time, but there is no set answer. Some toddlers take to it instantly, while some 6- or even 7-year-olds are left rather bemused. Quite often, the best attractions for young children are the hotel swimming pool or the long moving walkways from the car park! Some love the Disney characters at first sight, while others find their size frightening. There is simply no predicting how they will react, but Simon's eldest boy (then 4½) loved just about every second of his first experience (apart from the fireworks). A 3-year-old may not remember much, but you can be sure that they WILL have fun and provide YOU with some great memories, photos or video.

Here are a few tips, put together from personal experience and with advice from other parents:

The journey: try to look calm (even if you don't feel it) and relaxed. Small children soon pick up on any anxieties and make them worse! Pack a bag with plenty of little bits for them (comics, sweets, colouring books, small surprise toys, etc) and keep vital 'extras' like Calpol (in sachets, if possible), change of clothes, small first-aid kit (plasters, antiseptic cream, baby wipes), sunglasses, hat and sunscreen in your hand luggage. If they are fussy with their food, you may want to take a

> **BRIT TIP:** Pushchairs are essential, even if your children have been out of them for a year or two. The distances involved around the Theme Parks wear kids out quickly, and a pushchair can save a lot of discomfort (for dads especially!). You can take your own, hire them at the Theme Parks or even buy one relatively cheaply at the Auchan supermarket in Val d'Europe.

bottle of their favourite squash, etc. Ribena is unheard of in European supermarkets, for example.

Once there: take things slowly and let children dictate the pace, to a large extent. Remember to carry your small first-aid kit with you. Things like baby wipes always come in handy and it is a good idea to take spare clothes, which you can leave at

> **BRIT TIP:** The summer heat can make children irritable in no time at all, so take breaks for drinks or go to attractions which have air-conditioning.

the Luggage Check at both parks. Going back to the hotel for an afternoon snooze is a good idea – the late afternoon and early evening are usually the best times to be at the parks in terms of cooler temperatures (in summer), lower crowds and pure enjoyment. Both parks have a Lost Children meeting place (see page 111).

In the summer: carry suncream and sunblock at all times and use it

© Disney

Plaza Gardens

frequently, in queues, on buses, etc. A children's after-sun cream is also a good idea and don't forget to offer plenty of water or non-fizzy drinks. Tiredness and irritability are often caused by mild dehydration.

Eating out: look for the all-you-can-eat buffets as these are a great way to fill the family up (you may get away with two meals a day) and cater for picky eaters. The Lucky Nugget Saloon, Plaza Gardens Restaurant and Billy Bob's (the latter in *Disney Village*) all offer some serious buffets. Try to let your children get used to the size of the characters before you eat at a restaurant where they visit.

Having fun: try to involve your children in some of the decision-

making and be prepared to go with the flow if they find something unexpected they like (the relatively simple Pocahontas Indian Village playground in the *Disneyland Park* is a good example). With young children, you are unlikely to see and do everything, so just take your time and make the most of what you can all enjoy together.

> BRIT TIP: Baby Care Centres (for changing, preparing food and feeding, with nappies and baby food for sale) can be found behind the Studio Services, just inside the entrance to the *Walt Disney Studios Park*, and next door to the Plaza Gardens Restaurant in the *Disneyland Park*.

Travellers with disabilities

Disney pays close attention to the needs of guests with disabilities, and even has a discounted entry price. There are few rides and attractions that cannot cater for them, while wheelchair availability and access is almost always good. As the *Walt Disney Studios Park* is so recent, much thought and care has gone into the arrangements for people with various disabilities (from the wheelchair-bound to those with autism and epileptic concerns), and it is worth taking time to familiarise yourself with all the ways in which you can take advantage of the facilities. The Cast Members should be fully prepared to help and assist, ensuring you get the full value from all the thoughtful extra touches.

All Disney hotels (except *Disney's Davy Crockett Ranch*) have rooms accessible for guests with disabilities, while they also publish a free *Guide for Guests with Special Needs*

Lucky Nugget Saloon

© Disney

2

(outlining all the necessary information for an enjoyable visit), which is available at hotel receptions and Guest Services at both parks. The guide can be sent to you in advance from: *Disneyland Resort Paris*, Guest Communication, PO Box 100, 77777 Marne-la-Vallée, Cedex, France.

Guidebooks in Braille are also provided and guide dogs are allowed in (although they are not permitted on certain attractions). Start by going to Guest Services at either park and asking for a copy of the *Guide for Guests with Special Needs*. You will also be given a **Blue Card** that allows you to access the special entrances for guests with disabilities (usually through the ride's exit – the main queue lines are not designed for wheelchairs), plus special seating for the shows and parades. However, you must be able to show a doctor's note or disabled pass to qualify for one of these passes.

Visitors with hearing disabilities are not terribly well catered for, apart from a handful of attractions that have sub-titles on video screens rather than bilingual commentaries or headphone translators. The multi-lingual nature of the resort makes it difficult to use a close-captioning system effectively as in Disney's American parks and they seem to be still some way off from cracking this problem.

Disney for grown-ups

It may sound daft to include something specifically for adults but it is an often overlooked aspect that you don't need to have kids in tow to enjoy *Disneyland Resort Paris*. In fact, we've often felt the place is actually too good for kids! There is so much clever detail and imagination which the majority of youngsters miss in their eagerness for the next ride, it is usually the grown-ups who get the most out of the experience. In fact, there are just as many couples without children and young adults on their own visiting the Theme

Wonderful World of Disney Parade

Top 10 things to do in Disneyland Resort Paris

Here is our guide to the 10 things you MUST do on any visit to this wonderful resort:

1 Have a character meal
2 Dine at the Blue Lagoon restaurant
3 See the daily parades (especially if Fantillusion is running)
4 Take a stroll around Lake Disney
5 Have dinner at Planet Hollywood and then check out the live music at Billy Bob's Saloon in *Disney Village*
6 See Buffalo Bill's Wild West Show
7 Have a drink in the Redwood Bar and Lounge at Disney's Sequoia Lodge
8 Go shopping at La Vallée
9 Try the Panoramagique balloon ride at *Disney Village*
10 See Moteurs... Action! Stunt Show Spectacular in *Walt Disney Studios Park*

Parks (especially from countries like Holland and Germany), making it a legitimate holiday for all ages. Certainly, when you look at some of the sophisticated dining on offer and the evening entertainment at places like Billy Bob's and Hurricanes in *Disney Village* (although Billy Bob's often has an early evening session into which kids are allowed), it is easy to see the attraction for those aged over 21.

Paris obviously makes a wonderful honeymoon destination and newly-weds are just as likely to visit one of Disney's parks as the Eiffel Tower. Restaurants like the Blue Lagoon and Auberge de Cendrillon in the *Disneyland Park*, The Steakhouse in *Disney Village*, the Hunter's Grill Restaurant at *Disney's Sequoia Lodge* and the superb California Grill at the *Disneyland Hotel* all offer a genuine romantic touch to dining à la Disney.

Being practical

When it comes to the practicalities of your holiday, your obvious needs include **passports** for all the family (double-checking the name on your passport matches with that on your travel tickets) and remember that all children must have their OWN passport these days. Passports must also remain valid for 3 months after entering France, but no visas are required. For UK passport enquiries, call 08705 210410.

Travel insurance

You can get free or reduced cost treatment in all European Union countries. However, you must possess the new European Health Insurance Card (EHIC) which replaces the E111 on 1 January 2006. You can apply for the EHIC, which is free, online at www.dh.gov.uk/travellers, by phone on 0845 606 2030 or 0845 605 0707, or by post – you can obtain a form at the Post Office. You need to know your NHS/National Insurance number. The EHIC does not cover all medical expenses, however, or the cost of bringing a person back to the UK in the event of illness or death, so it is essential to have adequate travel insurance cover as well.

Having said you should not travel without good insurance, you should also not pay over the odds for it. Tour operators can be expensive or may imply you need to buy their insurance policy when you don't. In all cases make sure your policy covers you for: **medical treatment** up to £1million; **personal liability** up to £1million; **cancellation or curtailment** up to £3,000; **personal property** up to £1,500 (but check on expensive items, as most policies limit single articles to £250); **cash and documents**, including your passport and tickets; and finally that the policy gives you a **24-hour emergency helpline**.

Shop around at reputable dealers like **American Express** (0800 028 7253), AA (0800 085 7240), **First Assist** (0800 169 4078), **Club Direct** (0800 083 2466), **Columbus** (0870 033 9988), **Direct Travel** (0845 605 2700), **Options** (0870 876 7878), **Primary Direct** (0870 220 0634), **Worldwide Insure** (0870 112 8100) or the **E-Insurance Directory** (0800 458 6104).

Medical matters

When it comes to anything of a medical nature, it is worth knowing there are two fully English-speaking hospitals in Paris. The **American Hospital in Neuilly** is located at 63 Boulevard Victor Hugo, 92200 Neuilly-sur-Seine (Métro Porte Maillot); tel (in Paris) 01 46 41 25 25 or 01 47 47 70 15. And the **Hertford British Hospital** can be found at 3 Rue Barbès, 92300 Levallois-Perret (Métro Anatole France); tel 01 46 39 22 22. For an after-hours chemist, the **Drugstore Champs-Elysées** at 133 Avenue des Champs-Elysées (Métro Charles de Gaulle-Etoile), tel 01 47 20 39 25, is open until 2am daily, while the **Pharmacie Dhery** at 84 Avenue des

Disney for seniors

If Simon's parents are anything to go by, the over-60 age group can also get a huge amount of enjoyment from *Disneyland Resort Paris*.

The greater ease of getting here (as opposed to the American parks) is high on their list of plus factors, while the convenience of just about everything being within walking distance or a short bus or train ride scores highly, too. They preferred the *Disney Village* and hotel areas during the day when crowds were rare. Within two days, they were fully *au fait* with the whole resort and extremely comfortable with the set-up. Here is their own Top 10 of attractions suitable for the over 60s:

1   Cinémagique (*Walt Disney Studios Park*)
2   Star Tours (*Disneyland Park*)
3   Pirates of the Caribbean (*Disneyland Park*)
4   Moteurs ... Action! Stunt Show (*Walt Disney Studios Park*)
5   Studio Tram Tour (*Walt Disney Studios Park*)
6   Phantom Manor (*Disneyland Park*)
7   Animagique (*Walt Disney Studios Park*)
8   Tarzan Encounter (*Disneyland Park*)
9   'it's a small world' (*Disneyland Park*)
10 Flying Carpets Over Agrabah (*Walt Disney Studios Park*)

They would even go as far as listing the walk around Lake Disney as an attraction in its own right, while they also felt the more show-based style of the *Walt Disney Studios Park* suited them better than the rather more hectic ride-orientated nature of the original park. However, they still acknowledge the essential magic of the latter as totally unmissable.

Champs-Elysées (by Métro Georges V), tel 01 45 62 02 41, is open around the clock. There is also a pharmacy at the entrance to the big Val d'Europe shopping mall, closest to the RER station entrance, open from 10am–9pm Monday to Saturday.

Emergencies

In the event of an emergency, dial 17 for the police, 18 for the fire brigade or 15 for 24-hour medical emergencies. The public ambulance service can be called on 01 45 13 67 89. For a 24-hour doctor's service, call 01 47 07 77 77.

Safety first

Crime has never been a major issue at *Disneyland Resort Paris*, but it still pays to keep your common sense with you all the time, as you would in any city (especially in the vicinity of the RER station, where pickpockets sometimes operate).

Keep your hotel door locked at all times (even if you are just popping down the corridor) and don't leave things like cameras or camcorders on view in the car when you leave it parked. Both parks have a Lost and Found office and Guest Services can advise you of any additional security requirements (only the *Disneyland Hotel*, *Disney's Hotel New York* and *Disney's Newport Bay Club* have rooms that are equipped with safety deposit boxes).

The Paris **lost property office** is located at the Préfecture de Police, 36 Rue des Morillons, 75015 Paris (Métro Convention); tel 01 55 76 20 00. It is open Mondays and Wednesdays 8.30am–5pm, Tuesdays and Thursdays 8.30am–8pm and Fridays 8.30am–5.30pm. If for any reason you need to contact the British Embassy in Paris, it can be found at 35 Rue du Faubourg Saint-Honoré, 75383 Paris; tel 01 44 51 31 00.

Disney's Fantillusion Parade

© Disney

Disney's Sequoia Lodge at Christmas

Money

As ever on a foreign holiday, it is advisable not to carry too much cash with you. Travellers' cheques are easier to replace if lost or stolen (make a note of the serial numbers), but generally speaking cash and credit cards are almost universally accepted (although not by many small hotels and cafes in some areas of France). You can also use Switch, Visa and Mastercard at the several cash dispensers around the resort.

The currency, of course, is the euro. At the time of writing, £1 = €1.46, or €1 = 68 pence, so roughly speaking £5 would be a touch more than €7. For those who have yet to encounter the euro, there are eight coins – 1 and 2 euros, and 1, 2, 5, 10, 20 and 50 cents – and seven notes in 5, 10, 20, 50, 100 and 200 denominations.

In France, a 15% service charge is sometimes added to restaurant and hotel bills but the usual practice of tipping is simply to leave a few euros at the end of a meal. A taxi driver would expect a 10–15% tip, while a porter would expect €1 a bag.

Phone calls

If you need to **phone home**, avoid using the hotel phones as they are fiendishly expensive (and Disney hotels are no exception). Your mobile phone will probably also have expensive connection charges for calling from abroad (or even for receiving calls). It is better to use a public payphone and pay via your BT Chargecard or another kind of phone card. To call the UK from France, dial 00 44 and then the UK number (omit the first 0 from the area code).

The Wishes fireworks show at Disneyland Park

Tourist info

And, if you are out and about in France, look for the local **Offices du Tourism and Syndicats d'Initiative** for maps, advice and info on the local sights and attractions. Most tourist attractions are open 10am–5pm, with one late opening day per week, but, surprisingly, many close on public holidays (although not in *Disneyland Resort Paris*).

Know before you go

As hard as we work to keep this guide as up to date and accurate as possible, there are always going to be things that change after our deadlines, or areas we can't cover fully in such a relatively small volume. But you can stay on the ball by using the internet as much as possible and there are a good number of websites that can help you.

First and foremost is the official *Disneyland Paris Resort* website, www.disneylandparis.com, with the opportunity to book online and save money, while by far the most comprehensive and useful of the 'unofficial' sites is www.dlp.info/Guide/, the English translation of a superb German fan site. This includes excellent sections on the resort's history, current shows and parades, hours of operation, rumours, downloads and newsletters, plus the latest practical advice, and a chat and discussion forum.

Another excellent fan site is

Top 10 'Hidden Secrets' of Disneyland Resort Paris

Look out for the many special 'extras' which may not be so obvious to the busy visitor. Here is our guide to the best:

1 La Tanière Du Dragon – the 'Dragon's Lair' under the Castle at the *Disneyland Park*, which many people miss.

2 Lighting effects – you can change the lights inside Studio 1 at the *Walt Disney Studios*, in front of Club Swankadero and in the Liki Tiki Lounge.

3 Take a phone call – pick up the phone next to Walt's bureau inside the Photo Shop on the corner of the *Disneyland Park*'s Town Square and listen for a message!

4 Get breezy – approach the giant fan at the exit to the Armageddon attraction in the Studios park; it works via a motion sensor.

5 Heavy rock – sit on the large stone underneath the suspended bridge in Adventure Isle (*Disneyland Park*) – it rocks from side to side!

6 Puppet parade – be outside 'it's a small world' on the hour for a fun parade of ride characters.

7 Take a ride – sit on the motorcycle outside the Café des Cascadeurs in the Studios and be startled by the sound effects!

8 Get a haircut – in Dapper Dan's, the period barber's shop on Main Street USA in the *Disneyland Park*.

9 Make it rain – stand under the Umbrellas de Cherbourg next to the Backlot Express restaurant in the Studios.

10 Make some music – try out the working keyboard in the back of the technician's van outside Rock 'n' Rollercoaster starring Aerosmith, again at the Studios.

A question of characters – where are they?

The biggest question on most visitors' lips (especially those with children!) is usually 'Where can we find the characters?' There are invariably some who leave frustrated because they simply miss out on this essential photo and autograph opportunity. Therefore, to give you a head start on your character hunting, here is a quick rundown of where you can usually meet Mickey and Co:

Disneyland Park: at the top of Main Street USA for the Main Street Park Opening at 9–9.30am (or 10–10.30am on later opening hours) every day; Meet Mickey just in front of the upper exit of the Liberty Arcade; at regular intervals in the Central Plaza area in front of the Castle; in the morning on the stage of Le Théâtre du Château; periodically outside Colonel Hathi's Pizza Outpost in Adventureland; from time to time outside 'it's a small world' in Fantasyland; at breakfast at Walt's – An American Restaurant or the Plaza Gardens Restaurant; at lunch in the Lucky Nugget Saloon and tea at the Plaza Gardens.

Walt Disney Studios Park: in the entrance courtyard in front of Studio 1 for the first hour of the day, and periodically thereafter; at Meet Mickey in Animation Courtyard; every now and then throughout Animation Courtyard itself; during the daily Disney Cinema Parade.

Disney Village: at one of the character meals which are served throughout the day at Café Mickey (7.30 and 9.30am for breakfast, noon–2.30pm for lunch and 3–11pm for dinner), and at Sunday brunch at The Steakhouse (midday–3pm).

Disneyland Hotel: at breakfast and dinner at the Inventions Restaurant.

All Disney Hotels (including Disney's Davy Crockett Ranch): in the lobby area at regular intervals throughout the morning.

For all character meals, you need to make a reservation either when you book your Disney package, through reception at your Disney hotel or in advance by phoning (from the UK) 00 33 1 60 45 60 45 (just 01 60 45 60 45 in France) up to 2 months in advance.

To check when and where to meet the characters in the parks, always call in at **City Hall** at the *Disneyland Park* or Guest Relations at the *Walt Disney Studios Park*.

www.dlrpmagic.com, while, for some of the best photos and news of the resort, visit the excellent www.photosmagique.com. Log into www.dlpfoodguide.com for the ultimate guide to dining Disney-style. Also, on the *Walt Disney World* website to which we contribute – www.disboards.com – is a special forum on *Disneyland Paris*, as part of their busy discussion boards and chat room. Who knows, we might 'see' you there! Other general tourist information websites are: http://uk.franceguide.com, http://english.pidf.com, www.parisinfo.com and www.paris.org.

Well, that should give you enough food for thought in the planning stage for now. Let's move on to another vital subject in your preparations, that of actually Getting There…

Let us plan your holiday ...

In conjunction with the *Brit's Guide* website – www.askdaisy.net/disneylandparis – our Personalised Itinerary Planner will help you get the very most out of your holiday. We will design an itinerary tailored to your individual plans for the parks and attractions of *Disneyland Resort Paris* and the immediate area.

You will receive the most comprehensive package of specialised holiday info anywhere, and it represents the secret to the most fun, in the most hassle-free way at Europe's No 1 tourist attraction. Just check out the full details on www.askdaisy.net/disneylandparis and we'll do the rest.

You must apply for the Planner at LEAST 21 days before you travel and you must know your ticket requirements in advance.

Key Contacts

Here are the principal contact numbers for all the main agencies at *Disneyland Resort Paris* (to call from the UK omit the first 0 and prefix 00 33 to the number, e.g. to call Seine-et-Marne Tourist Office, dial 00 33 1 60 39 60 39):

Airport Shuttle Bus (info only): 01 49 64 47 08
Annual Passport Hotline: 01 60 30 60 69
Billy Bob's Buffet: 01 60 45 70 79
Buffalo Bill's Wild West Show: 01 60 45 71 00
Café Mickey: 01 60 45 71 14
Disney Village: 01 60 30 20 20
Disney Village Tourist Office: 01 60 43 33 33
Disneyland Park First Aid centre: 01 64 74 23 03
Disneyland Park Lost Children: 01 64 74 24 00
Euro Disney SCA: 01 64 74 40 00
France Tourist Office, London: 09068 244123 (60p/min) or
    info.uk@franceguide.com
Golf Disneyland: 01 60 45 68 90
Guided Tours: 01 64 74 21 26
Hotel New York: 01 60 45 73 86
King Ludwig's Castle: 01 60 42 71 80
Lost and Found: 01 64 74 25 00
Mail Order Service: 01 64 74 44 30/44 86/48 88 (or by email at
    dlp.mail.order@disney.com)
Park Guest Relations: 01 60 30 60 30 (or by email at
    dlp.communication.visiteurs@disney.com)
Resort Restaurant Reservations (up to 2 months in advance): 01 60 45 60 45
Seine-et-Marne Tourist Office: 01 60 39 60 39 or cdt@tourisme77.fr
Sequoia Lodge Hotel: 01 60 45 51 00
Shareholders Info & Club: 01 64 74 56 30 (or by email at
    dlp.actionnaires@disney.com)
The Steakhouse: 01 60 45 70 45
UK bookings: 08705 030303
UK Bureau: 020 8222 1000

Write to Disneyland Paris Guest Relations at *Disneyland Resort Paris*, Communication Visiteurs, BP 100, 77777 Marne-la-Vallée, Cedex 4, France.

Most Disney hotels and restaurants can be reached on the general reservation numbers, but several also have their own direct numbers.

Getting There

(or, Trains, Planes and Automobiles, plus Coaches and Ferries!)

In many ways, your choice of when to go to *Disneyland Resort Paris* pales into insignificance compared to the issue of how you get there. The options for travel on what is, after all, just a relatively short journey, are almost as wide-ranging as the resort itself.

Obviously, your location in the UK plays a large part in deciding what is best for you. The Eurostar service may be a wonderful method of transport but is not ideal if you live in Newcastle or Bangor. Equally, going by coach and letting someone else do all the driving has a lot of appeal but it can seem a long way of doing things if you live in the South East (where Eurostar and Eurotunnel are quicker options). Flying is increasingly popular and affordable with the low-fare airlines, and the advantages are especially noticeable from regional airports like Newcastle, Aberdeen, Bristol and even Southampton.

So here is an outline of each of the main possibilities, along with their pros and cons.

By car

With the opening of the Channel Tunnel in 1994, the dream of quick, reliable transport to the Continent became a reality. A permanent link was established along with a whole new realm of Channel-hopping possibilities. Some 85 million people have used the longest undersea tunnel in the world – 50km (31 miles) in length, 39km (24 miles) of them under the sea itself – in the first 10 years of operation. In 2004 alone, 2.1 million cars, 63,000 coaches and 7.2 million Eurostar passengers travelled through the Channel Tunnel to France.

BRIT TIP: If you exceed the speed limit by more than 40kph (25mph), the French police have the power to take your driving licence immediately, so you won't be able to drive. For serious offences they can confiscate your car.

And, while it obviously opened in direct competition with cross-Channel ferry businesses, it actually served to increase quite significantly

Eurostar

© Disney

the total traffic between the UK and Europe. Not only did the day-tripping habit pick up (and the number of British-orientated supermarkets in the Calais vicinity), but driving holidays to France, Belgium, Holland, Spain, Germany and even Italy also received a major boost. So, just two years after the opening of the *Disneyland Resort Paris*, it stands to reason the tunnel would become a prime route in getting people there (in fact, one of the many reasons why Disney eventually settled on the Paris site was because of the forthcoming tunnel link).

The combination of the tunnel and the well-established ferry links from Dover, Newhaven and Portsmouth now provide a wealth of opportunity for routes into France by car and coach, and more people travel by car than any other mode of transport. France is also blessed with well-organised and relatively smooth-flowing motorways (certainly compared to our M25), many of which are toll-road autoroutes (*autoroutes des péages*). In 2005, the tolls amounted to just €18.20 one way to use this quickest and most convenient of routes (A26 from Calais, then A1, A104 and A4 – see maps below and opposite). Basically, it is 105km (65 miles) on

Autoroutes des Péages

Tickets are issued at the beginning of each of the paid motorway networks. Payments are then calculated on the distance you travel and must be paid on leaving the motorway. You pay at the *péages* (or toll gates) with either cash or credit card. For short journeys locally it is a good idea to keep some small change handy to avoid the hassle of using your credit card. Payments also vary according to your vehicle, with different price bands for cars, vans, cars with trailers, lorries and motorbikes.

the A26, 153km (95 miles) on the A1, 25.6km (16 miles) on the A104 and then another 11.5km (7 miles) on the A4 before the turn off (Exit 14) for 'Les Parcs Disneyland'.

From Calais ferry port, you are directed straight on to the A26 (via the E15 – follow the clear signs for Paris, Reims), while from the Channel Tunnel, you have a short 6km (31/2 mile) stretch south-west on the A16 (follow the signs for Calais) before picking up the A26.

It is advisable to navigate by the directional signs rather than the route numbers, hence from Calais

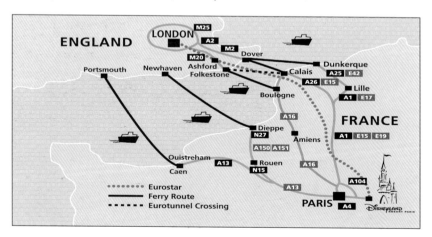

BRIT TIP: Watch out for the A26 junction with the A1, as the signposting is not terribly clear here and it is easy to miss. The motorway turn-off signs are all in white (and set off to the right-hand side) and you need to follow the big blue overhead destination signs for Paris.

on the A26, initially follow the signs for Saint-Omer, Arras, Reims, Paris; at the junctions with the A1, follow signs for Paris, Arras Est; immediately after Charles de Gaulle Airport, follow signs for Bordeaux, Nantes, Lyon, Marne-la-Vallée, Paris Est, Bobigny; once on the A104, look for Lyon, Meaux, Marne-la-Vallée and 'Les Parcs Disneyland'; at the junction with the A4, follow signs for Meaux, Reims.

The only other area to watch out for is switching from the A1 to the A104 at Charles de Gaulle Airport,

although there is a sign for 'Les Parcs Disneyland' just before and after the airport, directing you on to the A104. Immediately after the airport, the autoroute splits, and you need to be in the right-hand lanes for Marne-la-Vallée; it then splits again, and the right two lanes bring you on to the A104 heading south (see map below).

BRIT TIP: Although *Disneyland Resort Paris* is officially located in Marne-la-Vallée, the whole area along the A4 here is also designated Marne-la-Vallée, hence it is easy to get sidetracked. Once on the A104, follow the signs for 'Les Parcs Disneyland'.

It should take you a shade under three hours to drive from Calais, with the speed limit up to 130kph (80mph) on the autoroutes. You can save the toll money by taking the Routes Nationales (or N-roads), but

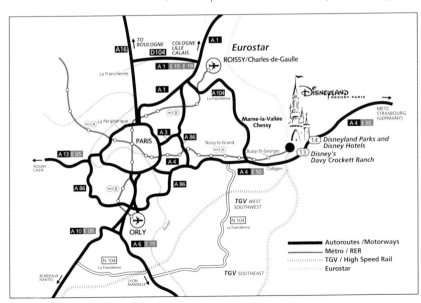

BRIT TIP: The autoroute speed limit is 130kph (80mph), but this drops to 110kph (68mph) when it is wet. It is 110kph (68mph) on non-toll motorways and 90kph (56mph) on other roads, 80kph (50mph) when wet, and 50kph (30mph) in towns.

that would add nearly an hour to your journey. The toll road system in France is split up into eight privately owned networks, but the one from Calais to Marne-la-Vallée is all under the control of SANEF (www.sanef.com). Check out www.autoroutes.fr for more details on your journey and a handy route planner, while the Eurotunnel website www.eurotunnel.com has some helpful route advice as well (see page 51). Another useful site is www.multimap.co.uk.

The first toll booths you come to on the A26 are after about 61km (38 miles) between Exits 4 and 5, and here you simply collect a ticket from the machine, which records the point at which you join the A-route system, and then you pay at the toll booths just north of Charles de Gaulle Airport (just after Exit 7). These are the only tolls you will pay on the direct Calais–Marne-la-Vallée route.

From the ferry port at Boulogne, follow the 'Toutes Directions' signs and these quickly bring you on to the A16 via a new stretch of dual carriageway. Once on the A16, head south for 200km (125 miles) until it becomes the N1, then follow N1 around until it hits the junction with D104 (after about 7.5km). Take D104 (La Francilienne) for 16km (10 miles) to the A1 just north of the airport. Go south on the A1 and follow the same directions as above (A104–A4). Tolls will be about €16.30 and the journey will take around 2½ hours.

If you take the Portsmouth–Caen ferry route, your journey will be around 265km (164 miles) via the A13, the Paris *périphérique* and the A4, and the tolls will be €15.90.

Once in the Marne-la-Vallée area, your main route to and from the Theme Parks is likely to be the A4, a busy stretch of motorway at peak periods (especially into Paris itself) but otherwise an easy-to-use arterial. There are no toll booths along this section at all, hence you can use the A4 as frequently as you like at no extra cost. Once you turn off at Exit 14 for the Theme Parks, everything is well signposted to the hotels and main car parks. A huge, ring road encompassing the whole resort (plus Val d'Europe), called the Boulevard de l'Europe, makes an interesting drive as you can get some unusual glimpses of the Theme Parks from it.

Eurostar

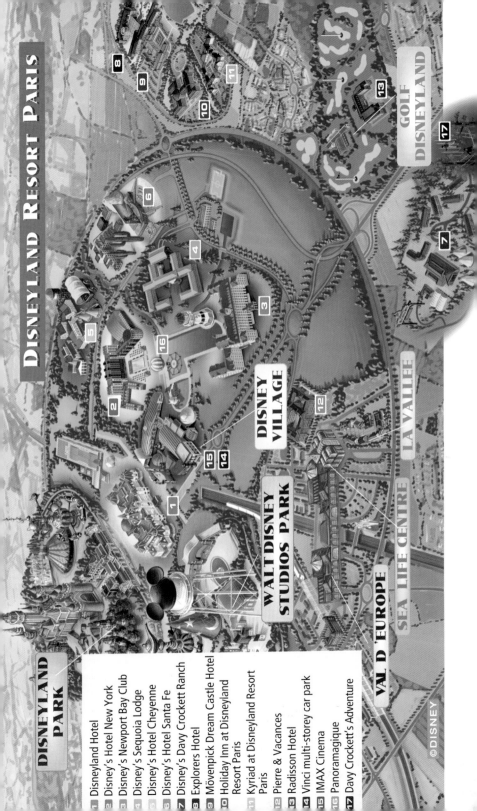

DISNEYLAND RESORT PARIS

DISNEYLAND PARK

DISNEY VILLAGE

WALT DISNEY STUDIOS PARK

GOLF DISNEYLAND

SEA LIFE CENTRE

VAL D'EUROPE

LA VALLÉE

1 Disneyland Hotel
2 Disney's Hotel New York
3 Disney's Newport Bay Club
4 Disney's Sequoia Lodge
5 Disney's Hotel Cheyenne
6 Disney's Hotel Santa Fe
7 Disney's Davy Crockett Ranch
8 Explorers Hotel
9 Mövenpick Dream Castle Hotel
10 Holiday Inn at Disneyland Resort Paris
11 Kyriad at Disneyland Resort Paris
12 Pierre & Vacances
13 Radisson Hotel
14 Vinci multi-storey car park
15 IMAX Cinema
16 Panoramagique
17 Davy Crockett's Adventure

©DISNEY

Driving in France

There are no major differences in the traffic rules in France (other than driving on the right-hand side!), but driving with dipped headlights is compulsory in poor visibility – so don't leave home without a pair of headlight beam adjusters. It is also advisable to take a set of spare bulbs, while a red hazard warning triangle is compulsory (for vans and cars with trailers) in case of a breakdown. You should take your vehicle registration document and insurance certificate, as well as your driving licence (it is a legal requirement to have it with you whenever you are behind the wheel). Check with your insurance company to ensure you have full cover while driving in France. Green cards are no longer required, but some insurance companies issue them anyway as they are a sure way of convincing local police you are properly insured. Road signs are pretty much universal, but additional signs or warnings to watch for are:

Allumez vos phares/feux	Switch on your lights
Attention au feu	Fire hazard
Attention travaux	Beware roadworks
Cedée le passage	Give way
Chaussée déformée	Uneven road surface
Essence sans plomb	Unleaded petrol
Fin d'interdiction de stationner	End of prohibited parking
Gazole	Diesel
Interdit aux piétons	Forbidden to pedestrians
Rappel	Remember (often on speed limit signs)
Route barrée	Road closed
Sens unique	One way
Sens interdit	No entry
Supercarburant	Lead replacement petrol
Verglas	Black ice

Children under 10 are forbidden to travel in the front seat. On-the-spot fines, or deposits (in cash – you should also get an official receipt), can be demanded for not wearing seat belts (compulsory front AND back), drink-driving, driving on a provisional licence and speeding offences (and French police are pretty hot on the latter). The use of mobile phones while driving is strictly prohibited.

Parking and rest zones are situated every 10–20km (6–12 miles) on motorways, with 24-hour petrol stations about every 40km (25 miles). If you break down, pull up on the right, put on your hazard lights and place a red warning triangle 30m (33yds) behind your vehicle (compulsory for vans and cars with trailers). Emergency telephones (orange) are usually every 2km (just over a mile) apart on motorways. If

BRIT TIP: If a French driver flashes his lights at you, it means he intends to go first, NOT that he is giving you right of way.

you break down and can't leave your vehicle, there are regular road patrols on all autoroutes. In addition, you must not park on yellow kerbs.

French motorway service areas (or *aires*) are generally 24-hour operations and offer a combination of facilities way beyond anything in the UK in terms of quality. There are two types of *aire*: one has full fuel, catering and shopping facilities, while the other is a picnic area with toilets. These are often pretty places to stop – but bring your own toilet paper (for some reason, it is not a standard French provision)! Both AA and RAC members can take advantage of their organisation's European Breakdown Assistance service, which is highly valuable when travelling on the Continent. Look up www.theaa.com (tel 0870 600 0371) or www.rac.co.uk (tel 08705 722 722).

> BRIT TIP: Buying petrol in French motorway service stations is as exorbitant as the equivalent in the UK. You can save 12–15% by filling up at the nearest hypermarket (*hypermarché*) in Calais or Le Havre. Savings on diesel can be even greater.

For **maps**, the AA's France Series 7 (£3.99) covers the full route from Calais to Marne-la-Vallée, while you would need 2 and 7 to cover the journey from Caen. Online, the website www.viamichelin.co.uk also offers some valuable maps and info. All autoroutes have an information radio station. In northern France, English-language bulletins are on 107.7FM on the hour and half-hour.

By ferry

Of course, if you are taking the car, you need to decide which method of cross-Channel travel you prefer, the various ferry services from one of three south coast ports, or the Eurotunnel service from Folkestone. If you opt for the more traditional ferry route, you can go from Dover, Portsmouth and Newhaven. Here's how they break down.

Dover
To start with, Dover is an easy port to get to by road, either straight down the M2/A2 in north Kent or (my preferred route) via the M20/A20, both of which come off the M25 London orbital. It is about an hour-and-three-quarters drive from central London (given a relatively traffic-free run) and you need to head to the Eastern Docks for the main ferry operators, or the Western Docks for the hoverport, off Union Street, which caters for all Hoverspeed sailings. Dover is a thoroughly modern, well-organised port and should get you aboard your ferry with the minimum of fuss.

The main passenger terminal includes a bureau de change, bank and cashpoint, an AA shop, a cafe and newsagent, information desks, phones, toilets and baby-change facilities. Also, once you have driven into the terminal area itself, there are two mini food villages offering another cafe, a Burger King, a bar, bureau de change and cashpoint, a shop, plus toilets, baby-change facilities and telephones. You should arrive at least 30 minutes before your sailing time and have passports ready as you drive in.

If you have booked in advance (which is highly advisable), you proceed straight through to your ferry operator's check-in. If you haven't got a ticket, you can park up in the short-stay parking area at the main entrance to the passenger

At the front gates

terminal and buy one from the Travel Centre (6am–9pm). Alternatively, you can now pass straight to check-in and purchase a ticket there. There are NO services by any operator on Christmas Day.

Five main companies operate from this busy cross-Channel hub:

P&O Ferries is Dover's biggest and most sophisticated operator, with up to 25 crossings to Calais a day, 364 days a year. They operate some of the newest and biggest ships on this route and, if you haven't travelled on a cross-Channel ferry for a while, you will probably be pleasantly surprised by the comfort and quality on offer these days. The crossing time from Dover is 75–90 minutes,

P&O *Pride of Dover*

although you mustn't forget to put your watches forward an hour on arrival in France.

Once through the Eastern Docks' main reception area, follow the signs for P&O Ferries, which will take you to the check-in booths (where you will usually need to show your passports – all British subjects MUST have a full, valid 10-year passport that will not expire for at least 3 months after you return. Non-British subjects should check their visa requirements in advance). At check-in, you are allocated a numbered embarkation lane to proceed to, from where you will be directed on to the ferry when it is ready to board. While waiting here, you can take advantage of the food villages and facilities.

BRIT TIP: Visit their website www.poferries.com to take advantage of their 'Best Fare Search', which offers cheaper fares the earlier you book.

Once settled aboard, you have a good choice of bars, shops, lounges and cafes in which to while away the time. All P&O Ferries' ships now include an International Food Court (usually the busiest area on board, especially just after embarkation), a First Base fast-food counter, the Harbour Coffee Company, Silverstones Sports Bar and a shop selling sweets and other snacks. Langan's Brasserie offers a more upmarket choice for a meal in mid-Channel and, if you have opted for Club Plus when you booked, you also get the benefit of the Club Lounge and its personalised service, as well as priority embarkation and unloading at the other end. (NB: P&O have discontinued their ferry routes from Portsmouth to Le Havre, so this is now their main

Join the Club

P&O Ferries offers three distinct extra services, which can be pre-booked or, in the case of the **Club Lounge**, booked on board (although it then costs more). The Club Lounge is an exclusive quiet lounge, complete with comfy leather armchairs, where you are greeted with a complimentary glass of champagne and offered tea and coffee, biscuits, fruit and newspapers by its own waiter/waitress service. There is also a business area where laptops can be used.

The **Priorité** service is a pre-booked priority loading system, which allows you to be embarked early and unloaded first, which is highly worthwhile when speed is of the essence. The two can then be combined in a **Club Plus** service, which provides use of the Club Lounge and the priority loading/unloading as well. At the time of writing, the prices were: £10/person each way for the Club Lounge, if booked in advance (£12 if booked on board); £12/vehicle each way for Priorité; if opting for Club Plus, £10/person each way plus £6/vehicle. For two people, Club Plus would be £46 return.

at up to 50% off UK high-street prices. Top brand designer sunglasses at up to 20% cheaper include Gucci, Prada, Ray Ban and Police. Wines start from just £10 for six bottles, and an extensive range of spirits is available at 2 litres for £20.

BRIT TIP: You can save money on P&O Ferries by booking a night crossing. Some on-board services are closed (there is no Club Lounge and Langan's Brasserie, for example) but prices are reduced for these 'Nite Lites' crossings.

For more info, visit their website www.poferries.com (there is an extra discount for booking online) or call 08705 980333.

SeaFrance is the only French ferry operator on the Dover–Calais route, offering 15 daily return crossings, 364 days of the year. In early 2005, it launched its latest super-ferry, the *SeaFrance Berlioz*. Sister ship to the award-winning *SeaFrance Rodin*, both offer crossings in just 70 minutes and provide 10 of the daily crossings, while the other five are handled by the older ships *Cezanne* and *Renoir*.

crossing for the whole of the UK's south coast.)

For the young ones, there are new children's entertainers on board the five Dover–Calais ferries for the school holidays, along with soft play areas. And provisions for the very youngest members of the family now extends to free Heinz baby food. There is also a good video games centre, the Megadrome, to keep older children amused.

For shoppers, some of the biggest savings are available on fragrances,

Davy Crockett Ranch

© Disney

Across the fleet, SeaFrance provides a decent range of restaurants and onboard activities. Le Relais, a self-service restaurant, Le Parisien, a French café, and Le Pub are on every ship, while *Rodin* and *Berlioz* also offer a fine-dining restaurant, Le Brasserie, serving gourmet French cuisine. All ships have a well-stocked shop, with major discounts on high-street prices, and at least one major lounge area. The two super-ferries add extra-smart lounge facilities, a good children's play area and video arcade.

Prices fluctuate depending on the month of travel and, again, early booking is strongly advised, with discounts often available. In October 2005, SeaFrance launched a new website, which displays prices next to each crossing, so that passengers can see which one will suit them best. For more info, visit www.seafrance.com or call 08705 711711.

Norfolkline provides an alternative to the occasionally hectic Calais crossings, with up to 10 sailings a day to Dunkerque, just over 40km (25 miles) further along the French coast from Calais. The crossing time is a slightly long (by Calais standards) 2 hours but the Dunkerque port facilities are well run, usually uncongested and easy to negotiate. In late 2005, Norfolkline was also in the process of introducing three new, modern ferries, each of 34,500 tons, capable of trimming the journey time to 110 minutes and adding significantly to the onboard facilities. They include relaxation areas with massage chairs, a separate VIP lounge, gaming areas, cinema, two playrooms for children, a full-service restaurant, fast-food restaurant and bistro. Freight drivers also have a separate restaurant and relaxation area.

For the tourist market, Norfolkline continues to focus on the needs of the motorist by carrying only cars, caravans and trailers, motorhomes and motorcycles, not coaches and foot passengers. The gift shop (at French duty-paid prices) offers fairly standard fare but is worth a visit, especially on your return trip, to grab a last-minute bargain or two.

Norfolkline advises checking in 1–2 hours before your departure time. From Dunkerque, Marne-la-Vallée is just over 300km (186 miles) away – follow the signs for the A16, then take the E42 to the A25 all the way to Lille and pick up the A1 to Paris. For more info, visit www.norfolkline.com or call 0870 870 1020.

SpeedFerries is the new kid on the block in Dover. The company has established a new style of ferry operation, similar to the low-cost airlines, with year-round direct service to Boulogne rather than Calais. The earlier you book, the cheaper the fare, which increases as a sailing fills up. Price is also independent of the length of stay. Lead-in price in autumn 2005 was

BRIT TIP: With a new direct link to the motorway A16 from the port of Boulogne, this now offers the fastest road link to Paris. The history-rich town of Boulogne also makes a good stopping point for its 13th-century Old Town and the modern National Sea Centre, plus an array of outstanding seafood restaurants. The town is only a few minutes' walk from the port, but has limited parking so it is better to park and walk in. Visit www.tourisme-boulognesurmer.com.

Thank you ferry much

We asked Britain's leading cruise and ferry website, **Seaview** (**www.seaview.co.uk**), to pass on their top tips for getting the most out of your cross-Channel journey – at the best price. Here's what they said:

Don't leave your booking until the last minute. Prices rarely improve by waiting.

Don't try to pull a fast one by buying a day-trip ticket when you plan to stay longer. Ferry operators have a knack of finding out and take a very dim view.

Most ferry companies make it easy to book online and offer discounts for doing so.

If you book online, keep the confirmation email with its unique reference number. Short crossings are often ticketless, so a booking reference is vital. And look after it – you'll have to produce it at the ferry terminal.

Read the reservation details carefully – twice! Mistakes do happen.

Make sure you give the correct details when booking, such as names as they appear in passports, exact length of car, etc. It can save vital minutes at check-in.

If there is a person with disabilities in your party, enquire about priority on-and-off arrangements.

Try to book a sailing time that you can make without having to dash, but don't panic if you miss it. Nowadays, there's usually room on the next sailing. If you are ahead of schedule, there's a chance you'll be put on an earlier sailing.

If you are taking your dog on holiday, the train is best. Eurotunnel has areas for dogs to excuse themselves before travelling and, unlike the ferry, they have the pleasure of their owners' company on the journey.

If you sail with SeaFrance, go for the new *Berlioz* or virtually new *Rodin*, by far the best ships in the fleet.

If you prefer P&O Ferries and can afford the extra, treat yourself to the Club Lounge. It's comfortable, usually quiet and soft drinks, coffee and tea, etc are complimentary. And maybe pamper yourself with a visit for a meal at Langan's Brasserie.

Be aware that, should an emergency arise, Apex bargain tickets are non-refundable, while full-price tickets usually are.

Remember you lose an hour on arrival in France, so take this into account when you are considering sailing times.

an eye-catching £25 one-way for a standard car and up to five passengers. The super-fast catamaran *SpeedOne* makes the journey in just 50 minutes, with five return trips a day. It is also designed only for cars (and small vans and motorhomes); there are no foot passengers, coaches or trucks.

The onboard experience is surprisingly stylish, with spacious air-conditioned lounges, as well as a cafeteria, coffee and wine bar, sundeck, children's play area, video arcade and a shop. There is even a drive-in SpeedShop at Boulogne which you can visit for all your duty-free shopping. To book, visit www.speedferries.com or call 0872 200570 (there is a £10 phone supplement, so the internet is cheaper). On returning to Boulogne, simply follow the signs to Boulogne Port (not the town itself).

Hoverspeed is the fifth main Dover operator, with a couple of significant advantages over the others. Hoverspeed operates two 81m (296ft) Seacat fast ferries, carrying up to 150 vehicles and 640 passengers, from their own dedicated terminal, and runs up to 10 return trips a day in just under an hour each way. With no freight or coach traffic, it's a more streamlined operation and, with a check-in time of just 30 minutes before departure, there are no lengthy queues and no berthing problems at Calais.

You can grab a snack at Upper Crust or Caffe Ritazza before boarding, while Hoverspeed also offers an excellent shopping service either on board, at the company's own dedicated store in Calais or even in advance on their website. Unlike the ferries, the Seacat is not a vessel loaded with restaurants, shops, etc. There is still space to wander around and some open deck space at the back, but it gives more of an airline-type service, with airline seats (albeit with more leg room!) and cabin crew. You can also upgrade (at £15 a head) to first class, which has

Legend of the Lion King at Videopolis

© Disney

its own pre-departure lounge in Dover and Calais, a private on-board seating area with at-seat service, complimentary breakfast, lunch or dinner served on board according to the time of departure, priority loading and unloading, complimentary newspaper and refreshments. To book, call Hoverspeed on 0870 240 8070 or visit www.hoverspeed.com.

Newhaven

Between Brighton and Eastbourne on the Sussex coast is this small but busy ferry port featuring the French company **Transmanche Ferries**, the only ferry service on the Newhaven–Dieppe route all year round. Newhaven is on the A259 coast road, but is best reached (from London) via the M23, A23, A27 (at Brighton) and A26. Transmanche is due to have two new ferries in 2006, with all modern on-board amenities, covering the journey in 4 hours, with up to three crossings per day. You can add a cabin to your booking, for £14 during the day or £20 on night crossings, or just opt to stay in the lounge or cafeterias. Both ships have a shop and a video lounge, while one of them also has a full-service restaurant. To book, call Transmanche on 0800 917 1201 or visit www.transmancheferries.com.

From Dieppe, it is 257km (160 miles) to *Disneyland Resort Paris*; follow the N27, A151, A150 and N15 before picking up the A13 and the route from Caen.

Portsmouth

For the closest port to Paris, head for Caen with **Brittany Ferries**. The French capital is little more than 2 hours from the Normandy port (see map on page 38) and Portsmouth is a lot more accessible from the Midlands and West Country than Dover or Newhaven. The down side is that it is a much longer journey. Brittany's new fast-ferry service can do the crossing in 3½ hours, but their older classic ferry offers two journey times, around 5½ hours on day sailings and 7 at night. However, the overnight crossings do have an advantage in that you arrive in France at 7.15am, and can be in the heart of the Disney magic by 10am. There are up to four return sailings a day (one a day with the fast ferry, which operates from mid-March to mid-November), leaving Portsmouth at 7am (fast ferry), 8.45am, 3.15pm and 11.15pm, and the port facilities are all new and well organised.

> BRIT TIP: There is a Carrefour hypermarket in Caen and also one in Herrouville, not far from Ouistreham, if you need to do some last-minute shopping before your return trip home.

Portsmouth itself is also served by excellent road links, with the port situated at the base of the M275 with its own exit on to the motorway. It is actually closer to London than either Dover or the Channel Tunnel and is arguably Britain's best-connected ferry port. The new Newbury bypass on the A34 has also cut down the journey time from the

Midlands, West and North. The Caen terminal is located at Ouistreham, the newest ferry port on the Channel, 15km (9 miles) to the north of Caen (open 6.30am–11pm), and is well designed to provide a smooth return journey, with easy access and good facilities. To reach Paris, simply follow signs to Caen along the D514 and D515, then pick up the city ring road (N814) and go south-east for 3.5km until you hit the A13. Then it is autoroute all the way to Paris, some 210km (131 miles), with €15.90 in tolls. Stay on the Paris *périphérique* and you will skirt the city to the south until you pick up the A4 to *Disneyland Resort Paris*. On the return to Caen/Ouistreham, follow the signs for 'Car Ferry'.

For websites to help you with ferry crossings and road access after you arrive, the following are helpful, starting with the essential www.seaview.co.uk. Then there's www.ferrybooker.com (with lots of useful info on driving in France, the ports and working out your route), while www.doverport.com and www.portsmouth-port.co.uk give you the full story of these two main UK ferry ports. When it comes to driving, www.autoroutes.fr, www.viamichelin.com and www.sytadin.tm.fr/ (for Paris traffic reports) are extremely useful and worth checking in advance.

View from Panoramagique

By Eurotunnel

Need to get to Calais fast, conveniently and with a choice of services 24 hours a day? Well, Eurotunnel is the answer. This versatile shuttle service from Folkestone in Kent has up to four departures an hour at peak times, with the crossing time just 35 minutes. In fact, from the time of loading to driving off at the other end can take just 45 minutes, making easily the quickest vehicle crossing time of any cross-Channel service. Finding Eurotunnel also couldn't be easier as the terminal is just off Junction 11A on the M20, about a 45-minute drive from its intersection with the M25, and is well signposted.

BRIT TIP: For the latest travel, weather and road news for the area, call Eurotunnel's information line on 0800 096 9992.

After arriving at the Eurotunnel terminal, proceed straight to check-in and quote your booking reference number. You can just arrive on spec, but you will be allocated a space on the next available shuttle, and may have to wait a while. It will also usually be more expensive than booking in advance. In busy periods, a booking is highly advisable to avoid a wait of more than an hour. You are requested to arrive at least 35 minutes before your booked departure time. You can stop off in their extremely smart and spacious main terminal building, grab a bite to eat and do a bit of pre-trip shopping. Once checked in, you drive through both British and French passport controls (there are no checks on arrival, as with the ferry). Please note that LPG vehicles are NOT allowed to travel on Eurotunnel.

BRIT TIP: Don't forget the documentation for your vehicle, insurance and any breakdown cover you have for the journey.

For an even quicker and smoother passage, travel **FlexiPlus** and benefit from a priority lane at check-in and a guaranteed space on the next available shuttle. There is an exclusive lounge (open 6am–10pm) to allow you to freshen up, enjoy a light meal, complimentary tea, coffee and newspapers, and use the phone/fax. There is even a take-away free snack service. The extra speed, convenience and service which this provides is highly worthwhile, especially on a short trip.

For direct access to the lounge, go straight to passport control, then follow the FlexiPlus signs (in the UK, keep to the right hand lane, in France, keep to the left). Stay in the respective lane until you reach the Eurotunnel FlexiPlus barrier, then use the token given to you at check-in to gain access to car parking for the lounge. You will also be given a paper hanger at check-in, which you need to display on your mirror. From the lounge, you will be given priority boarding on the next available shuttle.

Once you're ready to board, you just drive straight on to the shuttle where you stay in your car. You can get out to stretch your legs in the carriage (and there are toilets usually in every third carriage). On arriving at the other end, you drive off (in Calais/Coquelles) practically straight on to the A16 autoroute. From there, you head for the A26 (sign-posted initially to Calais, and then to Saint-Omer, Arras, Reims and Paris) before picking up the A1 at Arras (see map on page 39).

On the return journey, you come

off the A16 at Junction 13 (look for the signs for *Tunnel Sous La Manche*). If you have time to spare here, you can visit the huge **Cité Europe** shopping mall, which has some 200 shops and offers the usual great deals on things like wine, beer, spirits and food, plus clothing at stores such as Etam, Naf Naf, H&M, Sergio Tacchini, Zara and Quiksilver, as well as other well-known chains such as Footlocker, Toys R Us and Pier Import.

> BRIT TIP: Check out www.day-tripper.net for more details on Cité Europe, the bargains to be had and an excellent map of the area.

All in all, the Eurotunnel operation really is as simple as it sounds, and the ease with which you are suddenly off and running in France comes as quite a surprise the first time, so don't forget to drive on the right! It is also a relatively cheap option, with Short Stay Saver fares (2–5 days) from £78 per car (at 2005 prices) and Standard Fares (more than 5 days) from £98. A 5-Day FlexiPlus costs £149 each way and a standard FlexiPlus £199 each way

> BRIT TIP: An excellent route-planning facility can be found at the website www.eurotunnel.com. Just type in your route details from your home and you get easy-to-follow instructions to your destination. It even provides the total cost of the tolls en route. Click on 'Passenger Travel' and then 'Travelling Abroad'.

(you can also 'mix and match' FlexiPlus and Standard fares).

The other great benefit of Eurotunnel v The Ferries (apart from it suiting more independent-minded travellers) is the fact that the shuttle service is never affected by the weather, and you are certainly not likely to get seasick on their train! For more info, visit www.eurotunnel.com or call 08705 353535.

By Rail – Eurostar

The fastest direct route from London to Paris these days is via the smooth Eurostar operation from London's Waterloo station (and Ashford International in Kent) to Gare du Nord in the French capital or, even better and highly recommended, direct to Marne-la-Vallée itself (which is much quicker than flying). This is literally the fast-track service to *Disneyland Resort Paris* (2 hours 50 minutes from London to Mickey!), a high-speed train link in great comfort, style – and massive convenience.

> BRIT TIP: If you haven't already bought your RER ticket to get from Gare du Nord to Marne-la-Vallée (which you can do at any Eurostar station), avoid the often-crowded main ticket offices on the Paris station concourse. Instead, wait until you reach the last, smaller ticket office just before the entrance to the (Green) Line D of the RER as there is rarely much of a queue here.

Put aside any preconceptions (and real misgivings) of the British rail system, because this is how modern rail travel really *should* be. You are

BRIT TIP: We recommend changing RER trains at Châtelet Les Halles, as you simply need to switch platforms rather than go up and down a potentially confusing set of escalators – the RER signposting takes a bit of getting used to.

guaranteed a seat (no mean feat for some regional rail services), the trains are clean and comfortable and their time-keeping is second to none in the UK (okay, that latter is not saying a lot, but Eurostar really does have an excellent punctuality record). The opening of the first section of the new high-speed rail link trimmed 20 minutes off the rather pedestrian journey from London to the tunnel itself, while the whizz through northern France remains a breathtaking experience. The second part of the high-speed line is due to open in **2007**, when Eurostar's home station will move to London St Pancras and the journey will be even shorter.

Add to this the excellence of all the station terminal facilities – at Waterloo, Ashford, Gare du Nord and Marne-la-Vallée – and you have an operation of the highest order and user-friendliness. For anyone living within 2 hours' drive of Ashford International, this is an extremely worthwhile alternative to Waterloo as the journey time is barely 2 hours to Paris or Marne-la-Vallée and the ease and efficiency with which you can park at the station and walk across to catch your train makes for a hassle-free journey, especially with children.

Eurostar operates a daily service direct to Marne-la-Vallée, departing Waterloo at 9.39am and Ashford at 10.31, arriving in the heart of the Disney magic at 1.29pm. There are also up to 16 services a day to Paris's Gare du Nord station, as well as direct services to Lille, Brussels, Avignon and the French Alps. Connections are also possible to more than 100 destinations in France, Belgium and Holland (NB: there are no Eurostar services at all on Christmas Day. Sunday train times also vary slightly – consult www.eurostar.com for the latest timetables).

If you choose the Gare du Nord route (or are unable to take advantage of the Disney direct service), you should find it relatively

Geysers in snow at Frontierland

© Disney

Rainforest Café at Disney Village

© Disney

RER-ing to go

Using the RER system to get to and from *Disneyland Resort Paris* is a doddle. This largely overground train link takes about 35–40 minutes to get from the resort into central Paris and runs until after midnight every night. While the trains may not be the cleanest (the graffiti menace has been here with a vengeance!), they run at regular intervals every hour and scrupulously to time. The RER goes underground through central Paris, where it links up with the **Métro** underground system. You do not need to use the Métro – or the well-organised bus system, which links with both – unless you are on a serious sight-seeing tour of the city.

    Marne-la-Vallée is at the end of the (Red) Line A4, which runs basically east–west through Paris. Gare du Nord is at a junction of the (Green) Line D which runs largely north to south and (Blue) Line B, which bisects the city from north-east to south-west, and has the **Charles de Gaulle Airport** at the end of the B3 link (north-east). **Orly Airport** is on a special branch line – the Orlyval – connecting to the Antony station on the (Blue) Line B4.

easy to transfer to Marne-la-Vallée via the RER train link on Line D (although the trains are seriously crowded in the rush hour). Just follow the (Green) signs to Melun. From Gare du Nord, you change trains at Châtelet Les Halles to switch from Line D to Line A for Marne-la-Vallée.

    Another alternative (and a worthwhile tip if you miss the direct service) is to take one of the Eurostar trains to **Lille** and change there for a TGV train to Marne-la-Vallée (about 65 minutes). You do not even have to change platforms at Lille, just wait (usually no more than half an hour) for the French high-speed train and you're off straight to the heart of the Magic once more.

    Of course, the high-speed nature and regularity of the Eurostar service also means you can opt for just a **day trip** to *Disneyland Resort Paris*. Taking the 5.34am from London Waterloo would put you in Paris by 9.23am. The direct return service is at 6.43pm, arriving back in Ashord at 7.37pm and Waterloo at 8.27pm, but if that does not suit you, the last train from Paris to London is usually around 9pm, which means you could still have until 7.30pm in the Theme Parks before leaving.

Champs Elysées

Ticket types: With the Eurostar service to Paris and Lille (or any of their other regular destinations), you have the choice of three classes (revamped in September 2005), **Standard**, **Leisure Select** or **Business Premier**. If you are used to your local train service, Standard will feel like travelling first class (the individual seats are comfortable with decent elbow room, carriages are roomy and there is easy access to the two buffet cars), while Leisure Select and Business Premier offer a genuine high-quality service.

BRIT TIP: A special fare applies for both wheelchair users and a travelling companion on Eurostar – priced at the lowest available Standard class fare – and there are toilets and an area adapted especially for them in Leisure Select or Business Premier. Blind people travelling with companions also benefit from the same deal.

Leisure Select fares start from £139 return and offer a 3-course meal at your (extra-width, reclining) seat and complimentary newspapers and magazines. There is plenty of space if you need to work en route (or keep the kids amused with board games, etc), and uniformed staff are on hand. Baby-changing facilities and bottle-warming is available, along with activity packs for children if you ask at the terminals. Plenty of ramps, passenger conveyors and lifts are provided as well.

On the direct Waterloo–Ashford–Marne-la-Vallée route, Standard fares start from £59 return for adults and £50 for children under 12. Leisure Select fares start from £139 and £80 (children under 4 travel free

without an assigned seat). There are always two buffet cars per train and a smattering of Disney fun to whet your appetite, with Disney Cast Members on board to assist with hotel arrangements and provide some entertainment for the children and (occasionally) a character welcome at Marne-la-Vallée to get your visit off to a flying start.

Business Premier, as you would expect, is the most expensive and affords complete flexibility for travel any day of the week from London to Paris, as well as other perks like a 10-minute check-in and exclusive lounge access. However, if you are interested solely in getting to *Disneyland Resort Paris*, you would be better choosing the Leisure Select or Standard fares. With the London–Paris Leisure variety, all trips (except the Weekend Day Return) must include a Saturday night stay. But there is NO stay-away condition if tickets are booked more than 21 days in advance.

Eurostar fares compare extremely favourably with airline prices (even the low-cost carriers) and, for the extra convenience of arriving right in the heart of the Disney fun, they take some beating.

BRIT TIP: It is possible to travel one way in Leisure Select and the other in Standard. It is definitely worth travelling in Leisure Select on the way home to give yourself room to wind down after all that exhausting fun!

Eurostar services: At the main Eurostar **terminals**, you should find everything efficient and easy to use. At London's **Waterloo** mainline station, the Eurostar services operate from the lower level at the front of the concourse. Here you will find their purpose-built facilities offer a good range of shops, cafes, bars, currency exchange and a left luggage area. At **Ashford International**, the main concourse offers a pleasant cafe, plus shops, currency exchange and left luggage, while passing into the departure lounge gives you more chances to grab a drink or bite to eat, another shop and currency exchange, plus a Eurostar information desk. The multi-storey car park here holds 2,000 cars and parking is £9.50 a day (an alternative, open-air car park is available nearby at half the price, although it involves about a 100m/100yd walk to the station).

If you are returning from **Gare du Nord**, the Eurostar service is upstairs on the first level (it's surprising how many people don't notice this when they arrive), where there is again a good range of cafes and shops once you pass into the departure area. You have to check in at least 30 minutes before your departure to allow plenty of time for security screening.

BRIT TIP: At Ashford International, if you go through to the second cafe as you enter the departure lounge you will find less congestion there.

Marne-la-Vallée is the least exciting of the main Eurostar terminals (but then it can afford to be with its situation). You arrive at the lowest level of the station and take the escalator or lift up to the main concourse. If you are heading straight for the Theme Parks, there should be a Disney Cast Member (or even a character or two!) to direct you to the nearest exit. If you are heading for your hotel first, go out of the main doors straight ahead of you, and the bus stop for all the

Disney hotels (except *Disney's Davy Crockett Ranch*, which has no bus service) and those of the four Selected Hotels (the Explorers, Movenpick Dream Castle, Holiday Inn and Kyriad) are immediately in front of the station.

BRIT TIP: To find the *Disney Express* baggage service office at Waterloo, turn right immediately after check-in and it is located by escalator 23A.

The Eurostar service includes the considerable bonus of the **Disney Express** baggage arrangement, which enables you to go straight to the Theme Parks on arrival while your bags are taken to your hotel. This has to be organised before you travel either through your tour operator or at the Waterloo terminal if you have booked Disney accommodation independently (you need to be able to show confirmation of your hotel booking to do this at Waterloo).

Once you have the correct baggage tags (and Disney Cast Members will be on the direct service to assist you and provide the right tags if you have not been sent them with your tickets), you simply attach them to your luggage and take them to the first floor *Disney Express* baggage office when you arrive at Marne-la-Vallée.

For our money, this is the most

BRIT TIP: Unless you are going Leisure Select, it is worth taking a packed lunch with you on Eurostar to circumvent the relative lack of child-friendly food on board.

efficient and stress-free form of travel we have encountered, especially in Europe. And, when travelling with children, it provides a fair degree of parental ease of mind (as well as the bonus of children's general fascination with trains). The on-board buffet food could be better (especially for children) and smokers will not be happy to know that Eurostar is a completely non-smoking service, but those are extremely minor quibbles.

By Air

If the Eurostar route is the most time-efficient way of getting to the heart of the Magic, where does that leave air travel? Well, if you live anywhere outside the South East, it provides the best alternative, especially using the two main Paris airports of Charles de Gaulle and Orly. The proliferation of low-cost airlines in recent years has broadened the choice considerably (although Air France still takes some beating for its all-round service).

The many regional airports around the UK all have at least one service daily to the French capital and, with the likes of EasyJet, KLM, flybe and bmi (and bmi baby) all offering variations on the low-cost

Fantasyland façades

© Disney

> **BRIT TIP:** Beware the low-cost carriers who use Beauvais as their 'Paris' airport. Beauvais is more than 60km (37 miles) north of Paris and there is NO way to get people to Marne-la-Vallée other than a hired car. The one exception is Ryanair, who provide a shuttle bus to Porte Maillot RER and Métro station in west Paris for €12/person.

alternative, it means your choice of flights has never been greater. Add the scheduled services of Air France (from eight UK airports) and British Airways (who use 10) and you have a total of 22 regional flight gateways to Paris, including Jersey, Nottingham, Bristol, Southend, Belfast and Aberdeen.

Paris Charles de Gaulle Airport (CDG) is by far the bigger (and more complex) of the two Paris air terminals (it is the main international terminus, whereas Orly is more for domestic flights). Situated some 23km (14 miles) to the north-east of the city centre, it actually consists of no less than three main terminals, CDG 1, CDG 2 and the smaller satellite arm CDG T3. The CDG 2 terminal is subdivided into Halls 2A, 2B, 2C, 2D, 2E and 2F, with the RER and TGV stations

> **BRIT TIP:** It's about a 10-minute walk from the RER station to the Air France departure gates in Hall 2F at CDG 2 and from the station to Halls 2A and 2B. However, there is also a shuttle bus every 7 minutes.

situated between 2C–2D and 2E–2F. At CDG 1, the RER station is located next to Terminal 3.

While both CDG 1 and CDG 2 have their own RER stations, the T3 terminal is linked to CDG 1. There is also a free shuttle link between CDG 1 and 2 that runs every 7 minutes or so (at CDG 1 on the shopping level, at CDG 2 at Exit 10 of Hall A, Exit 12 of Hall D and Exit 2.08 – departure level – of Hall F).

The **VEA Navette** shuttle offers a direct service from CDG (all terminals) to the hotels of *Disneyland Resort Paris* 8.30am–7.45pm daily (until 10pm Fridays and Sundays). It is a fairly plodding coach service, taking a good 45 minutes to reach the first stop, but it does have the great benefit of being door to door and runs at 20–40-minute intervals throughout the main part of the day. It costs €14 for adults and €11.50 for children 3–11 (under 3s free). To contact the VEA service in advance, call 00 33 1 60 31 72 00 or visit www.vea.fr/uk/index.asp. From CDG 1, you get the VEA shuttle at the departure level, Gate 16. Using CDG 2, the shuttle is at Gate A11 from Hall 2A; Gate C1 from Hall 2C; Gate D12 from Halls 2B and 2D; and Gate 0.05 of the Gallery, Level 0 exit 0.09 from Hall 2F.

> BRIT TIP: The VEA Navette shuttles will take credit card payment, so don't worry if you don't have any euros to hand yet.

Alternatively, you can take the **RER** service on Line B all the way in to Châtelet Les Halles (about 40 minutes), then change there for Line D to Marne-la-Vallée (another 35–40 minutes). It is a simple enough route at off-peak times but much harder to negotiate with luggage in the morning or evening

rush hour. For RER info (in English), call 00 33 1 36 68 41 14 or visit www.ratp.fr and click on the International Passengers button.

Another alternative is to take the **TGV** train from the airport to Marne-la-Vallée, which can work out slightly cheaper than the VEA shuttle (although services are fewer). There are 10 trains between 6.51 and 11.19am, then basically one an hour 1–6pm and another 12 up to 9.34pm. At off-peak times, the ticket is €13.80 one way but it rises to €20.90 at peak times. The big benefit though, is that it takes just 15 minutes and you can walk out of the station to pick up the shuttle bus to any Disney hotel right outside. For the return journey to the airport, there are 13 services 8.12am–12.45pm, then another 12 3.01–10.16pm. (Be warned – if you miss the Charles de Gaulle stop, you will end up in Lille or even Brussels!) You can also get taxis outside all the terminals, although it will cost around €60 one way to any Disney hotel.

At **Paris Orly Airport**, 15km (9 miles) to the south of the city centre, it is divided more simply into Sud (South) and Ouest (West) terminals, and there is a free shuttle service operating every 5 minutes or so over the 2-minute journey between the two (from the South terminal, look for Exit K, and from the West terminal, go to the

Disneyland Hotel gardens

© Disney

departure level and Exit W). With good direct links into the city, Orly makes a reasonable alternative to Charles de Gaulle, although the **RER** route is a little more complicated (take the airport link to Antony, on Line B, then go to Châtelet Les Halles and change to Line A for Marne-la-Vallée). At Orly South, take Exit G on the ground floor (platform 1 to Paris), and at Orly West, take Exit G also.

BRIT TIP: For information on both Paris airports – including terminal maps, flight times and services – visit www.aeroportsdeparis.fr and click on the English button in the top right-hand corner.

Much the better choice though, is to use the direct **VEA Navette** shuttle bus service to all the Disney hotels (8.30am–7.30pm daily, until 9.30pm on Fridays, journey time 45–50 minutes) for €14/adult, €11.50 for children 3–11 (under 3s free). At Orly South, take Gate H for the VEA bus and at Orly West, take Gate C. A taxi from Paris Orly to any of the Disney hotels will cost about €30–35.

When it comes to the airlines themselves, **Air France** is, not surprisingly, the biggest carrier in terms of daily flights, using both main Paris airports. At Charles de Gaulle, they fly into CDG 1 and CDG 2 (Halls A, B, C, D, F). **British Airways** flies to CDG 1, as does **bmi** (from Belfast, Edinburgh, Glasgow, Leeds/Bradford, Heathrow, Manchester and Teesside), **flybe** (from Exeter) and **bmi baby** (from Cardiff and East Midlands). **British European** operates to CDG 2 (Halls D and F), plus occasionally to Orly West.

EasyJet (from Liverpool, Luton and Newcastle) flies into CDG T3 and **KLM** (from Stansted) operates at CDG 1. There are few direct flights to Orly from the UK, although Air France flies there from London City Airport. EasyJet also uses it as a base, but only for operations elsewhere in Europe, not the UK.

Choosing a tour operator

While it is perfectly possible – and sometimes cheaper – to book a DIY holiday by putting together your own hotel and travel arrangements, the tour operators to *Disneyland Resort Paris* have developed an extremely sophisticated, not to mention exceptionally good value, raft of packages that make booking with them (especially if you book direct) highly worthwhile. Add in the number of internet travel companies like ebookers.com and lastminute.com, plus new specialists like themeparkholidays.com (see page 65), and there is again a bewildering variety on offer.

The best thing to do is to shop around and get an idea of the prices for the different types of package. Most of the tour operators in this market are the big well-known chains, who all feature some of the

BRIT TIP: For all the up-to-date *Disneyland Resort Paris* issues go to the UK Discussion Boards on the No 1 Disney-related website, the DIS (www.wdwinfo.com). Either click on Discussion Forums, or go to www.disboards.com and visit the Disneyland Paris section. We may even be there to offer you some advice ourselves!

keenest pricing thanks to their ability to deal in bulk (Cresta, Paris Travel Service and Leger Holidays are all part of the MyTravel – formerly Airtours – group), but several out-and-out Paris specialists are worth considering.

When it comes to simple price comparisons, it is more the method of travel that makes the main difference, hence a coach-based trip is usually the cheapest on offer, followed by Eurotunnel or ferry self-drive, then Eurostar and finally flying. But there are often special deals to be found – particularly at off-peak times – and it definitely pays to keep your wits about you when looking for a bargain. So you need to know what the general going rate is before you plunge in!

Here is a look at the main eight national tour operators on the Disneyland beat. With all of them, Disney accommodation usually comes with unlimited entry Theme Park passes for your visit.

Cresta Holidays: One of the biggest of the mainstream operators who offer the full range of options, Cresta has been voted the Top Short Break Specialist by the UK travel trade for the past 12 years, so they have a good idea of what they're about. They also aim to be one of the most flexible outfits in the business, hence they can combine just about any aspect of the resort, hotels and travel arrangements to suit your requirements. Their brochures are also among the clearest and most readable on offer.

Cresta features the full range of Disney accommodation, three Disney Selected or Associated Hotels and 13 off-site hotels, all of which offer 'free night' bonuses, and many of which are chosen for their proximity to the RER line that takes you directly to the station at *Disneyland Resort Paris*. They also have a few great little extras, like a

£50 early booking offer and a Planet Hollywood privilege card, entitling you to a 20% discount from your total bill.

The smart Explorers Hotel (see page 87) is heavily featured in Cresta's 2006 programme and their lead-in price for the excellent value hotel (based on a 2-night stay) is an eye-catching £179 per adult and £79 per child, self-drive via P&O, inclusive of breakfast and unlimited Theme Park entry. Plenty of Kids Go Free offers are available in the first quarter of the year. Contact Cresta on 0870 161 0910 or visit www.crestaholidays.co.uk.

Transport: Self-drive via Eurotunnel, P&O Ferries, Hoverspeed; Eurostar; flights (Air France, British Airways, bmi, flybe and several no-frills carriers).

Leger Holidays: The biggest coach-tour operator to *Disneyland Resort Paris*, Leger has a countrywide network of routes, with more than 450 joining points, taking customers to Dover and crossing the Channel for what is then a 4-hour drive to the resort (with one refreshment stop). They operate a mixture of their own branded coaches plus those of well-known companies from all over the country. All are modern and comfortable with toilets and drinks.

Leger has produced their largest programme to date for 2006, with increased departures of coach, self-drive, Eurostar and air packages, providing the widest possible choice for all budgets. They package it all extremely well using the Explorers Hotel (see page 87) as their base price accommodation, which comes in slightly cheaper than Disney's most budget-orientated offering, the *Hotel Santa Fe*. They feature primarily 3-, 4- and 5-day packages, with the option to upgrade to *Disney's Hotel Cheyenne*, *Sequoia Lodge* or *Disney's Newport Bay Club* (and some free upgrade offers for early bookers). The Kids Go Free season (for 3–11s) from 2 January to

30 March is available with all four transport options (based on one adult to one child). Self-drive alternatives use the Explorers Hotel and *Disney's Davy Crockett Ranch*. Leger's innovative flight programme features Air France for the first time, flying from Heathrow, Birmingham, Manchester Newcastle, Southampton and Edinburgh, as well as low-cost carriers from Liverpool, Leeds–Bradford, Doncaster, Luton, East Midlands and Cardiff. Transfers are provided with all flight packages to Paris Charles de Gaulle airport.

Once in the resort, the coach can be used for excursions into Paris (a worthwhile extra on the 5-day tour). The 3-day coach package offers a 2-Day Park Hopper ticket; the 4-day package features two full days in the parks, with departure after breakfast on the fourth day; and the 5-day coach offers two park days and a full-day Paris tour on the fourth day, or the option to stay in the parks for a third day (extra day's park admission is not always included).

Arrival time aims to be between 8 and 10pm on the first evening. The return coach journey usually leaves after breakfast on the last day (early evening on 3-day packages). Leger Holidays operates year-round, but the summer is easily their busiest period (although the Kids Go Free season is also popular), and the 5-day package has really caught on

Outside the Disneyland Park

well since the opening of the *Walt Disney Studios Park*. The addition of the Explorers Hotel has given them an extra boost in the value-for-money stakes and has also proved extremely popular. Another new addition for 2006 is their 'Silver Service', the luxury coach experience with extra facilities such as fewer seats for extra legroom (the coach carries just 36 passengers), drop-down tables and foot rests, onboard entertainment system and a comfortable rear lounge.

Leger has 12 main departures over the 6 weeks of the summer holidays,

View from the Eiffel Tower

Cinderella and Prince Charming

and more than 62 departures throughout 2006. The majority use P&O Ferries from Dover but some dates are served via Eurotunnel. We have described a typical Leger 5-day break in Chapter 2 (see page 19), which shows how hard it is to fit everything in! Their brochures highlight the Disney special events like Bonfire Night, Halloween and Christmas extremely well. Call Leger Holidays on 0845 458 5167 or visit www.livethemagic.co.uk.

Transport: Coach via P&O Ferries or Eurotunnel; Eurostar; self-drive with P&O Ferries or Eurotunnel; flights (Air France and various low-cost carriers).

Paris Travel Service: This tour operator was the first British one to sell *Disneyland Resort Paris*, hence they have had more than 13 years to hone their offering. They have some of the most knowledgeable staff and arguably the most comprehensive brochure, with every possible combination of travel (including fly-drives) and every type of accommodation – all seven Disney properties, the four neighbouring Selected Hotels and a good selection of nearby off-site options. They can also tailor make two-centre holidays, allowing you to enjoy a stay in Paris before or after your Disney stay.

Their documentation and ticketing are first class, and there are some useful 'extras', like a free kids' autograph book (a really neat touch) and an array of special offers (like Kids Eat Free with P&O Ferries, Free Kids' Character Breakfast and Buffalo Bill's Wild West Show, Free Kids' entry to Sea Life and a privilege card for Planet Hollywood). There's a £50 early booking offer, £100 off for booking more than one room at certain hotels and £100 off per couple for adults travelling together (without kids) outside of the school holidays. A third or fourth night free is offered on selected dates, as are price reductions for travel on Eurostar.

Buffalo Bill's Wild West Show

> BRIT TIP: Travel agents underline how MUCH is now on offer at *Disneyland Resort Paris*. 'This is no longer just a day out at a theme park,' they say.

The Kids Go Free season is again a big part of their programme, from January to March. Contact Paris Travel Service on 0870 010 2456 (brochure request) or 0870 191 7200 (reservations), or visit www.paristravel.co.uk.

Transport: Self-drive via Eurotunnel, P&O Ferries, Hoverspeed; Eurostar; flights (Air France, British Airways, bmi, flybe and several no-frills carriers).

Thomson: A member of the TUI travel group (which also includes travel agent Thomson Retail, formerly Lunn Poly), this company is well organised and extremely knowledgeable, with a keen reservations team. There are some great special offers (notably 3 nights for 2, 4 for 3 and 5 for 4, all including breakfast and an extra day to explore both Disney parks), free child places at selected times of the year and early booking offers and discounts. They stress early bookers will get the best deals with the increasing popularity of the resort

> BRIT TIP: The main Disney tour operators advise: 1 Book early (essential for high season); 2 Use Disney's FastPass system in the Theme Parks (see page 109); 3 Plan your day with the aid of park maps (and this book!), which give you all the show times, parades, etc; 4 Book your meals on arrival.

and advise to book *early* for school holidays. They offer meal vouchers as an optional extra, which helps with your pre-holiday budgeting and you can pre-book character meals and shows, which is extremely handy.

An immensely readable brochure contains all the Disney hotels and the full range of travel options, including scheduled flights, low-cost carriers, Eurostar and self-drive options. For those who prefer to arrange their own travel, Thomson offers accommodation only, with Disney park tickets included.

A selection of Near the Magic hotels are also available on a self-drive basis offering free child places year-round and free night offers at certain times of the year. These are situated either 5–20 minutes' drive from the Disney parks or close to the RER line into Marne-la-Vallée. Call Thomson direct on 0870 606 1496 or visit www.thomson.co.uk.

Transport: Eurostar; flights (Thomsonfly, bmi, Air France, British Airways, bmi baby, EasyJet); self-drive via Eurotunnel, P&O Ferries, Hoverspeed.

Thomas Cook Signature: This famous name in the travel agency business operates an extremely well-run *Disneyland Resort Paris* programme. From the clarity of their brochure to the quality of their ticketing material – which includes a 36-page information booklet – Thomas Cook Signature lives up to its reputation as one of the originators and innovators in the tour operating business. Their free kids' pack – for all children aged 3–11 (but not on accommodation-only bookings) – is one of the best we've seen, with a J-bag containing a disposable camera, ripper wallet, activity book, crayons, a pen and autograph book.

Their booking staff are extremely switched on when it comes to advising guests with disabilities. You can again pre-buy meal vouchers to use in the hotels, parks and *Disney Village*, and book character meals in advance (especially during peak periods), which can help with your budgeting. They also offer free nights at Disney resorts periodically, some Kids Go Free deals, and a free kids' character breakfast and Buffalo Bill's show ticket with every adult booking (for under 12s). Plus there are exclusive offers such as free Sea Life Centre tickets and Earlybird Money Savers.

Thomas Cook features the full range of Disney hotels and the usual off-site options (these vary little between operators). Aimed at self-drive customers (or fly-drives, with Avis car hire), the off-site hotels are near RER stations. There are also some 'free night' deals to be had at various times. On P&O Ferries, kids eat free with a paying adult in the International Food Court.

The flight options are extremely well detailed, from no less than 17 UK airports (although Aberdeen and Belfast flights go via either Gatwick, Heathrow or East Midlands). For more info, call Thomas Cook Signature on 0870 443 4452 or visit www.tcsignature.com.

Transport: Eurostar; flights (bmi, Air France, British Airways, EasyJet, bmi baby); self-drive via Eurotunnel, P&O Ferries, Hoverspeed.

Osprey Holidays: This Disney specialist caters for holidaymakers travelling from all over the UK, but has particular expertise in packages from Scotland. Osprey Holidays has been in the travel business for almost 50 years and produces a full-colour 20-page *Disneyland Resort Paris* brochure. With the choice of either Eurostar or flights, plus any of the Disney hotels and a large selection of central Paris ones (from their City Breaks), Osprey also gives free night offers at resort hotels, while, as with the other operators, you can pre-book meals, character meals and Buffalo Bill's show. Call 0845 310 3031 for reservations, or visit www.ospreyholidays.com.

Transport: Eurostar; flights (bmi, Air France, British Airways and various low-cost carriers).

Newmarket: Mainly a coach operator, you won't notice Newmarket in any travel agent, but you will find their Magical Breaks packages in many local and national newspapers. From Aberdeen to Plymouth, you are likely to see their newspaper-endorsed reader offers, and usually at eye-catching prices (even for Eurostar packages). They offer mainly off-site hotels (hence the budget-orientated operation) with good, reliable coach services (most of which use P&O Ferries from Dover).

Their Paris expertise dates back to the opening of the *Disneyland Park*, hence they have a knowledgable staff (including their own in-resort reps), and also do big business with special interest groups and schools' Study Experiences (for students of information and communications technology, plus other curriculum driven subjects).

With their coach tours (the vast majority), they have some 500 pick-up points all over the country and the coach acts as your transport throughout the trip at the off-site hotels, which tend to be in the greater Paris area (usually of the Campanile, Ibis, Novotel standard – a basic but comfortable 2- and 3-star). The only drawback is you are restricted to the coach's one trip to and from the hotel (you have to make your own way back if you want to return earlier).

All are on a bed and breakfast (of the continental variety) basis, and they feature either 3- or 4-day trips (with the latter growing increasingly popular). On coach tours, the 3-day trips feature two 1-Day Passports for the Theme Parks (you arrive mid-evening on the first day, have one full day there, then return in early afternoon on the third day), while the 4-day version has a 3-Day Passport included (as you have two full days for the Theme Parks, plus part of the final day before an afternoon return; Scottish departures leave earlier on the final day).

Going by Eurostar, Newmarket offers 3- and 4-day trips, arriving in the early afternoon on day one and departing in the evening on day three or four. They also now sell a selection of similar breaks in conjunction with the low-cost airlines from a wide range of regional airports, with accommodation provided at the Kyriad Hotel at *Disneyland Resort Paris*. For more information, call 0845 226 7755 or visit www.newmarket-group.co.uk.

Transport: Coach via P&O Ferries or Eurotunnel; Eurostar; flights (various low-cost carriers from range of regional airports).

Harry Shaw: Another popular and busy coach-tour specialist, this company's speciality is 1-, 2- and 3-day trips, with the possibility of overnight travel on some to give you extra time in the Theme Parks. The basic option is between off-site accommodation (usually a 2-star hotel in the Ile de France region),

Adventureland Bazaar

where the coach takes you to and from the parks, and four Disney hotels (*Disney's Hotel Cheyenne, Disney's Hotel Santa Fe, Disney's Newport Bay Club* and *Disney's Sequoia Lodge*). However, the one drawback with off-site hotels is you are tied to the coach's return times. Call 024 7654 5544 or visit www.harryshaw.co.uk.

Transport: Coach via P&O Ferries or Eurotunnel.

Cowboy Cookout Barbecue

Meet Captain Hook!

There are then various regional companies who all feature *Disneyland Resort Paris*, including: Midlands specialists **Travelsphere** (0870 240 2426, www.travelsphere.co.uk), **Applebys** of Lincolnshire (08704 434040; www.applebystravel.co.uk); East Anglia specialist **Galloway Travel** (01449 767844, www.galloway-travel.co.uk); Yorkshire's **Gold Crest Holidays** (0870 70000 007, www.gold-crest.com); Middlesbrough-based

Siesta International Holidays (0870 444 6464, www.siesta holidays.co.uk); Nottingham's **Skills Holidays** (08456 665544, www.skillsholidays.co.uk); Gloucestershire's **Travelscope** (0870 380 3333, www.travelscope.co.uk). For larger groups, try **Bob Cole Group Travel** (0870 027 5220; www.bobcolegrouptravel.co.uk) and **Gold Crest Holidays**.

Finally, for a company with a difference that is designed to help both the more independent-minded traveller, who knows how to get there but wants some good advice on tickets etc, and for those who need to be assisted, log on to the excellent **www.themepark holidays.com** website. Full of great info, practical advice and a wealth of detail on the Theme Parks and hotels (both on- and off-site), not to mention some great Disney photos, the site offers all the benefits of a travel agent at the click of a mouse. You can book direct, following the easy-to-use instructions, or talk to the site's knowledgeable team (not surprising, since it's the brainchild of a former senior Disney marketing manager) on 0870 240 2510.

Frontierland from the Thunder Mesa Riverboat

Top 10 Romantic Options for Disneyland Resort Paris

Although it's well-known as a family destination, *Disneyland Resort Paris* is also popular for honeymoons, anniversaries and other special 'couples only' celebrations. Here is our guide to the best things to do when it is just the two of you, so that you can really make the most of your visit.

1 Stay in one of the Tinker Bell suites at the *Disneyland Hotel*.

2 Or stay in the Roosevelt Suite at *Disney's Hotel New York*.

3 Failing either of those, *Disney's Newport Bay Club* offers a genuinely lovely Honeymoon Suite.

4 Take one of Cityrama's Illuminations evening tours of Paris.

5 Have dinner at the California Grill at the *Disneyland Hotel*.

6 Take an evening stroll around Lake Disney and stop for a drink at the Redwood Bar at *Disney's Sequoia Lodge*.

7 Have lunch at the wonderful Blue Lagoon restaurant inside the Pirates of the Caribbean ride at the *Disneyland Park*.

8 Book a couple's massage at the soothing Thai Spa inside the Mövenpick Dream Castle Hotel.

9 Enjoy a drink in the Fantasia Bar at the *Disneyland Hotel*, listening to the relaxing sounds of their pianist.

10 In winter, stop at *Disney's Hotel New York* to watch the ice-skating and grab a mug of hot cocoa from the nearby drinks stall.

Book direct

Of course, you can always book directly with Disney if you have an idea of what you want to do. The resort offers a full range of packages with all the usual methods of transport and they even have a good range of off-site accommodation, both nearby and in Paris itself. Disney's brochure is worth getting just for all the lavish photography and large-scale maps and they highlight all the extras, free nights and Kids Go Free deals. The pricing system and dizzying array of supplements for each of the different forms of transport can take some deciphering, but you basically have every possible permutation open to you. The brochure is designed so that you begin by choosing your accommodation, then how long you want to visit (from 1–4 nights), select any additional features (like character meals and shows), and finally decide upon the mode of transport. For details, call their hotline on 08705 030303 or visit www.disneylandparis.com.
Transport: Eurostar; flights (Air France, British Airways, bmi); self-drive via Eurotunnel, P&O Ferries, SeaFrance, Hoverspeed.

But wait, before you can make a fully informed choice, you need to have a good idea of the array of accommodation that awaits you, both in the form of the Disney resorts themselves and the usually cheaper alternatives for staying off-site. So, read on, and we will reveal all about how to choose your hotel…

4 Staying There
(or, How to Play the Hotel Game)

When it comes to where to stay in and around *Disneyland Resort Paris*, you will not be surprised to know there is a bewildering variety. Disney alone has six highly contrasting and entertaining hotels on site, while *Disney's Davy Crockett Ranch*, about a 15-minute drive away, offers an alternative for those with a car. There are then another seven hotels 'near the Magic', which benefit from being close to the resort and several dozen more within a 15–25 minute drive.

The key is the combination of location and price. All the Disney resorts offer the huge convenience of being just minutes from the essential Theme Park Magic, but their hotels do tend to be on the expensive side. If you are staying on-site, the chances are you won't need any other form of transport. But a car is also not always necessary if you stay off-site, as the wonderful ease of use of the RER rail line makes staying in somewhere like Bussy-St-Georges, Noisiel or even Bercy, towards the centre of Paris, a perfectly viable proposition.

The section on the various tour operators in the previous chapter reveals the great range of packages on offer. Virtually every operator also features off-site hotels, as the demand for the Disney ones is pretty high and is at virtually 100% at peak periods like summer and Christmas.

The area along the RER corridor still makes a handy base for tackling Disney (and Paris, for that matter), and the general standard of hotels is sound if unspectacular. Their star-rating system is pretty accurate and virtually every hotel works on a bed-and-breakfast basis (a continental breakfast with cereal, pastries, cold meats, cheese and tea/coffee – the Holiday Inn at Disneyland Paris is a rarity in that it charges extra for breakfast). It is advisable to stay off-site during the summer when Disney's prices are at their highest, while the price difference between on- and off-site properties is less in the winter months.

> BRIT TIP: The quoted price rates of hotels in France are always per room and not per person.

Staying **off-sit**e can actually provide more flexibility for your holiday if you want to use the hotel just as a base and not part of the holiday itself (the Disney hotels certainly play an important role in the holiday experience). You'll have more incentive to get out and about if you stay off-site and it's convenient for seeing more of Paris, while many hotels offer 'extra night free' deals.

You should certainly check in advance, however, whether or not you'll need a car. If you are not close

© Disney

Disney's Sequoia Lodge

to an RER station – or the hotel does not have a shuttle service to the nearest station – you will struggle without your own transport. However, many of the tour operators (notably Thomson, see page 62) now offer travel to the resort by Eurostar with off-site hotels near RER stations.

Disney Hotels

When it comes to getting the maximum out of your trip, you can't beat the full and all-encompassing experience of staying **on-site** (see maps on pages 41 and 74) as the majority of Brits do (curiously, only a small percentage of other nationalities choose this option, so Disney hotels are often mainly British in their guest ratio). Just the simple fact of being able to walk into the Theme Parks in the morning, through *Disney Village*, is one of the great pleasures of staying here. Even from *Disney's Hotel Santa Fe*, which is the furthest away of the six on-site resorts, it is no more than a 20-minute stroll and, on a sunny morning, it is a true delight. The old estate agent's adage of 'location, location, location' is just as true here!

There are also other significant benefits to staying *chez* Mickey for the duration of your visit, most notably the excellent **character interaction** you get at all six hotels, in the morning and evening. At least one character will always be 'on parade' in the hotel foyer and kids are virtually guaranteed to get their autograph books off to a flying start in this way (intriguingly, both the Explorers Hotel and the Mövenpick Dream Castle in nearby Val de France have developed their own popular characters, although they call them 'mascots', for guest interaction). Disney's **service and hospitality** adds significantly to everyone's enjoyment, while all resort guests get their own **Identification Card** that can be used as a charge card in both parks and at *Disney Village* (apart from the Rainforest Café, Planet Hollywood, McDonald's and the Gaumont Cinema complex).

Resort guests also benefit from **free parking** at the hotels, Theme Parks and *Disney Village*, the **free shuttle bus service, free entry to Hurricanes disco** in *Disney Village*, along with a whole range of **recreational activities**, from swimming pools and tennis courts to outdoor playgrounds, video games and even ice-skating (outside *Disney's Hotel New York*, but open to all Disney hotel guests for a small fee). There is a **shopping service**

Characters at Disney's Hotel Santa Fe

© Disney

Café Fantasia at Disneyland Hotel

for hotel guests, whereby you can have anything you buy in one of the Theme Parks delivered to the Disney shop in your hotel, for collection from 8pm that day. Each hotel also organises regular **children's activities** and all have Disney TV and a computer games console in their play area.

> BRIT TIP: The character dining options can be booked through your hotel concierge in the foyer (see Brit Tip on page 73), and it is advisable to do this as soon as you check in.

Finally, and highly important for those with children, there is the option to have a **character breakfast** at one of three locations – the Inventions restaurant at *Disneyland Hotel* for guests there, Café Mickey in *Disney Village*, or the Plaza Gardens Restaurant in the *Disneyland Park* (there is, as you would expect, an additional charge for this). These feature an American buffet breakfast with a wide variety of breads, pastries, scrambled eggs, ham, sausages, cereals, fruit juices and hot drinks, and are priced at €16 per adult and €12 per child (3–11) for Disney hotel guests (it counts as a supplement against the normal hotel breakfast). They are also available for non-Disney hotel guests, but the prices will be €25 and €17.

The two outdoor **tennis courts** at *Disney's Hotel New York* are also available to all Disney hotel guests (for a small fee for balls and racket hire), on production of your Disney resort ID card.

An additional (non-character) feature at peak times for guests at *Disney's Newport Bay Club*, *Disney's Sequoia Lodge*, *Disney's Hotel Cheyenne* and *Disney's Hotel Santa Fe* is the **Good Morning Fantasyland**

> BRIT TIP: Although there is no extra charge for the Good Morning Fantasyland breakfast, you need to specify whether you would like to do it when you book your package, as it is likely to be fully subscribed when you check in at the hotel.

breakfast, whereby hotel guests can opt to enter the *Disneyland Park* an hour early and board the Disneyland Railroad train (or just walk) to

Disney's Newport Bay Club

Fantasyland, where a basic continental buffet breakfast is served in one of the restaurants (usually Au Chalet de la Marionette). You will then be in pole position to ride the likes of Dumbo and Peter Pan on the stroke of 9am.

In nearly all cases, when booking a Disney hotel you are obliged to accept the Unlimited Access Pass as part of the package (or a 3-Day Passport if you opt for the minimum 2-night/3-day package), which obviously suits most people as it keeps you up and running in the Theme Parks from first minute to last. However, it may not be suitable if you plan on doing some non-Disney sightseeing as well, hence you need to weigh up whether an off-site hotel might be the better option. The main exception to the Disney hotel rule is if you are an Annual Passport holder, in which case you can book just bed-and-breakfast packages through the central reservations office on 00 33 1 60 30 60 69 from the UK.

Most **room sizes** will accommodate a family of four comfortably, but you are limited for choice with five or more (although some rooms can accommodate a cot if required). Basically, you have only three choices in this instance: *Disney's Davy Crockett Ranch*, where the cabins can house up to six people (but you must have your own transport); two connecting rooms in one of the six hotels; or one of the 15 family rooms, which can accommodate up to six at *Disney's Newport Bay Club*, although these rooms are more expensive and are at a premium, so you would need to book early. (Looking outside the resort, the Pierre & Vacances Residence Val d'Europe is an ultra-smart apartment block in the town which can accommodate up to seven, while the Explorers Hotel can take family groups of up to 10.) Rooms for guests with disabilities are available in all six hotels, but not *Disney's Davy Crockett Ranch*.

All rooms feature a telephone, international TV channels and radio and a shower/bath. *Disney's Hotel Cheyenne, Disney's Hotel Santa Fe* and *Disney's Davy Crockett Ranch* do NOT have air-conditioning (although the former two have ceiling fans), while only the *Disneyland Hotel* and *Disney's Hotel New York* have hairdryers fitted as standard in the bathrooms (the others have hairdryers available on request). The *Disneyland Hotel, Disney's Hotel New York* and *Disney's Newport Bay Club* all have mini-bars, as does *Disney's Sequoia Lodge* in its Montana rooms only, while the former trio also have room safes. All but *Disney's Davy Crockett Ranch* offer non-smoking rooms and a left-luggage service.

When checking in, you will be given your park tickets, any vouchers for various options you might have booked (for meals or Buffalo Bill's Wild West Show), park maps, an information guide to the hotel (these are well written and highly collectable), a *Disney Village* programme and your Resort ID card, while children also get a name badge to wear (if they wish!).

BRIT TIP: If you arrive at the hotel between midday and 2pm, have lunch there before heading off to the Theme Parks. You will get served much quicker.

Each resort hotel should be able to supply a cot on request and all feature **children's menus** in their main restaurants. **Room service** is available only at the *Disneyland Hotel* and *Disney's Hotel New York*, and the Admiral's Floor of *Disney's Newport Bay Club*. In all cases, check-in time is 3pm (although rooms are occasionally available from 1pm. Take advantage of the left-luggage provision and you can still head straight for the Theme Parks) and check-out is 11am. However, there is no official in-house **baby-sitting** service for any of the hotels, although there is a private firm who can arrange in-room baby-sitting for you via the front desk.

> BRIT TIP: If you have booked Eurostar's *Disney Express* service (see page 55), you simply leave your bags, cases, etc, in the left-luggage office at your hotel when you check out, and they will be transferred for you to collect at the *Disney Express* office at the station. Whether or not you've booked, *Disney Express* labels ARE available for your return journey for a few extra euros at the check-in.

But if the pros of staying on-site are substantial, what of the cons? Well, the price difference is the obvious thing to highlight here. You can save a good 20–30% by opting for one of the smaller hotels nearby, and the four (soon to be five) hotels of the **Val de France** area all represent significant savings while offering much of the convenience, facilities and service (in fact, we rate the Holiday Inn and Mövenpick Dream Castle as possibly the best all-round value of all).

Breakfast at the Disney resorts can also be something of a bunfight at peak periods; you are allocated a set time-slot (which may not be terribly convenient in the first place) but still often find queues just to get in, even at more upmarket hotels like *Sequoia Lodge* and *Newport Bay Club*. If

you're looking to be in the parks by 9am, you may struggle to get through breakfast in time, unless you have the 7.30am time slot (not everyone's idea of a holiday rise-and-shine!). The off-site hotels are also noticeably less frenetic (with the possible exception of the busy Explorers Hotel), and often provide a welcome break from the hustle and bustle in early evening.

Those in the Val de France area benefit from a beautiful countryside location, with a large lake that backs on to the main quartet, which provides a pleasant way to unwind after a day at the parks. However, the (free) shuttle bus service can be a bit of a trial at peak times (8.30–9am and at park closing) as it calls at all four hotels in turn, which means either an uncomfortable 10–15-minute ride or, occasionally, having to wait for another bus if the first one is full (the Mövenpick in particular suffers from this as it is the last pick-up point on the four-hotel circuit).

Having underlined the price differential, Disney's six hotels (amounting to 5,200 rooms, plus the 535 cabins and 60 caravan sites of *Disney's Davy Crockett Ranch*) do come with a range of prices to suit most pockets, from the more budget-priced *Disney's Hotel Santa Fe* to the opulent 4-star *Disneyland Hotel* itself.

We at *A Brit's Guide* have our own ratings system for the hotels, too, allocating €s in the following price ranges:

€€€€€	= More than €150/night
€€€€	= €100–150/night
€€€	= €75–100/night
€€	= €50–75/night
€	= Less than €50/night

We also award CCCs out of five for the extra facilities at each property. Hence you can be sure a CCCCC hotel should have all the creature comforts you can think of, including a swimming pool and a choice of restaurants, while a CC would be of the more basic, motel-type. Here are Disney's magnificent seven in detail:

Disneyland Hotel

The resort's signature hotel, right at the entrance to the *Disneyland Park* (and otherwise known as the Pink Palace), is a massive mock-Victorian edifice featuring the most comfortable and spacious rooms, sumptuous decor and one of the best restaurants in the whole area. The Disney theming is at its most discreet here (you have to look closely at the wallpaper to realise the in-built Mickey subtlety) and there is some elegant furniture sprinkled around (witness the four classic grandfather clocks along one corridor which display the times at each of the Disney resorts around the world – they also play Disney tunes on the hour and half-hour!). Standard rooms feature either a king-size bed and a fold-out or two doubles, plus a highly elaborate TV/video cabinet with mini-bar, and all have the high ceilings reminiscent of Victorian buildings.

The top two floors feature the exclusive **Castle Club**, with a

Disneyland Hotel

private lift (straight to the Theme Park!) and reception desk, a lounge bar for breakfast, afternoon tea and light refreshments, plus a fabulous view out over the *Disneyland Park*. There are then even more spacious Junior Suites (58sq m/624sq ft as opposed to the 34sq m/366sq ft of standard rooms), plus four Tinker Bell Suites (69sq metres/743sq ft) with a lounge and a separate walk-in shower as well as a bath and three one-off suites of truly exceptional order – Walt's Apartment, the (Cinderella) Vice-Presidential Suite and the (Sleeping Beauty) Presidential Suite.

Hotel l'Elysée's Val d'Europe bar

City Bar at Disney's Hotel New York

From the three-storey lobby right through to the sauna, the period theming is impressive but not overwhelming. There is a **Galerie Mickey** selling souvenirs and travel essentials, the main bar area **Café Fantasia** (with smart, inventive decor geared to the film of the same name) as well as two restaurants. **Inventions** is themed on the great technical inventions of the 20th century and offers an excellent international dinner buffet with Disney characters in attendance, in addition to the character breakfasts. The **California Grill** is the hotel's

BRIT TIP: Each Disney hotel has a concierge desk in the foyer specially for booking meals and shows in any of the hotels, parks or *Disney Village*. Try to plan day by day and visit the desk first thing in the morning to make your bookings – especially at peak times. If you can book for your whole stay straight away, you will be one step ahead of the masses.

fine dining establishment and the quality on offer here is superb, with a conservatory-style motif and a show kitchen at one end. At the other end, a lounge affords more great views of the Theme Park.

The indoor pool area is equally smart, with a medium-sized pool, a large Jacuzzi, a gymnasium and massage treatment rooms, as well as the sauna, steam room and solarium. The inevitable video games room – the Mad Hatter's Arcade – is fully geared up for kids of the requisite age, while the Minnie Club children's activity centre includes TV, video, computer games and play areas. The only thing it doesn't have is an outdoor play area, but then the *Disneyland Park* is right on the doorstep! However, there is a supplement for a standard room with a park view. In all, there are 496 rooms, plus 18 suites, and it really is the pinnacle of the on-site accommodation. **Official rating ****; our rating €€€€€, CCCCC**.

Disney's Hotel New York

Welcome to the Big Apple! It is not the fact this is a Disney hotel so much as it is wonderfully themed with an art deco, 1930s' view of New York that extends from the massive 'tower block' façade to individual touches in the rooms and the background jazz throughout the lobby and bar area. There is little overt Mickey-ness about it, but lots

Disney's Hotel New York at Christmas

of grand style and clever imagery, with the bonus for some rooms of a fabulous view over Lake Disney. It also has, we reckon, the most amazing suite of them all, the two-storey Roosevelt Presidential Suite, with floor-to-ceiling windows, wonderful furniture, a living room complete with piano and a dining room for up to eight guests. The upstairs double bedroom has a separate lounge and Jacuzzi.

> BRIT TIP: If you find the *Disney Village* a touch too frenetic in the evening, head for the City Bar at *Disney's Hotel New York* which offers the perfect surroundings for a relaxing and enjoyable drink or two.

Most standard rooms (31sq m/334sq ft), which have some lovely rosewood cabinets, sleep four comfortably, while others offer just one king-size bed. The Resort Suites (56sq m/603sq ft, one on each corner of each floor) have masses of space for a family of four, with a separate bedroom and living room. There is a beautiful Honeymoon Suite (62sq m/667sq ft) as well. With 565 rooms in all (including 27 spacious suites), the hotel features two restaurants (the intimate, formal atmosphere of the **Manhattan Restaurant** and the more relaxed, cosmopolitan style of the **Parkside Diner**), a delightfully elegant bar, a hair salon (the only one on-site), boutique and gift shop, two outdoor tennis courts (small fee for racket and ball hire) and an ice-skating rink (an eye-catching facility in winter).

For kids, there is the Roger Rabbit corner, with differently themed activities at different times

> BRIT TIP: *Disney's Hotel New York* is a product of American architect Michael Graves, who also designed the Swan and Dolphin Hotels in *Walt Disney World Resort in Florida*. So, if you enjoy the fun-style architecture of those two, *Disney's Hotel New York* is bound to appeal.

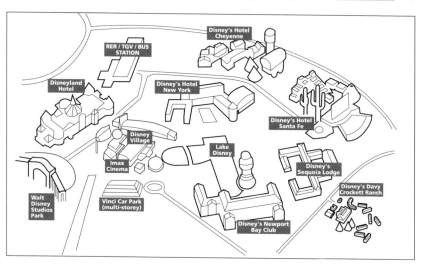

of the day, and the ubiquitous video games room. The one drawback here is that the hotel is also a big convention facility, and it can draw a sizeable business/conference crowd at times.

A bonus with *Disney's Hotel New York* is the swimming pool complex, which is easily the best of the on-site hotels. The extremely large pool has both an indoor and outdoor aspect, while there is also a Jacuzzi, sauna, steam room and a good-sized gymnasium, plus a pleasant outdoor terrace. After the *Disneyland Hotel*, it is also the closest to the Theme Parks, situated right at the opposite end of *Disney Village*, and is barely a 10-minute stroll from the gates of the *Disneyland Park*, slightly less for the *Walt Disney Studios Park*.

While it may be a touch too formal for some tastes (mainly due to the conference aspect), *Disney's Hotel New York* does have a terrifically exciting feel, especially for young adults and teenagers, and is in a perfect situation looking out over Lake Disney but still within an easy stroll of *Disney Village*. **Official rating ****; our rating €€€€, CCCCC.**

Disney's Newport Bay Club

Keeping with the American theme, *Disney's Newport Bay Club* has a New England seaside resort feel, with the largest spread of rooms of any of the on-site hotels (or any hotel in Europe, come to that). It may not appeal quite so much to children (it has possibly the most 'grown-up' style of all six hotels), but it is well equipped to cater for all the family, with two excellent pools (a large one outdoors and an elaborate one, with a pirate ship centrepiece, inside), a Jacuzzi, steam bath and fitness room, an outdoor play area, the usual video games arcade and a Children's

> BRIT TIP: Hairdryers and irons are available on request, free of charge, from the front desk at most Disney hotels, subject to availability and sometimes a deposit, except for the *Disneyland Hotel* and *Disney's Hotel New York*, where they are provided in the rooms.

Corner play area with organised activities on particular days. There is also a convention centre here, but the business aspect is less intrusive than at *Disney's Hotel New York*.

The two restaurants are semi-formal – the **Cape Cod** serves European cuisine with a touch of Mediterranean flair, while the similar **Yacht Club** specialises in fish, seafood and grilled meats (try the clam chowder for a true taste of New England) – and you are allocated either one for breakfast when you check in (if the hotel is full – if not, the Cape Cod is used on its own). There are two fine bars, **Fisherman's Wharf**, which opens from the foyer, and the more intensely nautical-themed **Captain's Quarters** piano bar, and both of them look out over Lake Disney. The large **Bay Boutique** offers a good selection of Disney merchandise and travel essentials.

The sheer size of the hotel (1,080 rooms, plus 13 suites) means the foyer can get terribly congested, especially from 9–10am when people are checking out. There is a separate reception desk for the **Admiral's Club**, which covers the lake side of the top two floors (hence wonderful views) and offers a more personal level of service, plus room service, and a quieter, more relaxed atmosphere (quite a bonus when the hotel is full). The majority of the spacious, 2-room suites (55sq m/ 592sq ft) are at this level, too, with the unusual octagonal Honeymoon Suite (45sq m/484sq ft) being quite stunningly romantic.

The main suites also feature some lovely colonial-style furniture and extra nautical touches. Standard rooms (27sq m/290sq ft) continue the refreshing blue-and-white colour scheme of the rest of the hotel, and all include mini-bars and room safes. *Disney's Newport Bay Club* is also at the furthest end of Lake Disney, hence it is a good 15-minute walk to the Theme Parks. But, on a pleasant morning, there is not a more delightful walk anywhere in the Ile de France. **Official rating ***; our rating €€€, CCCC.**

Disney's Newport Bay Club, lake view

Disney's Sequoia Lodge

If you like to be surrounded by gardens and greenery, head straight for *Disney's Sequoia Lodge*, as here you will be transported to one of the great American national parks. The main aspect of the hotel is a touch flat and monolithic but the interior and landscaping detail are quite breathtaking, with a fabulous use of stone and hundreds of imported trees and bushes for an authentic feel.

For the ideal winter retreat, the **Redwood Bar and Lounge** has a massive open fireplace and cosy furniture. The low, sloping, beamed ceiling and flagstone floor of the

BRIT TIP: Not sure of where to stay at Christmas? *Disney's Sequoia Lodge* is the perfect choice during the winter and takes on an enchanted atmosphere with all the festive decorations.

Hunter's Grill at Disney's Sequoia Lodge

lobby set the scene for an outdoor adventure with all the comforts of a luxury resort (well above it's 3-star rating, in our opinion). The judicious use of dark woods adds to the rugged feel and, when the weather is good, there is a lovely terrace where you can sit with a drink and survey Lake Disney.

The gift shop, **The Northwest Passage**, sells a standard range of toiletries, snacks, drinks and souvenirs, while the Little Prairie is the kids' corner, with a TV and video, games station and an elaborate character photo area (available 5 days a week to either take your own snaps or use the official Disney photographer). Then there is the usual video games room, plus an outdoor play area with slides and a sandpit, set among some beautiful gardens, full of unique (for Western Europe!) foliage, a waterfall and even a mock beaver dam. Stroll the paths along the 'Rio Grande' and you come to the hotel's pool lodge, an indoor/outdoor facility that features a water-slide, freeform leisure pool (great for kids), large Jacuzzi, sauna, steam room and gymnasium. There is a solarium that may be pre-booked at €7 for 10 minutes, as well as massages (€45 per half-hour).

The 1,011 rooms (including 16 suites) are split between the huge main building and five lodges spread throughout the gardens. Standard rooms (22sq m/237sq ft) have either a Lake Disney or gardens/car park view, large windows and a few extra touches like rocking chairs and rustic light fittings, which combine well with the dark wood furniture and the dark green bedspreads and curtains to provide that American backwoods ambience.

The cabin lodges offer exactly the same room space and facilities as the main building (Montana) rooms, apart from a mini-bar (so they are slightly cheaper). A lake view carries a supplement but is well worthwhile (and should be requested when you make your booking). The spacious 2-room suites (55sq m/592sq ft) all have a lake view and the Honeymoon Suite features an open-plan arrangement with no separating door between the bedroom and living room.

Disney's Sequoia Lodge has two mouth-watering diners, the **Beaver Creek Tavern** and **Hunter's Grill**. The former is the more family-orientated option, with a varied menu to suit those with a big appetite and includes their speciality of an extra large brochette of skewered lamb with a stuffed baked potato and mushroom garnish. The dessert buffet is outstanding and

> BRIT TIP: Our suggestion for the Hunter's Grill at *Disney's Sequoia Lodge* is the Ranger's Rotisserie – an endive salad, followed by a marinated roast chicken thigh, a herb sausage and spiced pork fillet, and then prime roast rump steak, sliced at your table, plus dessert. Outstanding!

Disney's Hotel Cheyenne

© Disney

there is a set menu for €21, with salad, choice of three main courses and dessert. Within the restaurant is a kids' area with a TV showing Disney cartoons.

The Hunter's Grill continues the hotel's outdoors theme in magnificent style, with a huntin', shootin', fishin' motif that boasts a feature kitchen serving up delicious rotisserie dishes. There are three main set options, including an excellent vegetarian menu, with a choice of desserts, all for €27.50 (without drinks). For both restaurants there is a separate children's menu (€10). Neither restaurant is open for lunch.

At first view, *Disney's Sequoia Lodge* may seem more of an adult environment, but children usually love the 'outdoorsy' feel and the great extras of the pool, gardens and play area, hence it makes a great family base but you may have trouble persuading the kids to leave when the characters are in residence! It takes 10–15 minutes to walk into the Theme Parks, or you can take the 5-minute free shuttle bus ride. **Official rating ***; our rating €€€, CCCC½.**

Disney's Hotel Cheyenne

Howdy partners, welcome to the Wild West – or Disney's version of it at least (far safer and a lot more comfortable!). This wonderfully imaginative hotel is usually a huge hit with children and is therefore a popular family choice (although it can be a little raucous at times when the kids re-enact Custer's Last Stand at regular intervals, armed to the teeth with rifles and bows and arrows from the hotel shop!). The theming is comprehensive and convincing, from the wonderful period-style entrance lobby (complete with two striking bronze horse-and-rider statues) to the

rooms and their rustic-style, kid-friendly bunk beds. It is also quite extensive, as all the rooms are low-rise (no more than two storeys) to give the Wild West cowboy illusion.

The level of creature comforts is not quite the same as elsewhere (no swimming pool or air-conditioning, no luggage delivery to the rooms and only a self-service restaurant), but there are some significant extras aimed at the kids, with optional pony and covered-wagon rides (spring and summer, for a small fee) and a Fort Apache outdoor play area.

The lobby is themed like a Goldrush-era claims office, with a Land Claims desk instead of a reception area, a huge stone fireplace and a mock hotel entrance at the opposite end of the vaulted-ceiling foyer, which also has a kiddie corner (with organised colouring, face painting and drawing on certain days) that has mini-saddles instead of chairs! The **General Store** is the standard gift shop and there is a video games room next door.

Western paraphernalia abounds, and the cowboy theme continues into the bar and restaurant areas, with saloon-style doors, wooden tables, chairs, balustrades and ceiling beams. The **Red Garter Saloon** features live country music in the evening and has an outdoor terrace.

The 750-seat **Chuck Wagon**, which also has its own **Saddle Bar** and wagon play area, is a cafeteria-style eatery dressed up like a Texan pioneer market place and serves a good mixture of international dishes, from barbecue-smoked chicken and beef to salads, pasta, risottos and fresh wok-fried Chinese specialities (set meal €22 for adults and children's menu €10).

Step out of the main building and you are in a true cowboy town, with raised, boarded sidewalks, dirt streets and blocks of hotel rooms all disguised as various buildings, such as the Guest House, Blacksmith and

Sheriff's Office. The 14 blocks are each named after a famous character like Doc Holliday, Jesse James, Calamity Jane and Running Bear. Blocks 17–19 (they are actually numbered from 10–25, omitting 13), Sitting Bull, Wyatt Earp and Billy The Kid, are closest to the main building and the bus stop for the free shuttle to the Theme Parks and *Disney Village*. There are 1,000 identical rooms (all 21sq m/226sq ft) spread out through the 14 blocks, which have internal access only and most feature a double bed and two bunks. The two guest launderettes are free to use, although you need to buy washing powder from the General Store.

The in-room theming is more limited here and the bathrooms slightly more spartan compared to the other resorts, but then it is designed for more budget-conscious visitors (no air-conditioning, just ceiling fans). The regular shuttle bus to the Theme Parks, *Disney Village* and RER station takes about 5 minutes, but you can walk it along a pleasant pathway that runs under the main road and up alongside *Disney's Hotel New York* in about 15. **Official rating **; our rating €€, CCC½.**

Disney's Hotel Santa Fe

Right at the budget end of the six-hotel spectrum is this extensive *pueblo*-style resort decked out in best American South West fashion, with Native American, Spanish and Mexican cultures providing the decorative motif, and a giant Clint Eastwood billboard (like a drive-in movie screen) welcoming you 'into town'. In truth, this is a glorified motel, but that doesn't stop it being fun for kids, good value for money and still well situated to enjoy all the Disney magic. It gets extremely busy in high season (breakfast sittings are pre-allocated from 7am) and is popular with coach operators, so it gets congested in the morning with large numbers of guests arriving and departing at the same time.

At first appearance, the hotel looks rather stark with its collection of square, concrete blocks up to five storeys high, but the Imagineers

4

> **BRIT TIP:** As at *Disney's Hotel Cheyenne*, breakfast at Disney's *Hotel Santa Fe* is of the most basic continental kind – cereal, croissants, pastries, juice, tea and coffee – but you can pay a supplement to add bacon, eggs and fresh fruit.

have been at work here, even if the fanciful 'volcano' is now a derelict grey hulk. There are four 'trails' through the resort (corresponding to the four different room sections – Artefacts, Water, Monuments and Legends) each with their own symbols and icons scattered around – from rusting desert 'vehicles' to outlandish meteorites, water trails, a geyser and even a crashed flying saucer! The smattering of desert scenery is also convincing and quite eye catching.

The main facilities are in the reception building, while the 1,000 rooms are spread out over 41 blocks,

> **BRIT TIP:** You need to request a room with bunk beds when booking accommodation at *Disney's Hotel Santa Fe* if that is what your children want (and which is usually a lot more comfortable for children aged 6 plus).

BRIT TIP: The petrol station next door to *Disney's Hotel Santa Fe* is one of the few places on-site where you can buy fresh milk – invaluable if your kids like the white stuff!

Disney's Davy Crockett Ranch

surrounded by small car parks, so if you are driving, this is the only hotel where you can park more or less outside your room. The 700-seat **La Cantina** serves up Tex-Mex food in a food-court-style servery, where you can make up your own meals (salads, tapas, fajitas, chilli burgers, nachos, roast pork, chicken, beef, spaghetti and meatballs) or choose one of the set meals (€22 for adults and €10 for children), and there is an ice cream and coffee bar. Imaginative touches have food served from the back of a flat-bed truck and drinks dispensed from 'petrol pumps' – worth highlighting as so many people miss them in their rush to get to the parks. The children's corner with organised colouring and drawing activities (in the evenings) is also here, with a computer console and Disney TV.

Next door to La Cantina is the

Rio Grande Bar, with live entertainment and karaoke on selected evenings. **The Trading Post** is the Disney gift shop, with a good range of souvenirs, snacks, drinks and basic toiletries. A video games room is available for the kids, plus an outdoor playground, the Totem Circle, which is handy if they have any energy left at the end of the day! Back in the lobby, characters meet 'n' greet in the morning, which is the ideal way to start the day if you

Disney's Hotel Santa Fe

have any young autograph hunters.

The identical rooms (21sq m/ 226sq ft) are cheerfully decorated, if a little spartan by comparison with the other hotels, but many also come with bunk beds instead of two double beds. As with all Disney accommodation, they can house a family of four (or four plus one in a cot), although they are a little short of drawer space.

Like *Disney's Hotel Cheyenne*, there is no in-room air-conditioning, just a ceiling fan. The two hotels are adjacent to each other, so it is perfectly permissible to pop 'next door' to enjoy some of the facilities there too, notably, the Fort Apache play area for kids, the pony rides and the Red Garter Saloon. The hotel is a good 20–25-minute walk from the parks, but once again, if the weather is clement, it is a lovely way to start the day as you stroll alongside the 'Rio Grande' and up by *Disney's Hotel New York*, around Lake Disney and through *Disney Village*.

Alternatively, the shuttle bus takes about 10 minutes, and while there is usually quite a queue in the morning around the parks' opening times, they run several buses at once on this route (as they do at all the bigger hotels). **Official rating **; our rating €€, CCC.**

Halloween at Disney's Hotel Cheyenne

Disney's Davy Crockett Ranch

If you drive down to *Disneyland Resort Paris* and are happy to use your car to get to the Theme Parks every day, staying at *Disney's Davy Crockett Ranch* is the best-value way to enjoy all the fun and still have a taste of Disney imagination with your accommodation. Here, in 'trapper country', are 535 cabins with 1- or 2-bedrooms accommodating up to six, plus 60

Indian Meadows at Disney's Davy Crockett Ranch

caravan and camper van sites, which all have water supply and connections for electricity and water drainage, plus their own picnic bench and open-air barbecue.

Set in 57 hectares (140 acres) of pretty woodland about a 15-minute drive from the Theme Parks (where parking is free with your resort ID card), you do get the feeling of being out in the cowboy wilds here (see map on page 86). The woods are dotted with imaginative touches such as Native American tepees, while all the main services and facilities are located in a wonderfully fun cowboy 'village' at the heart of the ranch. Here you will find a host of great activities and amenities, from the **Alamo Trading Post** (the gift shop and grocery store, 8am–11pm) to the great children's play area and even a farmyard and mini menagerie featuring reindeer and wolves.

BRIT TIP: The camping sites are particularly popular with the Brits and the Dutch, and they sell out well in advance at peak season, so you need to book EARLY in summer.

The 'village' is actually a fully-fledged resort in its own right, centred around the Trading Post and **Crockett's Tavern**, a log-cabin restaurant serving lunch (12.30–2.30pm) and dinner (6–10.30pm), with a take-away service, too. The buffet-style servery offers up a good variety of dishes, from salad, fish and chips, roast chicken and pasta to entrecôte steak and even a vegetarian meal, while there is a choice of four kids' meals (€10). Across the street is the authentic (if a little small) **Saloon** (5pm–midnight) serving beer, wine and cocktails, with live entertainment and karaoke

at peak times, plus outdoor seating and a large-screen TV in summer.

Bowie's Bike Barn (8am–6, 8 or 10pm seasonally), the information centre, houses the children's activity corner, with a computer play station, video console and organised face-painting and colouring, all set up around a large table with clever mini-saddles to sit on. Disney characters make an appearance every evening, while there is grown-up entertainment too, with themed evenings, line dancing and discos, plus organised sports, from jogging and aerobics to *petanque* and archery.

BRIT TIP: It is advisable, especially in summer, when the resort can hold around 4,000 people, to book a table for dinner at Crockett's Tavern. Lunch is rarely over-subscribed.

The Lucky Raccoon video games room adds that essential amenity for kids, and they are then spoiled for choice with the likes of horse and pony rides (4–11 only; €6–14), Davy's Farm (a petting zoo with goats, sheep, rabbits, birds and ducks), an outdoor play and climbing area, table tennis, volleyball, basketball, archery and mini-golf (the latter for €6 for nine holes). There are two free-to-use indoor tennis courts (one of which is used alternately for archery, table tennis and volleyball in winter) and a nature park with the Indian Meadows village and trails to see the reindeer park and wolf enclosure.

Cycling is another opportunity for children and adults, with a huge range of bikes, scooters and quadracycles for hire at €3–15 for an hour, to be used on the cycle trails throughout the resort and woods.

The final outstanding element of the resort is the **Blue Springs Pool**,

BRIT TIP: The reindeer actually 'work' in Disney's Christmas Parade at the *Disneyland Park*, but they get 10 months off, which they spend at the ranch!

an extensive indoor water park (8.30am–10pm) with a semi-circular paddling pool for toddlers, a large, free-form leisure pool that has a waterfall and long water-slide, fountains and squirt pond, and a huge Jacuzzi. You can rent towels for a small fee. Under 12s must also be accompanied by an adult at all times in the pool area. It is an exceptional facility and you may struggle to get the kids out, even with the lure of the Theme Parks!

Eight circular 'trails' house all the accommodation. Each trail has its own take-away cottage, where breakfast is served (7–11am) for you to take back to your cabin, caravan or tent. The 1-bedroom cabins (all 36sq m/388sq ft) each feature a spacious lounge with TV, a kitchen complete with two hot-plates, dishwasher, fridge, microwave, kettle, coffee machine and all the necessary cutlery, crockery and cooking utensils. There is also a breakfast bar area. The bathroom (fully stocked with towels) includes the toilet but the two are separate in the 2-bedroom version. Some have a pull-down double bed in the lounge,

BRIT TIP: The ranch's 60 two-bedroom cabins are all newer than the 1-bed ones, and come at a slight premium. They also go quickly (although more are due to be built), so it's best to book early.

others a convertible sofa, while the bedroom has a double bed and two bunks. Many of the 1-bedroom cabins do look their age (more than 12 years old), hence it is a basic 2-star property. Outside, they all have their own brick-built barbecue and picnic bench, plus parking.

The 2-bedroom version (39sq m/ 420sq ft) has the two bunk beds in their own room, ensuring Mum and Dad a little peace and quiet! The living quarters are arranged slightly differently and the general fixtures and fittings are that bit smarter, but the difference in price is minimal, so these are the better ones to go for. The caravan and camp sites are on Moccasin Trail (the others are named after similar Davy Crockett imagery – Wagon Wheel, Big Bear, Tomahawk, etc) and you will find toilets, showers and a launderette at the centre of this area. At peak times, a mini train/tram runs around all the trails, ferrying people between the accommodation units and the village area.

The site is completely secured against non-visitor traffic. You check in at the reception area at the main entrance, much as you would for a hotel, and they provide you with your keys, the all-important Disney resort ID cards and the security code to access the site, which you punch in at the gate just past reception. Then, when you depart, you can just drop the keys off in a deposit box, so you need not go back into the reception area.

The parks and *Disney Village* are about a 15-minute drive from the ranch, which is about 3km (2 miles) off Exit 13 of the A4 autoroute. To get there, simply come out of the property, take the second exit from the roundabout (signposted A4 Reims), and continue along the A4 to Exit 14 for 'Les Parcs Disneyland'. **Official rating ****; **our rating €€, CCCC.**

The new **Davy Crockett's**

BRIT TIP: To call ANY of Disney's hotels, simply dial the main switchboard – 00 33 1 64 74 40 00 from the UK, 01 64 74 40 00 in France – and ask for the hotel you require.

Adventure (see also page 189) is an adjacent forest park, open to the general public, with a series of five tree-top adventure trails of varying difficulty for all ages from 8 up. It promises up to 3 hours of challenging tree-climbing, rope bridges, giant swings, obstacle courses and the feature 16-m (52-ft) Tarzan Tree Jump. It costs €25 for those over 1.40m (4ft 6in) tall and €15 for those under. Look up more (in French only) on www.aventure-aventure.com.

Beyond Disney

Once you move beyond Disney for your choice of accommodation, things become simpler. There are few grand theme hotels (the Holiday Inn, Mövenpick Dream Castle and

Explorers Hotel

Midsummer's Eve at Davy Crockett's Ranch

Explorers Hotel at Val de France are the only exceptions) and no great variation in style or facilities (almost all are 2- or 3-star). Rooms tend to be small but comfortable and the majority will provide a good, basic continental breakfast. We have toured the Seine-et-Marne region extensively and looked at most of the hotels on offer and have been impressed by the generally high standard of cleanliness and friendliness we have found.

A lot of hotels in the immediate vicinity of Marne-la-Vallée are relatively new and so still quite smart and pleasant, while all hotels are inspected regularly to ensure they conform to their star rating. Quite a few have swimming pools, but you need to decide if you are likely to use a pool after a long day at the parks to make it worthwhile paying extra.

It is also possible to subdivide the off-site hotels into those which are Near The Magic (including the new sub-region of Val de France), and those which are a Short Drive away, and hotel chains that have accommodation in Paris itself (which is not necessarily a bad idea if you

Hotel du Moulin de Paris

want to see a lot of the city, as it is only 35–40 minutes to *Disneyland Resort Paris* by RER).

Near the Magic

When it comes to hotels that are within a figurative stone's throw of the Theme Parks, there are eight contrasting choices in the Val d'Europe area. These include four brand new hotels in an associated development just off the main ring road (which Disney refers to as its Selected Hotels). One of these, the Explorers Hotel, is primarily for the UK market, while all usually host a high percentage of British guests. Looking at them in detail, they are:

Hotel du Moulin de Paris: Built in 2001, this smart, well-run hotel in Magny-le-Hongre (a 5–10-minute drive from the Theme Parks) has been extensively refurbished, with all the 82 identikit bright, clean rooms getting a fresh, new look. They comfortably accommodate four, with a double bed, a single and a pull-out, or a double and two bunks (you need to request a room with bunks in advance). Cots are also available on request but maximum occupancy for each room is four. The bathrooms have a shower only,

no bath. Breakfast is served 7–10am in the airy conservatory-style restaurant, with dinner 7–10pm (and sandwiches 7am–midnight at the bar) and, in summer, an outdoor patio makes a lovely place to sit for a drink. A heated outdoor pool (May–September), sauna and small fitness room are all free to hotel guests.

If you arrive early and want to head to the Theme Parks, you can leave your bags in a luggage room.

A daily shuttle runs to and from the Theme Parks (returning half an hour after closing time) for €2 per person, while there is also a public bus to Marne-la-Vallée station. The hotel is on the Rue du Moulin á Vent, just off the Boulevard de l'Europe, the ring road that goes around *Disneyland Resort Paris*. More importantly, most packages here include your Theme Park tickets. Call 00 33 1 60 43 77 77 from the UK or visit www.moulindeparis.com. **Official rating ***; our rating €€€, CCC.**

Radisson SAS Hotel at Disneyland Resort Paris: Opening in December 2005, this ultra-smart new property of the Radisson group stands right on the edge of the Golf Disneyland complex in Magny-le-Hongre (and has impressive views

Radisson SAS Hotel

© Leonardo.com

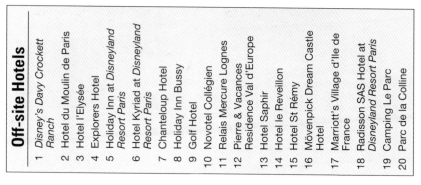

Off-site Hotels

1 Disney's Davy Crockett Ranch
2 Hotel du Moulin de Paris
3 Hotel l'Elysée
4 Explorers Hotel
5 Holiday Inn at Disneyland Resort Paris
6 Hotel Kyriad at Disneyland Resort Paris
7 Chanteloup Hotel
8 Holiday Inn Bussy
9 Golf Hotel
10 Novotel Collégien
11 Relais Mercure Lognes
12 Pierre & Vacances Residence Val d'Europe
13 Hotel Saphir
14 Hotel le Reveillon
15 Hotel St Rémy
16 Mövenpick Dream Castle Hotel
17 Marriott's Village d'Ile de France
18 Radisson SAS Hotel at Disneyland Resort Paris
19 Camping Le Parc
20 Parc de la Colline

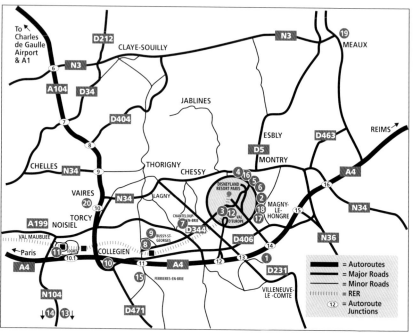

over the three 9-hole courses). With 250 fully air-conditioned rooms, including 20 suites and 139 family rooms for up to four people, it is set up to a large extent as a convention hotel, with excellent business facilities, so you can expect a busy but elegant style. But there should also be plenty to attract the Disney holidaymaker. There are two restaurants, the cosy **Brasserie Birdie** and the gourmet dining of **Pamplemousse Restaurant**, The Barley lobby bar (also serving snacks), a Play Club for children, and a Wellness & Fitness Centre, including a swimming pool, fully equipped gym and a variety of treatment and massage rooms. Call 00 33 1 64 17 31 42 or visit www.golfresort.paris.radissonsas.com. **Expected rating: ****, €€€€, CCCC.**

Hotel l'Elysée: At the heart of the Val d'Europe development, and therefore just a 5-minute RER ride to the Theme Parks, this ultra-smart 3-star property opened in July 2002. The Hotel l'Elysée features a grand reception lobby, underground parking and an extremely quiet ambience (a nice contrast after the hurly-burly of the Disney resort). The 152 rooms all accommodate four in a double and two single sofa beds (made up ready for your arrival), while there are four spacious junior suites and five rooms adapted for the disabled (two persons maximum). The rooms all have a mini-bar and safe and the marbled bathrooms are extremely smart. Cots are available on request, but they can't add up to a fifth person. However, there are inter-connecting rooms for larger families.

The hotel has a left-luggage room, a video games room for kids, an elegant bar and a high-quality restaurant (full English breakfast €9), while 24-hour room service is also available. Most packages here include park tickets and either a free parking pass or daily RER tickets (which are €1.50 each way). The last train from Marne-la-Vallée back to Val d'Europe is at 12 minutes past midnight each day. Call 00 33 1 64 63 33 33 for more details. **Official rating ***; our rating €€€€, CCC.**

Pierre & Vacances Residence Val d'Europe: Opened in 2003, this stylish apartment complex from the French chain of holiday residences has a good array of flexible accommodation which makes an ideal base for a longer stay in the region. With 292 apartments and studios, sleeping from two to nine (at a squeeze), this is a modern and well-furnished offering. All feature a fully equipped kitchenette (cooking hob, fridge, microwave and dishwasher) with a living room and either a one- or two-bedroom option, plus what they call a 'cabin' that has additional bunk beds. The studios offer living/sleeping space

for up to three, while the largest apartments can sleep three in the living room, four in the two bedrooms and two in the cabin. All have a bathroom and the larger ones have a shower room too.

> BRIT TIP: Towels are only provided in Pierre & Vacances properties for a fee, so it is advisable to bring your own. You are also required to pay a €200 deposit when checking in.

The resort-style set-up offers a launderette, indoor car park, luggage room, small gym and an outdoor heated swimming pool open year-round. A separate charge (on check-in) is made for TV and phone use. Continental breakfast is served daily (€8.50 for adults, €7.50 for children) in a corner of the big reception area. Call 00 33 1 60 42 82 00 or visit www.pierre-vacances.com. **Official rating ***, our rating €€€, CC.**

Val-de-France

This brand new region (as of 2003) consists purely of four neighbouring hotels which are well worth considering. Disney refers to them as its Selected Hotels, tour operators call them Near The Magic and they can be found just off the Boulevard de l'Europe, about a 10-minute drive from the Marne-la-Vallée station hub for drop-off to the Theme Parks and *Disney Village* (with regular free shuttle bus service). It *is* possible to walk in from here, but it takes at least half an hour.

Explorers Hotel: This highly imaginative 390-room hotel was built for tour operator MyTravel and its affiliate companies (Cresta, Paris Travel Service and Leger Holidays). It is designed primarily

BRIT TIP: The shuttle bus serves all four Selected Hotels and runs every 15 minutes (every 10 minutes at park opening and closing times). It operates 6.30am–11.30pm September–June and 6.30am–1am July and August and stops at all four in turn (Explorers–Kyriad–Holiday Inn–Mövenpick), which means the trip to the parks from the first stop can take a good 20 minutes when it's busy and vice versa on the return journey.

Hotel l'Elysée

with the British visitor in mind, hence there are some smart touches for families. It was the first fully themed off-site hotel (followed by the Holiday Inn and Mövenpick Dream Castle) and offers both extra-spacious rooms (with families of six to 10 in mind) and some superb children's facilities. It is much the same price to eat and drink here as in the parks or *Disney Village*, however, and their fine dining restaurant can be a touch expensive.

Designed like a grand French manor – the preserve of mythical explorer Sir Archibald de Bacle and his various 'discoveries' – it is a fun and spacious creation, from the busy lobby area (complete with a Kids

Corner with TV and a novel fountain) to the buffet-style restaurant with its outdoor terrace (wonderful on a sunny morning). Walk through the lobby and you have a startling view over the **Tropical Atrium** at the heart of the hotel, which is also home to the

BRIT TIP: Surprisingly, there is a €1 charge for a pool towel at the Explorers, so take your own towels. The pool also gets VERY busy in late afternoon.

Secret Lagoon Swimming Pool, a 20m (66ft) heated indoor pool with a separate toddlers' area. The wreck of the Seven Seas Raider pirate ship is beached at one end of the lagoon, allowing kids the chance to explore the decks and passageways or take to the water-slide. A second, more elaborate, dragon-themed water-slide was added in 2005, making this guaranteed fun for kids of all ages.

The **Plantation Restaurant** is the main diner, a market-style emporium offering breakfast

Explorers Hotel

(7–10.30am) and dinner (6–10pm). The excellent continental-style buffet breakfast offers a good selection for all the family (or you can choose a cooked breakfast for a few extra euros), while dinner is again a buffet option with a set menu from €18–22 for adults (€10 for children 3–11) or a good range of individual items (especially their salads and desserts).

BRIT TIP: Like the Disney hotels, you are given a time slot for breakfast each day. You collect these from reception when you check in and it is advisable to pick your times for your whole stay as the best ones go quickly.

For more informal dining, there is **Marco's Pizza Parlour** (noon–11pm) where you can order a take-away if you prefer and **Traders Café Bar** (noon–11pm) for snacks and a drink or two. The **Far Horizon Terrace** (5–11pm) offers an elevated view of the Atrium and the chance to sip a speciality tea or coffee, or a glass of wine or beer. The **Captain's Library** (6.30–10pm) is a themed full-service restaurant, once again offering children's meals, and with a small play area to keep them amused while Mum and Dad finish their dinner. While it is a touch expensive for an off-site restaurant (2-course menu from €21–24 including a glass of wine or €30 for a 3-course menu; kids menu for €12.50, including a surprise gift), the food here is outstanding for what is, in theory, a 3-star hotel. Finally, **Smugglers Tavern** (6pm–1am) is the hotel's main pub-style bar, with a corner given over to a large-screen TV for sports events. There are pool tables and dart boards, and snacks are available here, too. It is highly popular most evenings (you might want to request a room in a different block to the Tavern if you are early-to-bed types).

Traders Café is also brilliantly designed for parents to be able to sit back and watch their offspring expend some energy in the activity areas. Scally Wagg's Jungle Adventures is the big indoor soft-play area (in two sections, for 2–4s and 5–12s), with all the requisite ladders, ropes, slides and ball pools, while the Seven Seas Raider is also nearby. Then there is a two-part arcade/games room, the Kids Club for younger children (with ride-on toys and basic arcade games), and Harry's Action Zone for older ones, with the usual (noisy!) video games.

BRIT TIP: The Explorers' room configurations are the most family-friendly of any hotel here. The use of the 'bunk cabins' and single beds (instead of two doubles) give them huge flexibility, especially with older children.

The room choice is definitely a cut above usual hotel accommodation. Standard rooms, called 'Crew rooms', feature one

4

© Disney

Explorers Hotel

double bed and two singles, with a bath, shower and separate toilet (a useful idea), plus interactive satellite TV with video games, internet access and pay-per-view programmes and films, room safe, hairdryer and ceiling fan (no air-conditioning), plus tea and coffee-making facilities. Each Crew room can be connected to a 'bunk cabin' for two children. Extended families or groups of friends can take two interconnecting Crew rooms with the bunk cabin in between and sleep up to 10 (the bunk cabin doors can be closed).

There are then seven 'Captain's Suites' sleeping up to six in two bedrooms, plus three imaginative Themed Suites (Planet Hollywood, Jungle and Sweets), which add superbly equipped kids' quarters (you may struggle to get your youngsters out of this suite!). All 10 suites have a lake view and the vital addition of air-conditioning for the hot summer months. Finally, nine rooms are fully fitted out for guests with disabilities (arguably the best of their kind in the whole area). Additional features include free parking at the hotel, the parks and *Disney Village*, picnic lunches, currency exchange facilities, a Disney store, a concierge and information desk. However, the Explorers is a non-smoking hotel, apart from areas such as Smugglers Tavern.

The hotel is situated just across the resort-encircling Boulevard de l'Europe from *Disney's Hotel Santa Fe* and is the first of the four hotels of the Val de France district you come to. Call 00 33 1 60 42 60 00 or look up www.explorershotel.com. **Official rating: ***; our rating: €€€€, CCCC½.**

Holiday Inn at Disneyland Resort Paris: If you prefer that more upmarket touch, look no further than the newest Holiday Inn in the Seine-et-Marne region. Designed in French manorial style with a circus-themed flavour throughout (and quite stylishly done), this is a cut above the usual tourist fare (and, indeed, many other hotels in this well-known chain) and it scores high marks for families, too. At once both chic and cheerful, the hotel comes as a refreshing change from the usual identikit styling. It will appeal to all ages and boasts the extra service touches you would expect of a 4-star property, such as 24-hour room service and a business centre.

The 325 standard rooms (many interconnecting) feature a double bed and a curtained off section (like a circus big top) with bunk beds and a separate TV/games console for the kids. The 23 Kidsuites rooms have children's areas built into them in a more elaborate fashion. All rooms come with a main TV with international channels and internet access, plus room safe, hairdryer and tea- and coffee-making facilities. They are also fully air-conditioned.

BRIT TIP: Don't overlook the value of the Holiday Inn's family rooms and Kidsuites. If Simon's boys are anything to go by, you'll have difficulty getting your offspring out of the room because of 'their' area!

The hotel offers a sophisticated indoor leisure pool (with toddler area), smart fitness club and an extensive outdoor playground in the park-like gardens for the young 'uns, where they can burn off any excess energy. The new **Ringmaster's Corner** is a separate and imaginative children's area next to the restaurant, with chalkboards, tables and chairs, games, TV/video and even a kids' buffet (breakfast and dinner; €5 and €9.95). The main restaurant, **L'Etoile**, serves a pleasing mix of traditional French and international cuisine, while their buffet breakfast (with an extensive array of cereals plus hot and cold dishes) is possibly the best in the area – including Disney's hotels. The inner courtyard features an adjoining terrace to the restaurant and, for breakfast, this makes a wonderful start to the day if the weather permits. There is the inevitable Disney Store and an excellent bar/lounge, **Bar des Artistes**, which also serves a good array of family-orientated snacks (salads, sandwiches, omelettes, baguettes) for lunch and dinner.

> BRIT TIP: If the parks are especially hectic or you just want a quiet break for lunch, head to the Holiday Inn and take advantage of their relaxed and friendly service in Bar des Artistes.

The hotel has its own Bureau de Change, and the overall value for money here is top notch. As with the other hotels of Val de France, the VEA Navette airport shuttle for both airports calls three times a day and is available without reservation. Call 00 33 1 64 63 37 37 or look up www.ichotelsgroup.com. **Official rating: ****; our rating: €€€€, CCCC.**

> BRIT TIP: Sign up in advance online (for free) for the Holiday Inn's Priority Club programme and you qualify for early check-in if you arrive before the official 2pm opening time.

Hotel Kyriad at Disneyland Resort Paris: Right next door to the Holiday Inn is the new flagship hotel of the budget Envergure group. With a lovely country house style, it is an excellent option for those who want to watch the pennies but still get a taste of the Magic. The 300 airy and spotlessly clean rooms are all air-conditioned, which is a bonus at this end of the scale, and come with tea- and coffee-making facilities, hairdryer and room safe.

The standard room features a double bed and two bunks, while the twin room can be either two singles or a double bed. No room can accommodate more than four, but there are various connecting rooms bringing the number up to six or eight. The rest of the hotel is equally straightforward, with one restaurant (breakfast buffet at €6.50, dinner buffet at €19) and two bars in a friendly, relaxing ambience. The small children's play area in the lobby can get quite crowded in the morning. Although it is French owned and run, up to 60% of guests can be British at peak times, and the overall feel is fresh and cosmopolitan. Call 00 33 1 60 43 61 61 or visit www.envergure.fr/kyriadfr.html for more details. **Official rating: **; our rating: €€€, CC½.**

Mövenpick Dream Castle Hotel: This wonderful option opened in August 2004 and is another upscale property of the big Swiss catering and hotel group, aimed at a fully international market. Next door to the Explorers Hotel and similarly on the free shuttle bus route to the parks, the 400-room property (250 family rooms, 43 'Double Queen' rooms, 86 'King' rooms, including 10 fitted for disabled guests; and 21 suites) exhibits a beautiful castle style, from the elegant lobby (complete with twin 'thrones', a sword-in-the-stone replica and suits

BRIT TIP: We rate the Excalibur Bar at the Mövenpick Dream Castle one of the most enjoyable places to relax with a drink or two, and at a good price – their alcohol tariff is almost half that of bars in the *Disney Village*.

The authors at Mövenpick Dream Castle

of armour) to the well-fitted rooms (200 of which feature curtained-off bunk beds – a great family touch). There is also a neat children's play area in the lobby, complete with ball pool, plus pool tables. The restaurant choice is impressive, with the more standard offerings of **Sanssouci** augmented by the expansive style of **The Musketeers**, which features a spectacular themed buffet each evening (the desserts alone are worth stopping in for!). There is also a charming outdoor terrace which makes a lovely setting for dinner on a summer evening. Both restaurants serve breakfast at busy periods, meaning there are no frustrating queues in the morning, as there are at some hotels. Their

regular rate also includes a full American-style buffet breakfast (quite a rarity) and, as Mövenpick set great store by the quality of their cuisine, it is very good. The fully themed **Excalibur Bar** is a great place to enjoy a drink after a day in the parks and also serves light lunches and snacks.

Other notable features of the Dream Castle include a babysitting service, a fun swimming pool with a Jacuzzi, smart fitness/health facilities, video arcade and a garden

Hotel Kyriad

© Agence AHI/Agence Grossomodo

overlooking the lake which backs on to the other hotels in Val-de-France. They also have an array of their own characters, or 'mascots', which seem to keep children entertained in the lobby and at mealtimes. Uniquely, the hotel is home to a superb Asian/Thai-style massage spa, with a range of relaxing treatments (including couples' massage), a blissful tonic after a day pounding the parks! Call 00 33 1 64 17 90 00 from the UK or visit www.moven pick-hotels.com. **Rating: ****; our rating: €€€€€, CCCC.**

Chanteloup Hotel

A short drive from the Magic

Chanteloup Hotel: Tucked away in the pretty little village of Chanteloup-en-Brie, just to the west of Val d'Europe, is this small, family-run hotel. With just 64 small but smart rooms, each with a double bed and two fold-up bunks, plus a fitness centre, Jacuzzi and sauna, this is an ideal retreat after a day of frenetic theme-parking. It has a pleasant restaurant and a little foyer bar, and that's about it for the creature comforts, although there is a daily shuttle bus to Disney for €9/person return. To reach the hotel, turn off the A4 at Exit 13 and take the D231 past Val d'Europe for 4.5km (3 miles), then turn left into Chanteloup-en-Brie. For more info, call 00 33 1 64 30 00 00. **Official rating **; our rating €€€, CC.**

Holiday Inn Bussy: One of the few 4-star hotels in the area, this Holiday Inn is situated at the entrance to the modern town of Bussy-St-Georges, handy for both road and RER links to Marne-la-Vallée. It is a quiet, rather unprepossessing property, but it hides real charm and style, a long way removed from the usual rather brash image of the Holiday Inn group. The light airy foyer opens up to reveal a smart restaurant with a conservatory annexe and a small, intimate bar, with a couple of video games and a pool table. The outdoor (unheated) swimming pool is open until the end of September (or sooner if it turns cold), and has a lovely patio area that allows guests to dine outside when the weather is fine.

The 120 rooms are extremely comfortable, even for four, with the choice of a double, triple and quad (two doubles) configuration, plenty of cupboard space, and a marbled bathroom with hairdryer. Many rooms interconnect for larger family accommodation. They include satellite TV, internet connection, a

Novotel Collégien

trouser press and a kettle (but you need to buy tea and coffee sachets from reception).

The hotel hosts a lot of business conferences, hence it can be busy during the week, but it is only a 5-minute walk to the RER station (which is then 10 minutes to Marne-la-Vallée) and 10 minutes to the Theme Parks by car.

To get there, take Exit 11 off the A4 and follow the signposts to Bussy-St-Georges, go straight across two roundabouts, and the Holiday Inn is immediately on your right. Call 00 33 1 64 66 35 65 or visit www.hi-marnelavallee.com for more info. **Official rating ****; our rating €€€€, CCC.**

Golf Hotel: On the other side of Bussy-St-Georges is this distinctly countrified hotel, with a genuinely welcoming aspect, set on the edge of a golf course and with obvious benefits for the sporting fraternity. However, you don't need to be a golfer to stay here as the 93 light, airy rooms cater for everyone, with double, triple, twin and family rooms, the latter with a double bed and two fold-down or fixed bunks. Mini-bars and hairdryers are standard, as is internet access, and, there is plenty of storage space.

The large restaurant has big picture windows and an outdoor terrace, while there is a children's play area to the side and a large green for kids to expend any remaining energy on. The outdoor heated pool is open from May to mid-September and there is a small lobby bar for a quiet drink, plus two private tennis courts available for hotel guests. Given the surrounding greenery, you could easily think you were a million miles from the hectic Disney whirl, but you are only 10–15 minutes' walk from the RER station or 5 minutes on their free shuttle bus (on request). To get to the hotel, carry on past the Holiday Inn (see above), cross the Place du Clos-St-Georges, then turn right at Boulevard du Golf and the hotel is along on the left. Call 00 33 1 64 66 30 30. **Official rating ***; our rating €€€, CCC.**

Novotel Collégien: Slightly off the beaten track lies this smart hotel of the business-like Novotel chain (see page 101). Just south of the A4 and the town of Collégien, it is tucked away on a mini-industrial estate and has some surprisingly family-friendly touches, with a free welcome gift for children and a free character dining set at the restaurant. There is table football in the lobby, a heated outdoor pool (mid-April to end of September), and an extremely pleasant bar area (open until midnight). The 195 rooms (with one floor designated non-smoking) are all brightly furnished and feature a double bed and a fold-out sofa which will sleep two (smallish) children. Each room also has a mini-bar, Wi-Fi access and TV with English channels and pay-per-view films, while there are two pairs of connecting rooms and six adapted for guests with disabilities. Usefully, the toilet is separate from the bathroom.

A busy convention hotel for much of the year, it is given over completely to the tourism business in July and at weekends. You can find it just past the junction of the A104 and A4, heading south (to Croissy-Beaubourg), turn left off the D471, straight over at the traffic lights, and it is on the right. There is a free, secure parking area and you really do need to have a car here as it is 3km (2 miles) from the nearest RER station. Call 00 33 1 64 80 53 53 or visit www.novotel.com. **Official rating ***; our rating €€€€, CCC.**

Relais Mercure Lognes: Conveniently situated just off the A4 (but far enough away not to be bothered by traffic buzz), this neat,

Our Top 10 Places to Enjoy A Drink at Disneyland Resort Paris

1   The Redwood Bar at *Disney's Sequoia Lodge*
2   The Excalibur Bar at the Mövenpick Dream Castle
3   Fantasia Bar at the *Disneyland Hotel*
4   Billy Bob's Saloon at *Disney Village*
5   The Bar at The Steakhouse restaurant in *Disney Village*
6   Captain's Quarters Bar at *Disney's Newport Bay Club*
7   Sports Bar at *Disney Village*
8   City Bar at *Disney's Hotel New York*
9   Smugglers Tavern at the Explorers Hotel
10 Rainforest Café bar at *Disney Village*

4

modern offering of the budget Mercure group (see page 99) is in a quiet residential area in the new town of Lognes, not far from the RER station (about 10 minutes' walk). It offers 85 comfortable, modern rooms with satellite TV, Wi-Fi access, safe, well-designed bathroom and hair dryer. Family rooms for two or three children are in split-level duplexes, while the restaurant also caters well for kids (and offers a good buffet breakfast). There is a pleasant wine bar and outdoor terrace and a small fitness room and sauna.

The staff are unfailingly cheerful and helpful, and there is an internet terminal and Wi-Fi access in the lobby to check email (works with a France Telecom Telecarte, available from reception). Barely a 15-minute drive from the Theme Parks, the hotel is just off Exit 10.1 of the A4 (Val Maubuée Sud). Turn left at the first roundabout then right on to the Boulevard de Mandinet and it is on the next roundabout on the left. Call 00 33 1 64 80 02 50 or visit www.mercure.com. **Official rating ***; our rating €€€, CC½.**

Hotel Saphir: A one-off property, just to the south in Pontault-Combault, this has 179 exceedingly smart rooms for two to four people,

with the family rooms consisting of a double bed plus a single or a double sofa bed. While not the prettiest of hotels, it maintains a high standard of interior decor and service, and the heated indoor pool is an excellent (and rare) amenity, along with a sauna and fitness centre for an additional charge. The family-friendly restaurant is also well priced (set meals from €14 for adults and €8 for children) and there is also a pleasant bar. Call 00 33 1 64 43 45 47 for more info. It can be found just off the N104 travelling south at Exit 15. **Official rating ***; our rating €€€, CCC.**

Hotel le Reveillon: Further south, in the older confines of the town of Lesigny, this former monastery has been tastefully converted to hold 47 immaculate rooms on the edge of a beautiful golf course. Dating back to the 12th century, it also has a wonderful restaurant, and yet is still under half an hour's drive from the Theme Parks. It makes a great base for investigating some of the other villages of this area, but it is some way off the RER routes.

Family rooms offer an extra bed or bunks for children, and all feature satellite TV, mini-bar and hairdryer, while the superb traditional-style restaurant still has a children's menu. To get there take Exit 18 off the N104, then continue south on the Avenue des Hyveneaux and turn left after 1km (about ½ mile) at the signpost for Golf du Reveillon. Call 00 33 1 60 02 25 26 from the UK. **Official rating ***; our rating €€€, CC½.**

Hotel St Rémy: Finally, a hotel to suit couples, as this is a touch more detached and romantic than most,

Hotel St Rémy

set in the picturesque hamlet of Ferrières-en-Brie, but only 7km (4 miles) from Disney. Originally built in the 19th century, but tastefully restored and reopened in 2000, it has just 25 rooms (all en suite, with satellite TV and hairdryer) with some wonderfully elegant individual touches and style, wooden floors and antique furniture. Its fabulous restaurant still offers a children's menu (not Saturday lunchtime or

Sunday evening), but there is not a lot else to keep kids amused in this quiet location. A car is advisable, although Bussy-St-Georges is only 2km (just over 1 mile) away. The hotel can be found just off Exit 11 from the A4 – follow the signs to Ferrières-en-Brie and pick up the main Rue Jean Jaurès. Call 00 33 1 64 76 74 00 from the UK or visit www.hotel-st-remy.fr. **Official rating ***; our rating €€€, CC½.**

Camping

With the ease in which you can drive down to this region of France, it makes sense for people to look at camping alternatives, and one new campsite near the village of Touquin (13km/8 miles south of the town of Coulommiers) is worth highlighting in particular. **Camping Les Etangs Fleuris** is a wonderfully rural and secluded site with 170 pitches and a host of clean, modern facilities, including an excellent pool with one for children, a games room, bar and take-away, plus showers, toilets and a launderette. Their sporting activities include table tennis, mini-golf, *petanque* and fishing, plus horse-riding and nature walks nearby. The site also offers two kinds of two-bedroom mobile homes, all well furnished and maintained. It is about 45 minutes

Captain's Quarters Bar at Disney's Newport Bay Club

Parc de la Colline

from *Disneyland Resort Paris* and an easy drive along the D231. Canvas Holidays package the site with either a Channel crossing or flights to Beauvais or Charles de Gaulle, plus Theme Park tickets. For more details call 01383 629000 or visit www.canvas holidays.com.

Other sites in the Seine-et-Marne region include **Camping Le Parc**, 20km (12 miles) from *Disneyland Resort Paris* in 10 wooded hectares just outside the town of Villevaudé to the north-east (near Meaux). With 330 tent, camper van and caravan pitches, prices start from €16.60/night for a two-person tent without electricity but including shower use. It has a bar-restaurant, TV room and facilities for volleyball, tennis and basketball. Call 00 33 1 60 26 20 79 or visit www.campingleparc.fr.

Even closer is **Parc de la Colline**, near Torcy to the west, which has a mixture of mobile homes and chalets for up to seven people as well as camp sites, all with electric hook-ups. They even have their own shuttle bus to the Torcy RER station at €4.50 for adults and €2 for children and to *Disneyland Resort Paris* at €12.50 and €6. Call 00 33 1 60 05 42 32 or visit www.camping-de-la-colline.com.

For those looking to explore more of northern France, the popular and extremely well appointed site of **La Croix du Vieux Pont** at Berny-Rivière (near Soissons, about 80km/50 miles north of *Disneyland Resort Paris*) comes highly recommended. With three swimming pools, bar, restaurant and tennis court, plus a good range of mobile homes and pitches, as well as facilities for the disabled, it is featured by the likes of British tour operators Haven, Keycamp and Canvas Holidays. Call 00 33 3 23 55 50 02 or visit www.la-croix-du-vieux-pont.com.

La Croix du Vieux Pont

Gîtes and Clévacances

Two other notable local forms of accommodation are the individual B&B style of the Gîtes de France, with some 145 gîtes and 99 guest rooms in the Seine-et-Marne region, and the newer Clévacances, or town centre holiday homes.

Generally speaking, the village style of the **Gîtes de France** offers charming, rural tastes of the local

Clévacances

© CDT Seine-et-Marne

areas and their people, with anything from two to 10 rooms available to guests who enjoy becoming 'part of the family'. With so many to choose from throughout France, they have become a mini-industry and you can obtain a full guide to the area's *gîtes* from the Comité Departemental du Tourisme de Seine-et-Marne at 11 Rue Royale, 77300 Fontainebleau, France, tel 00 33 1 60 39 60 39 or visit www.tourisme77.fr. Log on to www.gites-seine-et-marne.com for more info about *gîtes*.

Clévacances are apartments, flats or suburban detached houses to let when not in use by their owners, from fully furnished weekly rentals to guest rooms. Prices range from €320–480 per week and they can be found throughout the Seine-et-Marne region, many very close to *Disneyland Resort Paris*. Reservations are usually handled directly with the owners and they are categorised for comfort by a number of 'keys' from one to five. To get a free booklet or request more information, write to Clévacances Seine-et-Marne, 11 Rue Royale, 77300 Fontainebleau, France, tel 00 33 1 60 39 60 39, or visit www.clevancances.com.

Hotel chains

Several French hotel chains offer good, cheap, basic accommodation for those on a budget both in Paris itself and in the Marne-la-Vallée area. Most are in the 1- and 2-star categories but a few offer a greater level of creature comforts. Here is a rundown of the most notable ones:

Formule 1: This is a basic, motel-type chain which keeps things pretty much cheap and cheerful (okay, forget about the cheerful bit). Built in boxy, prefab units, they are accommodation only (apart from an extremely simple continental buffet breakfast for €3.40 per person) but they are almost invariably the cheapest in any location with around 65 in the Ile de France region). They are surprisingly high-tech, with automated check-in and clean, functional but small rooms. However, the rooms do not have a shower or WC, there are only communal facilities on each floor. Part of the huge Accor hotel group, this is not the ideal place to go with a family because their service is so limited (and most rooms sleep only three) but for couples on a strict budget, they might be worth considering. For more details, call 0870 609 0961 in the UK or visit www.hotelformule1.com. **Our rating €, C.**

Etap: Similar to Formule 1 (and with 58 hotels in the region), but better with an in-room shower and WC. Non-smoking rooms are also available. Call 0870 609 0961 in the UK or visit www.etaphotel.com. **Our rating €, C.**

Campanile: Another motel-style group, they also don't have meals or bar service (although there is usually a restaurant attached to the property). Again, their hotels are all pretty uniform and stylised, but they are ideal for those on a budget, offer plenty of rooms for guests with disabilities and usually serve a great buffet breakfast. The rooms themselves are small but clean and comfortable. Part of the Envergure group (the second largest in Europe), the hotels rate officially as 2-star in France but provide a few extra, more thoughtful touches, such as in-room tea- and coffee-making facilities, making them a worthwhile place to stay. Rooms usually sleep only three and you need to reserve a child's fold-out bed in advance. Breakfast is around an extra €4/person at the associated restaurant and there are children's menus, too. Call 00 33 1 64 62 46 46 or visit www.campanile.fr. **Our rating €, CC.**

Kyriad: There are a lot more variations within this generally 2-star chain (which is also part of Envergure and a half-step up from Campanile) but it is still a basic family-orientated hotel, with decent rooms that comfortably sleep three and some that accommodate four (one double bed, two singles). Some hotels include mini-bars and hairdryers and provide pleasant individual touches such as a welcome snack tray. Their excellent-value restaurants all have children's menus. Call 00 33 1 64 62 46 46 in the UK or visit www.envergure.fr/kyriadfr.html. **Our rating €–€€, CC.**

Comfort Inn: A similar quality and style to the Kyriad and Campanile chains, the Comfort Inn hotels (part of the Choice Hotels International group) are mainly found in central Paris and offer an excellent-value selection. Their city location means there is quite a wide variety between the different style of each property but the basic standard remains sound. To book, call 0800 444444 (in the UK) or 08 00 91 24 24 in France, or visit www.choice hotels.com. **Our rating €€, CC.**

There are some 22 Paris Comfort Inns, and the closest one to *Disneyland Resort Paris* claims to be the **Comfort Inn Marne-la-Vallée**, but don't be fooled into thinking it is on the parks' doorstep – it is actually at Noisy-le-Grand, 1km (about ½ mile) from the Noisy-Champs RER station and six stops (about 15 minutes and 15km/9 miles) from Disney. However, it is still a good choice, just off Exit 10 of the A4 (the exit for Champs), a pleasant, recently built property, with well-equipped family rooms for three, four and five people (children 12 and under stay free with their parents). There are also non-smoking rooms and rooms for the disabled, plus a surprisingly good restaurant, where the buffet breakfast costs €7. Call 00

33 1 64 68 33 36 from the UK.

The Choice Hotels group also includes six of their more upmarket **Quality Hotel** properties in central Paris, with an official 3-star rating and some elegant touches.

Ibis: A more upmarket 2-star choice (in the Accor group), this chain is functionally comfortable in general, with standard rooms (international satellite TV is a bonus, as is in-room internet connection) that sleep three (with an extra fold-out bed) and compact bathrooms. All have a restaurant, bar and snacks available 24 hours a day (part of their commitment to a more personal service), with an outstanding self-service breakfast buffet from 6.30–10am, and a drinks and pastries service from 4–6am and 10am–noon. The restaurant choice varies from hotel to hotel. There are 45 Ibis hotels in the Paris region, including three in Marne-la-Vallée. To book, call 0870 609 0961 in the UK or visit www.ibishotel.com. **Our rating €€–€€€, CC.**

Mercure: This member of the Accor group has a 3-tier quality system, the basic Relais/Inn Mercure, the genuinely 3-star Hotel Mercure and the more upmarket Grande Hotel Mercure, with enhanced levels of service and comfort. Most rooms accommodate three, with some family rooms for four, all have mini-bars and hairdryers. Non-smoking and rooms for the disabled are also available.

The **Libertel** chain is also a Mercure affiliate, with a similar 3-star-plus style to the Grande Hotels. All have a decent restaurant (with a range of regional specialities), bar and a full-service continental breakfast. Their wine list is usually outstanding. The lobbies all feature a reading room, with a choice of international newspapers and magazines. They also specialise in weekend breaks and most of their

Holiday ownership

Inevitably, the explosion in hotel accommodation and tourist interest in the resort area has created the opportunity to 'buy' a piece of the holiday dream and there are several timeshare companies who would love you to sign on the dotted line. However, the only one we believe carries the right seal of approval is the extensive **Marriott's Village d'Ile de France** property, less than 2km (1 mile) from Disney. The first phase opened in June 2003 and consists of 141 two bed/two-bath townhouses with around 105sq m (1,260sq ft) of living space. The Marriott Vacation Club International has genuine international bona fides and strong Disney ties, so you can be sure of getting a quality product, with excellent back-up at a good price.

The Village has access to Disney's 27-hole golf course, plus its own dazzling array of facilities, including two swimming pools (one indoor lap pool and one outdoors), children's pool, whirlpool, health club (featuring a gym and aerobics room, sauna and steam room), children's facilities (games room, activity centre and outdoor playground), a bar/restaurant featuring local cuisine, a lobby lounge, a convenience store and deli (the Market Place, with a full array of fresh produce, wines and spirits, plus other essentials and even branded apparel). There are also 24-hour security and full reception services and a regular shuttle bus to the Theme Parks.

The two-storey townhouses themselves offer possibly the most luxurious accommodation in the region, with a king-size bed in the main bedroom, fully equipped kitchen (including microwave and dishwasher), a spacious living room (with satellite colour TV, DVD player and stereo, an additional TV in each bedroom), a utility room with washer/dryer and an individual terrace.

With Marriott Vacation Club, you purchase weeks within a particular season and you are free to reserve weeks within that season, while you may change dates within your purchased time period from year to year (and there are then more than 50 Vacation Club resorts worldwide you can exchange weeks for). For more details, contact Marriott on 0800 004477, by email at mvciparis.owners@vacationclub.com or visit www.vacationclub.com.

52 hotels are in central Paris. To book, call 0870 609 0961 in the UK or visit www.mercure.com. **Our rating €€€–€€€€, CCC.**

Novotel: More of a businessman's hotel (and another member of the Accor group), but full of mod cons to suit tourist tastes as well, this fully modern chain offers fresh, spacious and comfortable rooms (sleeping up to four), chic restaurants and bars, and extras like satellite TV, mini-bars and room service. Most feature outdoor swimming pools (although they close from the early autumn to the end of spring) and conference/meeting facilities. Conversely, while they can be busy during the week, they often offer some great weekend breaks when they are quieter. Children stay free with their parents, but breakfast is an extra €10–11. Call 0870 609 0961 in the UK or visit www.novotel.com. **Our rating: €€€€, CCC.**

Sofitel: The premium brand in the Accor group, each hotel is an individual, but all with a deluxe style in both the sumptuous rooms and the excellent restaurants, with the latter featuring some of the best cuisine in Paris. The full range of mod cons and facilities are accompanied by efficient, courteous service. However, the handful of

© Leonardo.com

Sofitel Paris

Sofitel hotels (18 of them) in the Ile de France are either in central Paris or by Charles de Gaulle Airport, hence their price reflects both their location and upmarket nature. To book, call 0870 609 0961 in the UK or visit www.sofitel.com. **Our rating €€€€€, CCCC.**

Well, that's about all the essential accommodation info you need for now. Having dealt with the preliminaries, it is finally time to… hit the Theme Parks!

Disneyland Hotel

© Disney

5 Welcome to the Parks
(or, Here's Where the Fun Really Starts!)

Okay, it's finally time to deal with the main business of being in *Disneyland Resort Paris* – the Theme Parks themselves. And there is a lot to take on board here. The *Disneyland Park* alone boasts some 45 attractions on its 57 hectares (140 acres), and there is something for all tastes and ages. The *Walt Disney Studios Park* has added a wealth of film and TV-orientated fun, although there is probably less to captivate the youngest visitors.

In all, there is at least 3 days' worth of pure adventure-mania spread between the two parks, and you need to have a pretty good idea of what's in store to get the most out of it and ensure you don't waste too much energy in the process! It is easy to get side-tracked by some of the clever detail or minor attractions and miss out on some big-time thrills, while equally there is a genuine treasure trove of small-scale Disneyana which would be a tragedy to overlook. Therefore, the following chapters will provide all you need to know to draw up your own plan of campaign for visiting each one.

If you have never visited a Disney theme park before, it is probably fair to start by reminding you that this is NOT a comparable experience to a day at any other European park. That is not to denigrate the likes of Alton Towers (which is actually on a similar scale), Thorpe Park or Chessington World of Adventures. All three possess some wonderful rides and offer good value for money. It is just that Disney builds and creates with a detail and a sense of wonder and fantasy that no one else can match.

You enter a truly magical world when you pass through the gates reading 'Le Parc Disneyland' in 1m (3ft) high lettering. And, for the duration of your stay, you will be beguiled by a realm which offers the most enchanting and thrilling range of attractions on earth.

Anyone who has already been to the *Magic Kingdom Park* in Orlando or *Disneyland* in Anaheim, Los Angeles, will have a good idea of what to expect. However, while the *Disneyland Park* bears a strong resemblance to both of those, a lot of the essential detail and many of the attractions are completely different. When the Walt Disney Company set out to build a new resort experience on the European mainland, they did not want a mere copy of existing ideas. Rather, they wanted to update, enhance and improve, go back to the Imagineering drawing board if you like, cherry-picking the best features of all their parks and re-inventing them in a dramatic, new setting.

The Paris version is, to our eyes, a more refined and artistic interpretation of the American examples. The Imagineers were well aware they were building for a

WHAT'S NEW IN THE PARKS

Disney is forever looking at new ways to engage visitors and provide additional experiences, so there is a constant flow of live entertainment and other changes. In 2005, they unveiled **Space Mountain: Mission 2**, a complete revamp and re-theming of this popular roller-coaster, and a sparkling new fireworks show **Wishes** in the *Disneyland Park*. Over at the *Walt Disney Studios Park*, they added **Lilo & Stitch Catch the Wave Party** and **Starring Cruella De Vil**, two live-action shows at peak times with lots of audience involvement. Now, for 2006 – and beyond – there are some exciting large-scale developments on the boil which will add some much-needed depth to the offerings at the *Walt Disney Studios*.

The *Disneyland Park* will be the first to benefit, around Easter 2006, with the opening of **Buzz Lightyear's Laser Blast** (replacing the old Visionarium show). This interactive ride-and-shoot fun is already a hit at other Disney parks and should be a popular addition here.

Then, in 2007, get ready for the eagerly anticipated **Toon Studios** at the *Walt Disney Studios*. This should be an attraction in its own right with an intensely themed cartoon world, involving all-new character meet-and-greets and other interactive elements, plus at least one new (much-needed) restaurant. Many critics have felt this park is rather thin on overall attractions, but the Toon Studios will add at least two more, with **Crush's Turtle Twister**, a highly elaborate Crazy Mouse-type coaster which promises to immerse riders in the world of *Finding Nemo*, the Disney-Pixar big hit. There will also be a **Cars** ride, with a Disneyfied version of traditional fairground bumper cars.

2007 will also be marking the **15th anniversary** of the *Disneyland Park*, so expect a raft of special birthday celebrations, with an all-new daily parade also in the works.

Finally, visitors to the *Walt Disney Studios* won't fail to notice the major construction project in the heart of the park. This is for the Paris version of the hugely popular **Tower Of Terror** ride (from the *Disney-MGM Studios* in Orlando), which is due to open in 2008. This near-60m (200ft) edifice will house one of the most amazing and dynamic rides in the Disney repertoire adding a new 'Twilight Zone' dimension to the park.

Of course, there will be other developments, additions and changes which beat our deadline, so be sure to check our website for the latest news: www.askdaisy.net/disneylandparis.

5

European market and have deliberately tried to tailor their designs in a less overtly American way. Of course, much of the fundamental magic inherent in their parks is quintessentially American, hence they maintain a strong essence of Uncle Sam much of the time. But there is also a greater awareness of Disney's European heritage (Walt Disney himself spent a good deal of time in France as a young man and his family traced their lineage back to French antecedents) and of the need to tell the stories in a way that makes sense to an audience consisting primarily of French, British, Germans, Dutch, Belgians, Spanish and Italians (and they are never just plain 'rides' or 'attractions' in a Disney park – everything has to tell a story and add to the overall theme).

The multi-lingual nature of the resort is therefore a key component to the overall feel and style of what's

> **BRIT TIP:** It pays to arrive a little early for the opening time at each park to put yourself in front of the crowds for the first couple of hours. This way you can enjoy some of the rides which attract serious queues later on.

in store, and some of the design influences of those various nations are also evident in the Theme Parks themselves (the Sleeping Beauty Castle in the *Disneyland Park* is partly modelled on Mont St Michel in Normandy, for example).

Sleeping Beauty Castle

The language challenge

It is also true to say the need to think in several languages provided the Imagineers with additional challenges which they had to meet in different ways, using sub-titles, translations and extra soundtracks. While this adds a unique feel to familiar attractions ('it's a small world' or The Adventures of Snow White, for example), it does irk a small minority of English-speaking visitors – although I have yet to meet any children who didn't enjoy Pinocchio's Fantastic Journey simply because the commentary happened to be in French!

To my mind, the answer is always to remember that we Brits are the visitors, and it pays to try to remember those few words of French we learned at school. At the end of the day, the resort is trying to appeal to the widest possible audience and, by and large, they succeed with extraordinarily cosmopolitan ability.

Set menus

A point worth highlighting for anyone unfamiliar with French restaurant culture is the usual provision of a fixed-price menu (*prix fixe*, in French) alongside the à la carte choice. Even at the standard counter-service burger-and-chips

Disneyland Park entrance

Main Street shop

type diners, there is a Menu Mickey, consisting of a main course (burger, salad, pizza or pasta), a choice of dessert and a soft drink. At the full-service restaurants, the cheaper the set menu (starter, main course and dessert), the more limited it is.

> BRIT TIP: If you fancy a beer at one of the counter-service restaurants around the Theme Parks, the best value is to choose the set meal option with beer instead of soft drink and you pay just €1 extra.

For both parks, we provide an At-A-Glance guide (on pages 114 and 150) which gives you some idea of what to expect to pay for food and souvenirs along the way, and it is worth pointing out that your costs can quickly mount up if you buy numerous snacks – a 50cl bottle of mineral water costs €2, a 25cl beer is €3.60, soft drinks variously €2, €2.60 and €3.40, a simple doughnut €1.80 and a large portion of chips €2.60. Kids meals, which consist of a main course, such as chicken nuggets or

pizza, chips, a yoghurt or ice cream, a small drink and a 'surprise' toy, are all €6. Even if you are totally unfamiliar with euros, you should be able to work out the kind of real cost you are looking at for a day in the Theme Parks.

Vegetarians are usually well catered for, as many of the outlets can provide something for the veggie appetite. The full-service restaurants all offer at least one vegetarian main course and good salads are not hard to find. They will also do their best to accommodate requests from guests who have particular dietary requirements; don't be afraid to ask.

Unlike the versions of the *Magic Kingdom Park* in other Disney resorts, this one does serve alcohol, but it is not cheap. A beer in one of the full-service restaurants is usually around €6, while a bottle of wine can vary between €18–50.

Ticket types

Moving along to more practical matters, you need to work out what type of ticket you should buy to make the most of your stay. With most packages that provide your accommodation, a length-of-stay pass is included. That means you can enjoy both parks from the minute you arrive until the time set for your departure. It obviously provides the

Hakuna Matata in Adventureland

BRIT TIP: If you want to leave a park and come back later, you must have your hand stamped at the designated exit gate and, on your return, show both the stamp (which can only be seen under ultra-violet light) and your entrance ticket.

peace of mind and convenience of knowing that you do not need to worry about the mechanics of which park to visit when, as you have the benefit of being able to hop between parks at any time.

However, there is a range of ticket types, including annual ones, which are worth considering if you are staying off-site or visit regularly.

1-Day Passport: This provides admission to either the *Disneyland Park* or the *Walt Disney Studios Park* for a full day's fun (which can be up to 11pm at peak periods). You may exit and re-enter that same park as many times as you wish throughout the day.

1/2/3-Day Park Hopper: This great-value ticket provides 1, 2 or 3 full days at the two parks, offering total freedom of movement between them on each day. The days do NOT need to be consecutive, which is invaluable if you are staying off-site and visiting other attractions in the region over, say, a week. Park Hopper tickets are also valid for a year from the date of purchase (but not if they are part of a package).

Fantasy Annual Passport: This provides entry to both parks, plus some useful extras like free parking, a free annual magazine, access to the official website with special offers and invites to special occasions (like new attraction previews), plus 25%

off special event tickets (such as the Halloween party) and 10% off at Disney restaurants and shops. However, there ARE blackout days at both parks when the Passport is not valid for admission. In 2006, these are 11–17 February; 16, 30 April; 7 May; 4 June; 25–27 October; 1 November; 26–30 December. For 2007 dates, check out this website nearer the time www.disneylandparis.com/fr/passep ort_annuel/nonadh/hp.htm. For some reason they only give the information in French.

Dream Annual Passport: This version offers unlimited year-round access to both parks, plus a number

Top 10 attractions

Here, purely for fun, is what we rate as our Top 10 attractions, first for the *Disneyland Park*:
1 Space Mountain: Mission 2
2 Pirates of the Caribbean
3 Big Thunder Mountain Railroad
4 Phantom Manor
5 Indiana Jones and the Temple of Peril
6 Disney's Fantillusion Parade
7 Wonderful World of Disney Parade
8 Tarzan Encounter
9 Legend of the Lion King
10 La Tanière du Dragon

And for the *Walt Disney Studios*:
1 Moteurs…Action! Stunt Show Spectacular
2 Cinémagique
3 Rock 'n' Roller Coaster starring Aerosmith
4 Disney's Cinema Parade
5 Armageddon: Special Effects
6 Disney Studio 1
7 Animagique
8 Studio Tram Tour
9 Disney Animation Gallery
10 Push, the talking trashcan

BRIT TIP: You can save money if you are tempted to buy an Annual Passport after a 1-day visit to one of the Theme Parks, as the cost of your used ticket will be deducted from the price. Visit the Annual Passport office at either Theme Park before you leave.

of exclusive advantages, discounts and events especially organised for Dream Passport holders, access to Fantasyland in the *Disneyland Park* one hour before official opening and preferential rates on Disney hotel rooms at certain times. These bonuses include 10% off in most shops, restaurants and bars throughout the resort, 15% off up to four tickets a day for Buffalo Bill's Wild West Show, free admission to Hurricanes nightclub in *Disney Village* for the passport holder and one guest, 50% off special event tickets such as the Halloween party, a birthday present for children 3–11, free parking for the Theme Parks or *Disney Village*, free pushchair and wheelchair hire in the Theme Parks, free luggage storage, 10% off *Golf Disneyland* fees, free annual magazine, priority information and reservation hotline, access to the official website with special offers and information and invitations to special occasions at the resort. There is also a Welcome Package with one-

BRIT TIP: If just one family member buys the Dream Annual Passport, the whole party can still benefit from the many discounts at the shops and restaurants in the parks.

off offers for 20% deductions at one restaurant and one day at Disney shops, a welcome gift and five FastPass tickets.

BRIT TIP: Fancy a dabble on the stockmarket? All shareholders of Euro Disney SCA (the holding company that runs the resort) benefit from a range of hotel, park, shop and restaurant discounts similar to those of the Dream Annual Passport holders.

There is a substantial difference in price between the two Annual Passports (see At-A-Glance guides on pages 114 and 150), but you can save a good deal over the course of a year if you plan on visiting the resort at least twice, and the possible savings against the multi-day Passports should also be obvious.

Unlimited Access Pass: For all Disney hotel guests, this pass for both parks is built into the price of your package and is valid for the duration of your stay. So, if you book a Disney hotel stay, either independently or through a tour operator, you will not need to buy any further tickets.

Unfortunately, there are no outlets that discount Disney tickets (as sometimes happens in America). With the exception of the annual Kids Go Free promotion, usually from January to March (which is a fairly sizeable 'discount'), there are no sources for cheap tickets, apart from occasional special promotions through Disney's business partners such as Esso and Air France. In quiet periods, there may be discounts to be found at the Disney hotels' concierge desks for events like Buffalo Bill's, but that's about it.

Where to buy tickets

So, if that's the reality, where can you buy your tickets, apart from joining the long early-morning queues at the ticket booths at the entrance to both parks? Well, you can call the UK booking centre on 08705 030303 or the 7-day-a-week French version on 00 33 1 60 30 60 30; visit any Disney Store in Britain or on the Champs Elysées in Paris; any FNAC store in Paris, the Virgin Megastore on the Champs Elysées;

> **BRIT TIP:** It is usually worth buying your tickets as far in advance as possible to avoid the probably annual price increase.

Liberty Arcade

the main RATP ticket offices on the Métro or RER; any Travelex Foreign Exchange Bureau (notably at the Eurotunnel terminal in Folkestone and at Portsmouth ferry terminal); on board P&O Ferries on Dover–Calais and Dover–Zeebrugge routes; or the Eurostar ticketing desks at the London Waterloo terminal or Ashford stations, or their Victoria station shop.

There are then the various official ticket brokers at travel agents and other outlets, some of whom can offer 4- and 5-Day Hopper Tickets. Two companies we are happy to

Disney characters in Frontierland

vouch for are Keith Prowse Attraction Tickets and ThemeParkHolidays.com. The **Keith Prowse** ticket agency (on 08701 232425 or online at www.keithprowsetickets.co.uk) run occasional 'extras' with their tickets, plus a range of Paris city excursions, dinner shows (including the Lido de Paris, Moulin Rouge and Crazy Horse cabarets), sight-seeing visits and cruises, and it is well worth getting a copy of their brochure. **ThemeParkHolidays.com** (on 0870 240 2510 or www.themepark holidays.com) are keenly priced and sell accommodation packages too.

Once you have your tickets, you can avoid the first bugbear of visiting either park – the ticket booths. These are located prominently outside both parks but, however many windows are open, there is nearly always a slow-moving queue. If you can avoid them, you will get a significant jump ahead of the crowds.

The final thing to remember before we get to the Theme Parks proper – especially the *Walt Disney Studios Park* – is you can always escape the crowds during the day by

© Disney

Alice's Curious Labyrinth

stepping out into *Disney Village* for a while. The great accessibility and convenience of the whole resort means that, if the Theme Parks are heaving, the *Disney Village* and the hotels are probably a lot quieter, hence it IS possible to find places without queues to enjoy a meal, a drink or just recharge the batteries (and, at peak periods, you WILL need a breather at times) before you charge back into the hectic whirl.

Ratings

All the rides and shows in the Theme Parks are judged on a unique *Brit's Guide* rating system that splits them into the Thrill rides and Scenic ones. Thrill rides earn T ratings out of five (hence a TTTTT is as exciting as they get) and scenic rides get A ratings out of five (an AA ride is likely to be over-cute and missable). Obviously, it is a matter of opinion to a certain extent but you can be sure a T or A ride is not worth your time, a TT or AA is worth seeing only if there is no queue, a TTT or AAA should be seen if you have time, but you won't miss much if you don't, a TTTT or AAAA ride is a big-time attraction that should be high on your list of things to do, and a TTTTT or AAAAA attraction should not be missed! The latter will have the longest queues so you should plan your visit around these rides.

FastPass

Disney has a unique FastPass (FP) system for some of its most popular shows and rides worldwide and it is worth taking advantage of it in the *Disneyland Park* (it is not available in the *Walt Disney Studios Park*, where queues are usually much shorter).

BRIT TIP: Some rides DO run out of FastPasses before the end of the day, so it is advisable to grab one for the likes of Peter Pan's Flight and Big Thunder Mountain BEFORE early afternoon.

5

Here's how the FastPass works: at all attractions with the FastPass service (which is FREE – many people don't realise this), there is a series of kiosks next to the main entrance where you insert your park entrance ticket. The kiosk immediately spits your ticket out, followed by a separate slip with a

Disney's Cinema Parade

© Disney

BRIT TIP: If you have young children, it is a good idea to put a note in their pocket with details of their name, your mobile phone number, hotel, etc. Cast Members are trained to take lost children to the Meeting Place and the provision of a note makes their job easier, too.

time 'window' during which you should return to the separate FastPass queue (usually at least an hour later, occasionally 4 or more). When your 'window' is open, simply return to the FastPass queue and enjoy the attraction with only a minimal wait. Unlike other Disney resorts, here you can get a FastPass for all five available FastPass rides at once (six when Buzz Lightyear opens in 2006) – if you can put in the necessary leg-work to visit them in one go! You CANNOT hold more than one FastPass for a particular ride, but you can at least get a selection of rides lined up and plan part of your day around them.

Previously, you could hold only ONE FastPass ticket at a time, which often meant a frustrating wait. You also need FastPass tickets for EVERY member of your party.

Some rides are restricted to children over a certain height and are not advisable for people with back, neck or heart problems or for pregnant women. Where this is the case, we have noted 'Restrictions: 1.32m (4ft 3in)' and so on. Height restrictions (which are strictly enforced) are based on the average 5-year-old being 1.02m (3ft 3in) tall, 6s being 1.1m (3ft 6in) and 9s being 1.32m (4ft 3in).

Those with neck or back problems, or mothers-to-be, are advised to avoid going on the following rides: Space Mountain: Mission 2, Indiana Jones and the Temple of Peril, Big Thunder Mountain Railroad and Mad Hatter's Tea Cups at the *Disneyland Park* and Rock 'n' Roller Coaster at the *Walt Disney Studios Park*.

The 'baby switch'

If you have small children, but don't want to leave them while you have a ride, you DON'T have to queue twice. When you get to the front of the queue, tell the operator you want to do a 'baby switch'. This means Mum can go on the ride while Dad looks after junior and, on her return, Dad can have his turn while Mum does the babysitting.

Many children also get a big thrill from collecting autographs from the various Disney characters they meet, and nearly all the hotels and shops sell some great **autograph books**.

Rides for wimps!

For those who are reluctant to hurl themselves on to the fastest rides, here (by special online request!) is a guide to a walk on the mild side with Disney. None of these will upset even the most sensitive of stomachs (although, with the exception of Space Mountain, Indiana Jones, Mad Hatter's Tea Cups and the Rock 'n' Roller Coaster, there are few rides designed to be really dynamic):

1　Disneyland Railroad
2　'it's a small world'
3　Le Pays des Contes de Fées
4　Le Carrousel de Lancelot
5　Peter Pan's Flight
6　Flying Carpets Over Agrabah
7　Casey Junior
8　Autopia
9　Thunder Mesa Riverboats
10　Dumbo the Flying Elephant

BRIT TIP: Kids, try to find the thickest pen you can for collecting autographs. Most of the characters find it a struggle to write with normal size pens in their great big hands.

If you have children of wide-ranging ages, check out the special section at the end of each park chapter to see which rides and attractions appeal most to which age groups. It is important in a resort of this size to concentrate on those areas which have most appeal for YOU and, while it is not possible to be 100% accurate, the advice here is fairly tried and tested, so you can get a pretty good idea of what is most likely to be popular with your offspring!

A full **Baby Care Centre** is provided in the *Disneyland Park* next door to the Plaza Gardens Restaurant at the top of Main Street USA on the right, where there are nappy-changing facilities and a feeding room, with baby food (and nappies) on sale.

The Meeting Place for Lost Children is also to be found here, with its own Disney staff. At the *Walt Disney Studios Park* the Baby Care Centre is behind the Studio Services in the Front Lot, just inside the entrance on the right-hand side and you can find your lost children there, too.

Park etiquette

Some final words of warning. Picnics are NOT allowed inside the Theme Parks (although you can take bottles of water), but there is an area set aside for picnics outside at the exit of the moving walkway from the main car park. Appropriate clothing must be worn in the parks – which means shirt and shoes – at all times. No bare chests – even for women! Smoking, eating, drinking, flash photography and video lighting are not permitted on rides, during shows or in queues.

So what are we waiting for? First stop, the *Disneyland Park*…

5

Pin trading

In addition to collecting souvenirs, you will probably also encounter the pin-trading phenomenon at some stage of your Disney adventure. This is hard to explain to the uninitiated as it has no real parallel in modern British culture. It is a particularly American idea and involves collecting – and trading – the many dozens of different enamel brooches which you can buy in almost every shop. They vary in price from around €8–15 and serious collectors carry them on lanyards around their neck, eagerly looking to barter and swap with other members of this not-so-secret society. Various Disney Cast Members also join in by displaying lanyards with pins to swap, and they are duty-bound to swap for anything they may be displaying.

We have to say, pin trading rather baffles us, but those who get hooked on it will attest to having great fun looking for potential swaps with fellow devotees (as well as spending a small fortune on their collections!). For more info, log on to the UK-orientated discussion boards of www.disboards.com and ask one of the regulars to explain how to get suitably enthused!

The Disneyland Park
(or, To All Who Come to This Happy Place, Welcome!)

It makes sense to start by taking an in-depth look at the original development here at *Disneyland Resort Paris*, the first Disney park in Europe, which opened its gates in April 1992. Although it is comparable to the *Magic Kingdom* in *Walt Disney World Resort in Florida* (America's biggest tourist attraction), be prepared for some surprises in both scale and content from the US version. The *Disneyland Park* is bigger by some 17 hectares (42 acres) than its Orlando counterpart and, while there may be fewer 'lands', the Paris version is more elaborate and involving.

The attractions range from the twee and fairly ordinary (Mad Hatter's Tea Cups and Autopia) to the wonderfully inventive (Phantom Manor and Pirates of the Caribbean) and on to the downright thrilling (Space Mountain and Indiana Jones and the Temple of Peril). The all-encompassing theming covers the

Key to Disneyland Park Map

Main Street, USA
1   Main Street USA Railroad Station
2   Town Square
3   Disneyland City Hall
4   Main Street Transportation Company Vehicles
5   Liberty Arcade
6   Discovery Arcade
7   Central Plaza

Frontierland
8   Fort Comstock
9   Phantom Manor
10 Thunder Mesa Riverboat Landing
11 Rustler Roundup Shootin' Gallery
12 Big Thunder Mountain
13 Pocahontas Indian Village
14 Critter Corral
15 Chaparral Theatre
16 Frontierland Railroad Station

Adventureland
17 Indiana Jones and the Temple of Peril
18 Adventure Isle
19 La Cabane des Robinsons
20 Skull Rock
21 Pirates' Beach
22 Pirates of the Caribbean
23 Passage Enchanté d'Aladdin

Fantasyland
24 Sleeping Beauty Castle
25 Le Carrousel de Lancelot
26 The Adventures of Snow White
27 Pinocchio's Fantastic Journey
28 Dumbo the Flying Elephant
29 Peter Pan's Flight
30 Fantasy Festival Stage
31 Fantasyland Railroad Station
32 Alice's Curious Labyrinth
33 Le Pays des Contes de Fées
34 Casey Jr – le Petit Train du Cirque
35 Mad Hatter's Tea Cups
36 'it's a small world'
37 Royal Castle Stage

Discoveryland
38 Space Mountain: Mission 2
39 Les Mystères du Nautilus
40 Orbitron – Machines Volantes
41 Star Tours
42 Discoveryland Railroad Station
43 Honey, I Shrunk the Audience
44 Autopia
45 Buzz Lightyear's Laser Blast
46 Videopolis/Legend Of The Lion King
47 Arcades Alpha & Beta

DISNEYLAND PARK

©DISNEY

The Disneyland Park at a glance

See full colour map on page 113.

Location	Off Exit 14 of the A4 autoroute, proceed to the clearly signed car park; or turn right out of the Marne-la-Vallée RER and TGV station; or through the *Disney Village* if staying at a resort hotel
Size	57 hectares (140 acres) in five 'lands'
Hours	10am–8pm autumn and winter weekdays; 9am–8pm spring, plus autumn and winter weekends, Christmas and New Year; 9am–11pm summer holidays
Admission	**Under 3** free; **3–11** €34 (1-Day Passport), €43, €77, €92 (1, 2 and 3-Day Park Hopper), **adults** (12+) €42 (1-Day Passport), €51, €93, €113 (1, 2 and 3-Day Park Hopper); **Annual Passports** (per person): Fantasy €119, Dream €159. NB: *All prices subject to increase from Easter 2006 (see www.disneylandparis.com)*
Parking	€8
Pushchairs	€6.50 (Pushchair shop to right of main entrance, just under railway arch)
Wheelchairs	€6.50 (Pushchair shop)
Top Attractions	Space Mountain: Mission 2, Star Tours, Peter Pan's Flight, Dumbo the Flying Elephant, Big Thunder Mountain Railroad, Legend Of The Lion King
Don't Miss	The Wonderful World of Disney Parade, Fantillusion Parade and Wishes fireworks (summer and Christmas seasons only), The Tarzan Encounter, 'it's a small world', La Tanière du Dragon
Hidden Costs	**Meals** — Burger, chips and coke €9.95; 3-course meal €28 (€15 for children) at Blue Lagoon
	Kids' meal — €6 (at all counter-service restaurants)
	T-shirts — €8.90–23
	Souvenirs — €1–600
	Sundries — Kids' autograph book €4.90; Space Mountain ride photos €14–22

Wild West (Frontierland), dark jungles and mysterious caverns (Adventureland), film and storybook fantasy (Fantasyland) and a kind of retro future world (Discoveryland), possibly the most imaginative of the lot. There is at least one (depending on the time of year) unmissable daily parade and a range of other live theatrical productions which all carry the Disney hallmark of imaginative family entertainment. In fact, plenty to make you go 'Wow!' plus a whole variety of attractions that will raise a big smile or two.

Prepare to be immersed completely in a convincing world of make-believe, where every tiny detail, from the uniforms of the Cast Members to the clever signage and even the rubbish bins, conforms to that land's theme, but be aware of some fairly blatant attempts to lighten your wallet along the way, notably at the many gift shops, especially after a number of the rides. By Disney's own reckoning, some 16,000 types of merchandise are on sale and, although 90% of it costs less than €15, it can quickly add up if you have children of the large-eyed variety!

BRIT TIP: Take advantage of Disney's free package pick-up service if you do a lot of shopping. When you pay, ask for the items to be sent to The Disney Store in the *Disney Village* for you to collect after 6pm. If you are staying in a Disney hotel, your shopping can be delivered to The Disney Store there for collection after 8pm.

Another slight negative to be aware of is the quality (or lack of it) in much of the counter-service dining. With only a couple of notable exceptions, the fare is not terribly imaginative and is not particularly cheap, either (around €10 a head, even for the most basic meal). In the course of three days, that can be almost €190 just in meals for a family of four, eating twice a day at park counter-service restaurants. Conversely, the handful of full-service restaurants DO offer some fabulous food – but at a price. Go for lunch at our favourite restaurant, Blue Lagoon, and you could easily be €86 lighter afterwards with four to feed. A cheaper alternative is to stock up at breakfast, keep going with snacks

BRIT TIP: If you want a real budget option for lunch, nip out of the parks to the RER station of Marne-la-Vallée and grab a baguette, sandwich or Croque Monsieur at the station cafe. The beer alone is €2 cheaper!

from the many hot-dog, popcorn, doughnut and drinks wagons around the Theme Park, and have your main meal in *Disney Village* or at the hotel in the evening (where buffet options are often better value).

You actually enter 'Le Parc Disneyland' underneath the *Disneyland Hotel*, the rather fanciful conglomeration of buildings known as the Pink Palace. You pass some extremely pleasant gardens (the whimsical Fantasia Gardens, with a number of character-shaped topiaries) and the inevitable fountains and ponds (good photo spot, this) before entering the main entrance plaza. The ticket booths are to the right of the entrance passage, but hopefully you already have your tickets and can head straight to the turnstiles. If you need Guest Relations or Left Luggage, bear to the right of the main hotel building and they are in front of you. Be aware that there is quite a walk from the main car park to the Theme Parks, even with the moving walkways. You should allow 5–10 minutes to get there, and pushchairs are a real boon if you have little ones.

Main Street USA

Once through the turnstiles, you enter a plaza in front of the main Disneyland Railroad station. Walk under the station and you are in **Town Square**, the main entrance to

6

Disneyland Park proper, and the lower portion of the first 'land', Main Street USA. This is a grand, turn-of-the-century version of small-town America, with a truly eye-catching array of shop and office façades all built in epic detail. It is not so much a thoroughfare as a living museum to generations of genuine Americana and it offers a fabulous glimpse into an idealised past of the United States.

Here you will get your first look at the most-photographed edifice in the whole resort – the Sleeping Beauty Castle (or Le Château de la Belle au Bois Dormant, to use its full French title). To your left is **Disneyland City Hall**, another guest relations office where you can

Main Street characters

> BRIT TIP: Can't find the characters? Go to City Hall and they will tell you where they will be. City Hall is your best friend for a variety of queries, from the location of baby facilities (there are none here) to meal bookings.

pick up park maps (if you haven't already got one at your hotel or in the many cubicles underneath the Railroad Station), book meals at any of the restaurants or just ask any park-related questions.

To your right is the **Main Street Transportation Company**, where several vintage and horse-drawn vehicles can take you along Main Street USA to the Central Plaza, the Theme Park's hub, from which radiate the other four 'lands'. If you have time (or children), it is quite fun to take one of the horse-drawn trams or vintage cars (including a police paddy-wagon), but it's quicker to walk (especially if you use either of the two covered arcades which run alongside Main Street USA).

One of the most eye-catching features, though, is the **Disneyland Railroad**, with a station (it has four; Adventureland is the only 'land' without a railroad stop) well positioned to catch the unsuspecting visitor. The Victorian-style station provides an elevated view down

Main Street vehicles

© Disney

Halloween Festival, Frontierland

BRIT TIP: Main Street USA is full of clever Disney memorabilia – look for photos of Walt and his wife Lilly in Lilly's Boutique; the two murals of other Emporium shops in the Emporium; and the plates set into the street which bear the legend Elias Disney Constructions. Many of the windows also bear witness to Disney Imagineers and VIPs down the years.

Main Street USA, but the signature steam train ride, which circles the whole park and includes a clever 'Grand Canyon' scene en route to Frontierland (and a glimpse inside Pirates of the Caribbean), has long, slow-moving queues for much of the day. AAA.

BRIT TIP: The Disneyland Railroad is a relaxing ride when many of the others are showing long queues but DON'T join it at Main Street where few people actually get off. Instead, try the stations at Frontierland or Fantasyland for the shortest wait.

Main Street USA is basically the Theme Park's principal shopping area, with a whole range of stores (including the gargantuan **Emporium**, which stocks just about every kind of souvenir known to mouse-kind!) and cafes. Also here is **Dapper Dan's Hair Cuts**, a wonderfully atmospheric vintage barber's with the kind of furnishings you would usually find only in an antique shop (or an apothecary's), where you can stop for a haircut and/or shave if the mood takes you (€18 each, or €26 for both; child's haircut €10).

If you need any film or photographic equipment, Town Square Photography, hosted by Kodak, should be able to help you out (although beware the prices here – it is much cheaper to bring basics like film, batteries and flashcards with you). In all, there are 12 cunningly arranged shops along this 100m (109yd) boulevard and it is worthwhile returning in the afternoon when the rides are busiest to check out some of the amazing detail here.

6

Lilly's Boutique in the Emporium

© Disney

BRIT TIP: Video camera battery running down? Don't fret – you can visit City Hall and they will be able to recharge it for you there and then.

You can also find 10 different snack bars and restaurants to provide everything from breakfast, to a gourmet lunch, afternoon tea and evening dessert. Pick of the bunch is **Walt's – An American Restaurant**, which offers an elegant lunch and dinner (set menu €25 or €29, €10 for children, €15 teens). This fabulous diner, designed like a 1900s' hotel, is a tribute to Walt Disney himself, his ideas and creations, and features a wealth of personal detail, photos and memorabilia. The *Disneyland Park* character breakfast also alternates between here and the Plaza Gardens Restaurant (see below).

BRIT TIP: Celebrate your birthday in style at Walt's. Order a cake at the start of your meal and it will be brought to you at the end with a great fanfare. It costs €22 and serves 4–8.

At the top of Main Street USA, the **Plaza Gardens Restaurant** offers an excellent series of all-you-can-eat buffets for breakfast, lunch and dinner in a plush, conservatory-style setting. The fun **character breakfast** (alternating with Walt's) is €25 for adults and €17 for kids (3–11) if you are not staying at a Disney hotel, or €17 and €12 if you are (it counts as a supplement because breakfast at your hotel is included; book in advance as it is popular). It is served in two sittings, at 8 or 9.30am. The lunch buffet

(€20 for adults, €10 for kids; drinks not included) consists of a huge cold spread – salads, meats, bread and fruit – and a whole array of hot dishes – casseroles, pasta, roast beef, sausages, hot dogs and several types of vegetable and rice – plus a mouth-watering selection of desserts. There is also an excellent **character tea-time** (3–4.30pm) every day, featuring all the Disney favourites, with a tantalising spread of cakes, pastries and desserts, plus one hot and one cold drink each (€13/person). For an extra €5 a head, you can enjoy the even more fun-filled character Birthday Party.

Otherwise, your eateries are mainly of the counter snack kind, with the **Market House Deli** (sandwiches, salads and pasta), **Casey's Corner** (all manner of hot dogs and soft drinks), **Victoria's Home-Style Restaurant** (pasta, quiche, pizza and salads), **The Coffee Grinder** (coffee, tea and cakes), **The Ice Cream Company** (hosted by Nestlé), **The Cookie Kitchen** and **Cable Car Bake Shop** (two sides of the same breakfast-orientated servery, with some delicious pastries and cookies) and the **Gibson Girl Ice Cream Parlour** (a full range of ice cream delights). Bear in mind not all of these are likely to be open at any one time (apart from the weekends in high season).

For shopping, you should definitely check out the **Emporium**,

BRIT TIP: As an example of the Imagineers' art, listen carefully outside Victoria's Home-Style Restaurant and you will catch the distinct sounds of someone using the bathroom in the 'guesthouse' above!

as well as **The Storybook Store** (books, stationery, CD and audio cassettes), **Harrington's Fine China & Porcelain** (some lovely china, crystal and glass giftware), **Disney Clothiers Ltd** (for a more upmarket selection of apparel) and **Main Street Motors** (dedicated to Winnie the Pooh and friends), while **Disneyana Collectibles** is a must for Disney collectors with its range of original books, film cels, lithographs and ceramic figures.

As an alternative to walking up the middle of Main Street USA, pick one of the two arcades at either side (the **Liberty Arcade** to the left, and the **Discovery Arcade** to the right) and wander right through away from most of the crowds. The Liberty Arcade features a clever tableau about immigrants arriving in New York (in French), while the Discovery Arcade is decorated with some clever period detail, which is worth a look later on.

BRIT TIP: Need to stay dry? Both Liberty and Discovery Arcades are fully covered and provide back-door access to most of the shops and cafes along Main Street USA. Very popular in winter!

At the top of Main Street USA on the right-hand side (just after the Gibson Girl Ice Cream Parlour) is a handy **Information Board** which displays the waiting times at the various attractions. Late arrivals should take note of this to get an idea of where to head first (and where to avoid for a while).

Main Street USA is also one of the prime locations to meet various **Disney characters**. Most days start with the official character 'opening ceremony', an early-morning

cavalcade featuring Mickey, Pluto and various other chums. Many of them stop to sign autographs in three locations – on a platform outside the Liberty Arcade (just past Casey's Corner on the left as you come up the street), in the Central Plaza and on the Royal Castle Stage just to the right in front of Sleeping Beauty Castle.

For Halloween, Main Street USA is transformed into **Spooky Street**, with a major pumpkin-inspired

Character Carnival

Although the Disney characters change from month to month, you can be fairly sure to catch them most of the time (especially 10am–midday) waiting at the following locations:

Town Square (in corner by Liberty Arcade): Any of Minnie, Pluto, Chip 'n' Dale, Donald Duck and Goofy.

Main Street USA (by Casey's Corner and Liberty Arcade): Mickey Mouse.

Central Plaza (Castle Hub): Disney Princesses.

Royal Castle Stage (in front of Castle): Winnie the Pooh (occasionally Tigger or Piglet).

Fantasyland (by Mad Hatter's Tea Cups): Some Alice in Wonderland characters, Pinocchio and Robin Hood.

Discoveryland (between Videopolis and Space Mountain): Any of Lilo & Stitch and Toy Story characters.

Adventureland (by Colonel Hathi's restaurant): Jungle Book and Lion King characters.

Frontierland (outside Cowboy Cookout Barbecue): some of Goofy, Pluto, Chip 'n' Dale, Country Bears and Pocahontas characters should be there.

6

makeover and some wonderfully clever visual touches. A giant pumpkin also appears in front of the Castle, with free face-painting for childred aged under 11.

Rope drop

If you arrive prior to the official opening time (either 9 or 10am), Main Street USA is not the place to linger as most of the crowd will flock to the **Central Plaza** in front of the Castle. This is REALLY where the action starts for a full day in the park, so don't be fooled into thinking they have opened early by letting you into Main Street USA. You need to have already planned your campaign from here to get a head start on the masses. Depending on which of the 'lands' in front of you appeal most, head in one of the four directions and wait for the opening hour 'rope drop' by the Cast Members at each entrance.

BRIT TIP: If you are among the first to reach Central Plaza and you manage to get to the main rides first, you will enjoy the *Disneyland Park* at its best – with short or non-existent queues at the most popular attractions.

Mad Hatter's Tea Cups

Carnival time!

If you fancy the appeal of cowboy country and the lure of a great thrill ride like Big Thunder Mountain or the scary fun of Phantom Manor, head up Liberty Arcade and, at the top, wait to turn left into Frontierland. For the mysteries of Adventureland (including the wonderful Pirates of the Caribbean ride), move into Central Plaza and wait at its entrance on the left.

Those with children in tow, who will demand rides in the company of all their favourite characters like Dumbo, Peter Pan and the Mad Hatter, should wait in front of the Castle for the chance to get into Fantasyland first. Or, if the appeal of big thrill rides like Space Mountain: Mission 2 (an interior, looping

Skull Rock

roller-coaster) and Star Tours (a brilliant simulator space ride) is highest on your 'To Do' list, then turn right in the middle of Central Plaza and await rope drop there.

> BRIT TIP: A perk with the Dream Annual Passport is entry to Fantasyland an hour before it officially opens. The Dumbo and Peter Pan rides often start half an hour early, so you can have a go on two of the most popular rides without queuing.

Once the ropes go down, the early-morning crowds will move (quickly!) in one of the four directions, so keep your wits about you. Study the park map for where you want to go – and benefit from a first hour or so without lengthy queuing. It also pays (and royally so in peak periods) to avoid main meal times if you want to eat without more long queues and frenzy. It is a notable fact of *Disneyland Resort Paris* that people tend to pack out the

> BRIT TIP: Park too busy? Don't forget it is relatively easy to head back out to *Disney Village* and grab a bite to eat at places like Planet Hollywood and Annette's Diner.

counter-service cafes rather than the handful of full-service, sit-down restaurants. This means 12–2.30pm is a seriously bad time (unless it is an extremely quiet period of the year) to head for places like the Fuente del Oro Restaurante, Pizzeria Bella Notta, the Cowboy Cookout Barbecue or any of the other 14 counter-service diners in the park. Try to have a snack prior to midday or look to eat in mid-afternoon and you will benefit from slightly shorter ride queues during lunchtime.

Alternatively, you could book lunch at the start of the day at one of the four full-service restaurants (Walt's, Auberge du Cendrillon, Blue Lagoon or Silver Spur Steakhouse) to guarantee a pleasant sit-down and some rest – especially with children.

Fuente del Oro in Frontierland

Pace yourself

When it comes to eating, be aware that inclement weather quickly causes long queues to pile up in the restaurants, even in *Disney Village*. If you can pre-empt that sudden rain squall by getting to a cafe first, you will be well placed to watch the rush come in when the deluge starts. Equally, if you have brought some good **rain gear** with you, it is a great time to enjoy some of the rides while the majority seek shelter.

The final piece of advice before we send you off on the great *Disneyland Park* adventure is to pace yourself. It is easy to try to do too much and end up a frazzled wreck by mid-afternoon! In summer, when the crowds are at their peak and the temperature can top 30°C, it can be a particularly tough business negotiating the rides, the long periods of queuing and the demands of tramping from one side of the park to the other in the name of entertainment. This is when you will most feel the benefit of a **solid plan**, booking your mealtimes in advance and giving yourselves a rest at strategic moments, whether it be finding a quiet corner for a drink or visiting a show that provides a welcome sit-down, preferably in the air-conditioned cool.

You will also need to **drink** a lot of water during the summer. The physical demands of the parks will quickly creep up on you unless you remember to rehydrate at regular intervals. It is, sadly, an all-too-common feature in mid-afternoon to see or hear grizzly children, often being berated by parents for not

BRIT TIP: Save euros by bringing a bottle of water with you and refilling it from the many drinking fountains around.

enjoying themselves (!), when all everyone needs is just to sit down for a few minutes, recharge the batteries and drink some water.

Most children (ours included) get a huge energy charge from being in the Theme Parks and the adrenalin keeps them going long after they should have keeled over. But that excited state can run out at a moment's notice and turn to angst if they are not regularly fed and watered – and it is easy to overlook the latter with so much going on.

In summer, it is advisable to carry a good **sunscreen** and use it liberally while you are queuing to prevent an unhealthy dose of the sun, which also exacerbates the tiredness factor – your biggest enemy.

Frontierland

Okay, enough of the warnings – let's get to the fun! There is masses in store, so let us take you on a full tour of the remaining four 'lands' in the *Disneyland Park*. Starting immediately to your left from the Central Plaza brings you to Frontierland, a true rootin', tootin' cowboy town that oozes child appeal and has plenty of visual creativity and stimulation for grown-ups too. It is a realm of pioneers and gold diggers, the Wild West in vivid 3-D, with a big helping of some of the epic scenery which the real-life version possesses in places like Nevada and Arizona.

As in virtually all areas of the park, Frontierland rewards the casual wanderer with some great little paths leading nowhere in particular but which reveal some interesting details or amusing scenery, such as the Indian village encampment or the hot springs (complete with Old Faithful geyser).

Once again, the loyal re-creation of the era can be seen in every building and façade, none better than the main entrance of **Fort Comstock**, which is an attraction in itself where you can see scenes from Legends of the Wild West. Here, you can climb the wooden stairs to the ramparts, visit the US Marshall and Fort Jail, and peer into the offices (see if you can spot Buffalo Bill) and stables. Kids will want to roam the ramparts and scan other areas of the park through the telescopes provided. It is a good place to let youngsters explore on their own, too. AAA.

Phantom Manor: Turn left after coming through Fort Comstock and head along the plaza past the Silver Spur Steakhouse for one of the most clever and amusing rides in the Disney repertoire. This elaborate haunted mansion is a variation on the theme established in Anaheim and Orlando, with a ghoulish entryway leading to an underground ride of wonderfully creepy proportions. Unfortunately, the introductory spiel and commentary are all in French, but it needs little real explanation as the gloomy entrance parlour (watch for a remarkable trick here) takes you down to this spook-tastic world.

> BRIT TIP: Queues build up at Phantom Manor from mid-morning and, although they rarely top half an hour, this ride is a good one to do early or during a parade, when it's quieter. Late evening is another good time.

Under 5s may find the mock-horror elements a bit too convincing but otherwise the whole experience is more fun than frightening. The story of an elaborate socialite wedding that went tragically wrong,

leaving the bride as one of the 999 ghosts, is a bit hard to follow, but the ride takes you right through the manor and into a realistic haunted town in best graveyard fashion. In the queue you can study the elaborate terraces and gardens outside the manor, while you exit into Boot Hill and some more pun-laced scenery that includes various graves – such as 'Here lies Shotgun Gus, holier now than all of us'. The more attentive will also notice the sounds of knocking from the largest of the mausoleums in the graveyard here. This can be a great source of amusement when people notice it for the first time on wild and windy nights! AAAA (TTTTT for youngsters).

Thunder Mesa Riverboat Landing: Backtrack slightly along the plaza and you can hop on a boat, offering a slow-paced and picturesque ride around much of Frontierland, including several sections which can be seen only from the water. The commentary is bilingual and it is quite a capacious ride, so there is rarely much of a queue. The two boats, the *Molly Brown* and *Mark Twain*, both provide an enjoyably authentic experience. This is a good ride to save for later in the day when both Phantom Manor and Big Thunder are busiest. AAA.

Fans of the old-style arcade shooting ranges can get a quick 'fix' at the **Rustler Roundup Shootin' Gallery**, where €2 (the only additional charge for an attraction in the Theme Park) will give you 10 shots at various audio-animatronic targets. TT.

Big Thunder Mountain: This is one of Disney's trademark roller-coasters. While others may thrill (or terrify!) with their topsy-turvy antics, Big Thunder sticks firmly to the straight and narrow and is as fun

6

and inventive as most people desire, with this abandoned 'gold mine' showing it still has some life in it in the shape of its runaway train. Again, you get a different version from other Disney parks, this one starts straight away with a dive into the dark under the lake before whizzing around the mock sandstone monoliths and mine shafts in exhilarating fashion.

> BRIT TIP: If you head to Frontierland first, Big Thunder should be your opening ride, followed by Phantom Manor. Then return to the mine-train coaster and grab a FastPass for another go later!

With three different ascents (and plunges), the proliferation of clever scenery all around you is never less than spectacular, so it usually needs at least two or three rides to take in all the detail (it looks great at night, too). This is one of the five FastPass (FP) rides, so it is well worth taking advantage of, as the queues often reach as much as an hour during peak periods. Afterwards, you can buy the souvenir photo of you on your ride (six package options, from €12–22). Restrictions: 1.02m (3ft 3in). TTTT.

Pocahontas Indian Village: If the youngsters are too short (or apprehensive!) to ride Big Thunder, head for this straightforward play area with a mixture of slides, swings and climbs geared towards under 6s. Unfortunately, this is one area that is affected by the weather as it closes when it rains, but, otherwise, it is a valuable place to allow the young 'uns to let off some steam. TTT (for the right age group!).

> BRIT TIP: The back of the Pocahontas Indian Village originally housed the Indian Canoes ride, which closed after little more than a year because of operational difficulties. Next door, you can also see the entrance to the former River Rogue Keelboats – another early failure.

Critter Corral: Continuing the tour of Frontierland brings you next to this fairly standard petting zoo aimed primarily, once again, at younger children. Here, they can pet rabbits, donkeys, sheep and goats,

Big Thunder Mountain

© Disney

Mickey's Winter Wonderland

Mickey's Winter Wonderland takes over in the theatre from mid-November to early March, with an equally clever ice-skating show featuring Mickey and all the gang (including a suitably hapless Donald Duck) that will keep youngsters enchanted for the full 25-minutes. It is a fairly straightforward song-and-dance pastiche, but once again the staging and lighting are impressive and its bilingual style ensures English speakers are not left out of the picture. AAAA.

Next door is the **Frontierland Railroad Station**, which is often the best place to catch the Theme Park's steam train and take the slow chug all the way around.

Your dining options in Frontierland feature two outstanding opportunities. The **Silver Spur Steakhouse** is a truly deluxe establishment, designed like a classic Western hotel, using rich,

6

Silver Spur Steakhouse

dodge the chickens and enjoy the other paraphernalia of the farmyard set-up. AAA (under 8s).

Chaparral Theatre: Opposite Critter Corral, this is one of the park's four main live entertainment venues. The attractions here are seasonal and Disney does tend to change them at regular intervals but, at the time of writing, the two offerings were: **The Tarzan Encounter**, a sensational 25-minute song, dance and acrobatic extravaganza showcasing the music from the animated film, with a cast of energetic 'apes' who find all manner of ways of leaping off, around and over the clever stage scenery. Tarzan and Jane (inevitably) make an appearance and, while it can be a bit loud for very young ears, it is a riot of colour and movement. There is also an audience participation section for children that is worth being ready for. AAAA (plus TTT).

BRIT TIP: If there is no queue, take the Railroad steam train for the best short cut to Fantasyland or Discoveryland. However, it is usually quicker to walk if you need the fastest way back to Main Street USA.

dark wood and plush upholstery. The subdued lighting provides an intimate dining style and there is a display kitchen at the back. Steaks are their stock-in-trade, but they also do excellent salmon, chicken and pasta. A set, 3-course meal is €25 for adults, a 2-course Menu Pony Express for children 3–11 is €10 and for teens €18 (à la carte dishes range from €14.90–25). Superb desserts add to the high quality on offer here.

Character-seekers will want to make a beeline for the **Lucky Nugget Saloon**, which offers a fabulous Tex-Mex buffet lunch from 12–3pm with characters, plus 6–10pm for dinner in high season. The restaurant is wonderfully styled like a two-storey Western saloon, with a stage and a long bar, and the food is a serve-yourself buffet (€30 for adults, €15 for 3–11s) featuring assorted crudités, chicken wings, nachos, salsa, fajitas, spare ribs, chilli con carne, pasta, pizza and a large choice of desserts (drinks not included). The character interaction here includes the seemingly omnipresent Chip 'n' Dale (or Tic and Tac as they are known in France), Pluto, Gideon (from Pinocchio) and Daisy Duck. If €90 for a family of four (plus drinks, which are not included in the set price) seems a touch expensive (as it does to us), check out the character tea opportunity at the Plaza Gardens Restaurant.

Otherwise, your dining choices include the evocative **Cowboy Cookout Barbecue**, a counter-service barn of a place featuring spare ribs, burgers, smoked chicken and chicken nuggets. The lovely smoky barbecue smell, the cowboy ambience and the Country & Western twang (with live music periodically) add up to a memorable dining experience, even if the food is only average. **Fuente del Oro Restaurante** goes down Mexico way for more counter-service, *cantina* style, with tacos, chilli con carne and other Mexican specialities such as fajitas and quesadillas (one of the better counter-service options, but very busy from midday to 2pm). Finally, the **Last Chance Café** offers more cowboy fare with typical Western decor, serving turkey legs, chips and sandwiches.

Shopping is suitably cowboy orientated, with **Tobias Norton & Sons – Frontier Traders**, a leather emporium featuring hats, boots, wallets and belts; **Bonanza Outfitters**, offering the full range of Western apparel; and the **Eureka Mining Supplies**, which stocks a selection of typical cowboy-style foods and toys, including the inevitable hats and guns.

Halloweenland

If you are here in October, remember Frontierland becomes Halloweenland for the month, with a dazzling array of spooky special effects, creepy scenery and haunted shows. A giant spider's web covers Fort Comstock, the Thunder Mesa Riverboat gets a ghoulish Mummy-style makeover, pumpkins, witches and scarecrows abound, various Disney characters turn up throughout Halloweenland's pathways and the daily Parade is taken over by Disney Villains like Cruella De Vil, Ursula, Maleficent and Jafar. Children (under 12) can get into the 'spirit' with a makeover at the **Halloween Face Painting Workshop** in the Castle Plaza (with a choice of Witch Pink or Pumpkin Orange!) or the **Hairdressing Workshop** for a 'hair-raising' style near the Pumpkin Paint Pit near Big Thunder Mountain. The 2005 Halloween season added an amusing extra element with the **Pink Witches** staging a daily battle with the **Pumpkin Men** along Main Street USA and into Halloweenland (and on the Parade), with guests being invited to take sides in the amusing bickering. The **Pink Witches Convention Academy** and the **Pumpkinwood Forest** are set up in opposition, while the **Witches Wake Stage** adds live music (near the Cowboy Cookout Barbecue) and kids are invited to grab some sweets at a traditional *Piñata*.

> BRIT TIP: The two extra Halloween Parties on 30 and 31 October are not widely publicised in the UK, so they are worth noting and seeking out if you are visiting at that time (or call 08705 03 03 03).

Two extra-spooky evening **Halloween Parties** are staged when the park is open 8.30pm–1am with unlimited access to the main attractions (in Halloweenland, Main Street USA, the Indiana Jones ride in Adventureland and Space Mountain: Mission 2 in Discoveryland), and the addition of live music on a special stage in front of the Castle plus a 'haunted' disco for a separate ticket price of €27 (in 2005). Our research assistant Robert Rees is a confirmed Halloween fan and highlights the great evening atmosphere for the Halloween Parties, made even more memorable by the amazing costumes many guests wear.

> BRIT TIP: Try to get a view of the Castle from one of the small side paths between Frontierland and Adventureland, as there are a number of unusual perspectives offering good photo opportunities.

The transformation of the whole 'land' – unlike anything attempted at the American parks – is hugely ambitious, but the Imagineers have pulled off quite a triumph here, making October a real must-visit month if you can.

Another unique feature of this section of the park is the latticework of paths which interconnect between Frontierland and Adventureland. This surprisingly small-scale landscaping is a notable element of the European influence behind the overall design, and the paths are almost interwoven to provide an alternative way of getting around as well as highlighting different aspects of the lands (but keep your map handy in case you get lost!).

Adventureland

Africa, the Caribbean and the jungles of Asia combine to provide Adventureland with a host of contrasting – and thrilling – experiences, all with lush landscaping. There are the fewest amount of attractions here, but the whole area has such a wealth of detail and fine architecture (take a close look at Skull Rock and the castle façade of the Pirates ride), it is easy to spend a good deal of time just wandering and admiring. Even if you don't eat at most of the counter-service diners, it is worth looking into places like Colonel Hathi's Pizza Outpost and Restaurant Hakuna Matata to appreciate the

BRIT TIP: Adventureland is the hardest 'land' to navigate, so hang on to your map to find your way from place to place.

Adventureland in spring

interior design that gives them a real storybook feel.

Indiana Jones and the Temple of Peril: If you come from Frontierland, turn left by Colonel Hathi's for this 5-star thrill ride. Not content with creating a ducking and diving coaster that seems to zip along much faster when you're aboard than when you're watching, the designers added a brain-scrambling 360-degree loop and have reconfigured it twice to run either backwards or forward (in 2005, it was again going forward). The theming is wonderful, with the queuing area leading you through an archaeological dig in best Indiana Jones fashion, before you reach the temple and your rickety mine wagon.

Before you know it, you are being thrown around a tight, twisting track with its sudden loop and dramatic swoops, only to come to the end of the track all too soon once your body has got the hang of it! This is definitely not the ride if you suffer from neck or back problems as there is quite a bit of vibration along the

way but it is also quite exhilarating and much more fun than it looks. Indiana Jones is a FastPass ride, which is handy for coaster lovers as

BRIT TIP: The scary aspect of the Indiana Jones ride and its position at the innermost end of Adventureland means it is often overlooked by many park visitors, hence it is a good ride to do during the busier parts of the day.

Indiana Jones and the Temple of Peril

© Disney

La Cabane des Robinsons

it rarely draws a big queue and means you can usually ride with only a 10–15-minute wait and then bag a FP for later on. Restrictions: 1.40m (4ft 6in). TTTT.

Retracing your steps slightly and turning left brings you into the central portion of Adventureland, known as **Adventure Isle**. The Imagineers have worked overtime here to create something different from a number of existing themes in other parks, and they opted for an overgrown adventure playground of the most elaborate kind. This is a delightful pot-pourri of attractions, mainly aimed at children but which are also eye-catching and detailed enough to appeal to adults as well.

La Cabane des Robinsons: The Swiss Family Treehouse is the first you come to on the Isle. The re-creation of the treehouse of the castaway Robinson family from the 1960 Disney film is only a walk-through attraction, and looks rather tired these days as the giant 'banyan tree' which was adapted to provide their shelter, food and running water is in urgent need of an overhaul. But queues are rarely a problem and there are great views from the top. AA. Rumour mill: there is talk of La Cabane being re-themed to a Captain Jack Sparrow hideout, with much of Adventure Isle getting a *Pirates of the Caribbean – Curse Of The Black Pearl* movie makeover.

6

Le Coffre du Capitaine

© Disney

> BRIT TIP: Adventure Isle is just about the only area of either park that is NOT accessible for guests who have disabilities. It is simply not designed for the use of wheelchairs.

Spinning off the treehouse is a high-level rope suspension bridge, **Le Pont Suspendu**, which takes you on to the five other sections of the Isle, **Skull Rock** (a labyrinthine stone edifice which towers over one end of the lagoon), **L'Ile au Tresor** (a series of lookout towers and spooky secret caves), **Le Ventre de la Terre** (a series of galleries under the tree), **Captain Hook's Galley** (a rather tame pirate ship which actually has little to explore) and **La Plage des Pirates** (or Pirates' Beach, a clever play area of slides and climbs expressly for the little shipmates). Kids will want to dash off and explore Ben Gunn's Cave, Ambush Alley and Dead Man's Bridge, and it is a good area in which to let them loose for a while. TTT/AAA.

Pirates of the Caribbean: Coming off at the top end of Adventure Isle brings you to one of Disney's trademark and truly unmissable rides. The original version of this attraction was installed in *Disneyland California* in 1967 and remains an Imagineering gem to this day, highlighted by the use of their pioneering work with audio-animatronics. These are a series of life-like (or robot-like, in some cases) figures which move, talk, gesticulate and, in this instance, lay siege to a Caribbean island! Your journey starts as you wind down inside the Pirate Castle, through secret streets and dingy dungeons, until you reach your boat for a plunge into the unexpected darkness of the pirate realm.

There are two minor plunges (and slight splashes – front seat passengers may get a little wet), the first of which drops you into the middle of the island siege, with the clever – and distinctly amusing – action going on all around, and a second which drops into the pirate treasure caverns. Skeletons and

dungeons abound, and it may be a little too intense for under 5s, but there is little that is genuinely scary and the whole effect is so amazing you will probably want to have several turns to appreciate all the detail involved. While it is a popular ride, queues rarely top half an hour here and move steadily, and it is a welcome place to cool down during the hotter months. AAAAA (TTTT for under 8s). NB: See if you can spot some of the elements 'borrowed' when this ride was used as the inspiration for Disney's hit film *Pirates of the Caribbean* in 2003.

If you enter Adventureland via the main entrance off the Central Plaza, you will come into the **Agrabah Bazaar** area. Sadly, this magnificent outdoor/indoor shopping and dining scenario straight out of 1,001 Nights largely closed down in 2002 and there is no sign yet of it being re-opened. In its place, you will find a couple of fairly hum-drum gift shops, plus the **Passage Enchanté d'Aladdin**, a walk-through exhibit of the Aladdin story with some amusing tableaux and clever lighting tricks. AA.

Adventureland is also home to one of our all-time favourite Disney restaurants, the **Blue Lagoon**, which is actually set inside the Pirates ride (so there are usually a few shouts of 'Bon Appetit!' from people setting off on the ride as you dine). You enter just below and to the left of the ride entrance, and the

> BRIT TIP: Plan a special meal, even with the kids, in the Blue Lagoon and you won't be disappointed. Book at City Hall or with your hotel concierge. A perfect pit stop in winter when it is heated to tropical temperatures!

setting alone is worthy of perusal. You eat on a mock 'outdoor' terrace under dim lights, authentically furnished, listening to sounds that evoke the feeling of an evening on some distant Caribbean island. The seafood-orientated menu is also a delight, with the likes of fricassée of tuna and swordfish, steamed emperor fish and mahi-mahi, Jamaican pepper fillet of beef and chicken curry. The set menu is €28 (€15 for teens, €10 for 3–11s), while starters range from €8.90–16 and main courses from €15–25, topped by the speciality dish Treasures of the Sea, a mix of crab claws, scampi, shrimps, whelks, scallops, winkles and oysters for a princely €39. The kids' menu includes sausage, tuna in tomato sauce with pan-fried vegetables, and a proper ground-beef burger that actually tastes like meat (although that may not go down well with those with a penchant for fast food!).

BRIT TIP: A 'secret' route goes from the park's main entrance all the way to the heart of Fantasyland, mainly under cover. Take the Liberty Arcade up Main Street USA, turn sharp left into Frontierland, walk straight through Fort Comstock and follow the covered walkway into Adventureland, skirt round the side of Les Tresors de Scheherazade (briefly in the open), then pick up the walkway alongside the restaurant Au Chalet de la Marionnette and you end up at the Peter Pan ride. It is also a quick way to get OUT of Fantasyland when the park is busy.

Your counter-service options here include **Colonel Hathi's Pizza Outpost** (pizzas, salads, lasagne and spaghetti – set pizza menu at €9.95 – all in best *Jungle Book* style) and **Restaurant Hakuna Matata** (a decent African safari adventure, with spiced chicken, fish nuggets, lamb kebab and a shrimp and tuna salad). **Café de la Brousse** and **Captain Hook's Galley** offer sandwiches, hot dogs, ice creams and drinks.

Shopping brings an additional array of possibilities here, with **Indiana Jones Adventure Outpost** (safari accessories and Indy souvenirs) and **Le Coffre du Capitaine** (as you exit the Pirates ride, and with a suitable range of sea-themed treasures and toys) the pick of the bunch.

Fantasyland

6

Having arrived in the Theme Park's largest 'land' via Adventureland, here you will find the biggest selection of rides and the most concentrated fun for under 8s. This is the stuff of pure fantasy and the whimsical creativity on show is first class, from the huge Castle down to the tiny detail of the clock façade on 'it's a small world'. Unfortunately, it is also the most crowded section of the Theme Park, with queues building up quickly from mid-morning and rarely abating until early evening (when it is open until 11pm). Parts of Fantasyland at the back close from 9pm to prepare for the evening fireworks, so don't think you have the place to yourself all of a sudden!

If you have young children, Fantasyland should be your first port of call as it is likely to offer the most candidates for 'favourite ride' and it is not unknown for families to spend virtually all day here. If you come for 'rope drop' (highly recommended), you should head straight through the Castle and try to do the Carousel, Dumbo and Peter Pan in quick succession, as these three are all terribly slow-loading rides where the queues build up almost immediately and remain painfully slow all day. Excluding Peter Pan but including the Mad Hatter's Tea Cups (another slow-loader), you might also be inclined to say 'We waited all that time for THAT?' at the end of the ride as they are not terribly exciting for grown-ups, being basically rethemed versions of standard fairground rides. However, children will almost certainly demand to ride Dumbo at least once and, if you have managed to get it under your belt without waiting half an hour or more (and the queue usually peaks at a mind-numbing hour), you will have done very well!

BRIT TIP: When Fantasyland is seriously busy, many people overlook the little area right at the back which is home to two excellent child-pleasing rides, Casey Jnr and Le Pays des Contes de Fées, where queues rarely build up but, if they do, move quite quickly.

Wonderful World of Disney Parade

Inside Sleeping Beauty Castle

Taking Fantasyland in a clockwise direction starting at the Castle, you have 12 main attractions from which to choose, plus seven restaurants and seven shops that include some of the most original gift items in the park.

Le Château de la Belle au Bois Dormant (Sleeping Beauty Castle): This is a draw in its own right having two contrasting things to see. **La Galerie de la Belle au Bois Dormant** is easy to miss as you scamper through, but is actually upstairs in the Castle and tells the story in picture-boards and words (in French) of Sleeping Beauty. Check out the beautiful Renaissance-style tapestries which line the walls and the stunning (and highly photogenic) stained-glass windows. You can also walk along an external balcony which provides a great view from both sides of the castle. AA.

Underneath *le château* and accessible via three different portals (including a back door of Merlin's shop, down a winding stone staircase), is the magnificent **La Tanière du Dragon**, or dragon's lair. Here, the creature that turned many a would-be saviour of Sleeping Beauty to toast lurks in steamy, underground splendour, wrapped in

Blanche-Neige et les Sept Nains

reptilian fashion around the stalactites and stalagmites, occasionally rearing his audio-animatronic head to threaten fire and brimstone on all those who dare to disturb his slumbers. In the semi-darkness, it really is a convincing beast (watch its chest 'breathing'!) and is usually far too menacing for under 5s. TTT (for under 8s).

Stepping through the Castle's rear gateway brings you to a courtyard and a great photo opportunity with the Sword in the Stone. Immediately in front of you then is **Le Carrousel de Lancelot**, a fairly standard horsey roundabout which youngsters love, even if queuing can take an age and Mum and Dad would rather be doing something (anything!) else. AA (TTTT for under 5s).

Blanche-Neige et les Sept Nains (The Adventures of Snow White): Right next door, this is a typically Disney kiddie ride which is a fairly dark journey into the cartoon world of the classic film. The soundtrack is in French, which detracts a little if you are unfamiliar with the story (but then, how many people is that likely to be?), and all kids can relate to this mildly scary trip into the realm of the Wicked Witch, her evil plans and the suitably happy ending. Under 5s may find parts of it menacing, but Simon's 4-year-old was okay once he had got over the initial worries of being in the dark and was happy to ride it again several times (shouting 'Boo!' at the witch!). AAA (or TTT for under 8s).

Pinocchio's Fantastic Journey: Following on is another dark ride, this time in the company of Jiminy Cricket showing his attempts to

6

Sleeping Beauty Castle

keep the wooden puppet-boy on the straight and narrow. Again, it is a touch intense for the real young 'uns (especially with the surprise menace of the whale), but most kids find it fun rather than frightening. The special effect at the end with the Blue Fairy is well worth seeing. AAA (TTT for under 8s).

Dumbo the Flying Elephant: Needing little explanation, this is a standard fairground whirligig with elephants as the flying 'vehicles' (albeit without the requisite flapping ears which were, in theory, Dumbo's trademark). The front-seat passengers get to make the elephant go up and down while circling gently round and round, and that's about it. There is little to look at while you are queuing (and the lines move painfully slowly) and the music is horribly repetitive, but kids seem to get a buzz out of piloting their elephant and it is a highly visible ride, so hard for parents to ignore! Head here first thing in the morning or expect to queue for an hour or so (the crowds do ease off a little during the parades, but there is no substitute for doing this early on). TT (TTTT for under 8s).

Peter Pan's Flight: Next door to Dumbo is Fantasyland's other serious queue-builder, which has the saving grace of being a FastPass ride (see page 109). Once you get to board your pirate ship, you rise up, up and away over the streets of London, turn right at the first star and straight on to morning, all the way to Neverland and a close encounter with Captain Hook and his inept pirates. It is another indoor dark ride (very dark as you go through the star-lit portion), but the overhead mechanism of your 'ship' and the elaborate scenery combine to create the right illusion. Usually a big hit with all the family and a must-do ride as far as the kids are concerned, try to take advantage of

the FP. Be aware the waiting time can easily top an hour here and much of the queuing area is out in the open, so your best bet, if the FPs have all gone (as often happens in high season by 2pm), is to leave it as late as possible or wait until a parade has just started. AAAA (TTTTT for under 8s).

Step out of Peter Pan, turn left and you come to the **Fantasy Festival Stage**, a showcase for various visiting school bands, singers and dance acts (billed under the heading of *Magic Music Days*) a number of times every month, as well as the venue for some of the Christmas festivities.

> BRIT TIP: When not in use, the Fantasy Festival Stage makes a handy place to sit in peace and quiet with a drink or snack.

To the left of the Festival Stage is the entrance to the **Fantasyland Railroad Station** and this will usually get you back to Main Street USA much quicker than walking, if there is no serious queue.

Now, all these attractions so far are relatively faithful copies of existing Disney rides in other parks, but the next one is a *Disneyland Resort Paris* original.

Alice's Curious Labyrinth: An interactive maze leading up to the Queen of Hearts' castle, this seems to have almost universal appeal for children up to about 12, with a whole range of *Alice in Wonderland* tricks and motifs along the way, including amusing signage, squirting fountains (kids *really* gravitate towards these, trying to catch the water as it 'jumps' from fountain to fountain), an encounter with the hookah-smoking Caterpillar and several scrapes with the Queen of

Hearts and her guards (in various audio-animatronic guises). It is fairly gentle stuff but keeps youngsters (and their parents) amused for a good 15–20 minutes and is an ideal place to visit when waits at Peter Pan and Dumbo hit an hour. AAA.

Passing further along and under the railway bridge brings you to the little area right at the back of Fantasyland which gets overlooked by some. But, if you have young children, this is somewhere you won't want to miss, both for the instant kiddie appeal and the shorter queues here. Both rides are copies from the original *Disneyland Park* in California, but they possess a timeless charm.

Le Pays des Contes de Fées: This is a gentle boat ride into a fairytale world of miniature depictions of stories like *Snow White*, *Peter and the Wolf*, *The Wizard of Oz*, *Beauty and the Beast* and *The Little Mermaid*. For the Aladdin section, your boat is 'swallowed up' by the giant lion's mouth cave from the story, which can be a little daunting for the youngest passengers, but the whole thing proceeds at barely walking pace, so you have plenty of time to ease any apprehensions. AAA.

> **BRIT TIP:** If you are at Le Pays des Contes de Fées at any other time than peak periods, the boat ride is usually a walk-on attraction and has the great benefit for youngsters of being able to take them straight back on for another go.

Casey Jr – le Petit Train du Cirque: Another guaranteed hit for the under 8 brigade. In reality, it is a fairly tame, junior-sized coaster, themed in eye-catching style after the circus train in Dumbo. Some of the cars are designed like animal cages, others are open and, of course, two can sit up front in the 'engine'. It glides along for some 5 minutes, encountering a couple of mild dips and gentle bends, but it gives just the right illusion of excitement to those of the requisite age (and any nervous parents!). Indeed, Simon's youngest – then aged 4 – must have set a record for riding this five times in a row with great glee, delighting in trying to sit in every different seat, front and back! AAA (TTTT for under 5s).

As you exit this two-ride mini-land, you pass the disused Les Pirouettes Du Vieux Moulin, a big-wheel type ride which proved unworkable with even moderate queues and which has quietly been abandoned. It still looks good in non-working mode but sadly that is all you get from it.

Mad Hatter's Tea Cups: Another standard fairground ride, this has been given a bit of *Alice in Wonderland* top-spin to make it seem a bit more than it actually is. Kids all seem to love the chance to ride in these manically whirling cups, which have a wheel to make them spin counter to the main rotation (Uuurgghhh! we say). We have to admit, going round in never-decreasing circles (or so it feels) was never our cup of tea at all, but it remains a seriously popular ride, so it is best to do this one early in the day or later in the evening. TTT.

Continuing our clockwise tour of Fantasyland brings you next to one of Disney's signature rides.

'it's a small world': Designed under the direction of Walt himself for the New York World Fair in 1964, this ride has stood the test of time amazingly well for children under 8 and remains a big hit to this day. The exterior façade is one of the most eye-catching in the park,

6

'it's a small world'

with all manner of moving and static elements that add up to a wonderfully artistic collage. Inside, all it really consists of is a slow-moving boat ride through a series of highly colourful scenes featuring audio-animatronic dolls singing and dancing in various national-themed displays, from Britain to Brazil and Africa to the Arctic. It has an insidiously catchy theme tune (we challenge you NOT to be humming it when you exit!) and a fabulously imaginative winter-wonderland final scene, but otherwise it just highlights the clever way in which Disney's Imagineers can take a routine kind of ride and give it a whole new style and appeal.

Once again, it proves if you give it the right scale and a proportionate amount of detail (with a little sprinkle of Disney 'pixie dust'), the ordinary can become quite extraordinary. Even many adults are captivated by the spirit and vivacity of this attraction, and it is one that bears multiple rides during the day. Queues here rarely top 20 minutes and move quite steadily, so this is a good one to do at most times, but especially in the afternoon (and when it might be hot). AAAA.

> **BRIT TIP:** Hang around outside 'it's a small world' on the hour and watch the wonderful clock (you can hear it ticking from quite a distance) come to life with a display of moving figures in best Toytown tradition.

Returning to the front right of the Castle brings you to **Royal Castle Stage**, which is home to **Winnie the Pooh and Friends**, a 25-minute show (in high season only) in the company of Christopher Robin and his bear of very little

Fantasyland topiary

© Disney

Le Pays des Contes de Fées

brain, plus Piglet, Rabbit, Eeyore and Tigger. It is simple, easy on the eyes (and ears) and is usually perfect for giving under 8s a half-hour break from the non-stop ride scenario. However, beware the hard stone benches (extremely uncomfortable by the end of the show!) and the lack of any shade in summer (remember hats and sunscreen). AAA.

When it comes to mealtimes, Fantasyland has a gourmet offering in **Auberge de Cendrillon**, with an elegant ballroom-type setting and an excellent French menu. Open 11.30am–4pm, it features ravioli, risotto, roast salmon, entrecôte steak and duck pâté as well as regular burger fare, and there is also a pleasant outdoor courtyard (where Cinderella's carriage stands). The set meal for adults is €28 and €10 for children (3–11). The other outlets are all counter-service types and fill up quickly for lunch at even mildly busy times: **Au Chalet de la Marionnette**, which has a rear entrance opening into Adventureland, features roast chicken, burgers, salads and chips, plus a range of German desserts; **Toad Hall Restaurant**, modelled in mock English country house style, á

la *Wind in the Willows*, serves fish and chips, pies, sandwiches and cakes; and **Pizzeria Bella Notta**, an Italian diner modelled on *Lady and the Tramp*, offers pizzas and pasta.

More venues for a snack, ice cream or drink include **March Hare Refreshments**, **The Old Mill** and **Fantasia Gelati**.

For shopping, the interlinked group in and around the Castle offers some worthwhile retail therapy, with **Merlin l'Enchanteur** (a clever little 'rock-carved' boutique featuring fine crystal, glassware – hand-made while you watch – and porcelain statuettes), **La Boutique du Château** (a Christmas-orientated offering), **La Confiserie des Trois Fées** (a great sweet shop in the company of the good fairies Flora, Fauna and Merryweather from *Sleeping Beauty*), and the epic **Sir Mickey's** featuring cuddly toys, jewellery, glass and ceramics, and children's clothes, toys, games and Disney souvenirs.

6

Belle's Christmas Village

© Disney

Discoveryland

When the Imagineers set about designing the park's fifth and final 'land', their challenge was to come up with a new variant on a fairly well-worn theme. In both Anaheim and Orlando, this area had been developed as Tomorrowland, an unabashed attempt to predict and present the future in an amusing way. There is a mock retro styling about the previous examples but that was felt to be an over-used idea when it came to *Disneyland Resort Paris* and the call went out for something new.

So, the Imagineers studied their European history and literature and came up with a new motif, that of a future world inspired by technology derived from such historical luminaries as Leonardo da Vinci and Jules Verne. That helped to determine the overall look and feel of Discoveryland (a new title too, as Tomorrowland was felt to be too narrow a definition), hence the styling is a kind of 'antique' future, with much of the architecture borrowing heavily from Verne's 19th-century images of the future.

The two principal icons – Space Mountain: Mission 2 and the Café Hypérion – are magnificent re-creations of Vernian visions and help to create a visual stimulus that is both bold and exciting (can you tell we quite like this area!). The fanciful exterior of Space Mountain is one of the greatest examples of the ride designer's art because so much of it is totally unnecessary to the ride itself; it is purely and simply a statement of style that epitomises the creativity inherent in a Disney Theme Park. And the rides here are pretty good, too!

Space Mountain: Mission 2: Completely re-themed and revamped in 2005, this breathtaking blast of a ride borrows from the

> **BRIT TIP:** If you don't visit Space Mountain early in the day and you can't get a FastPass, return in early evening to beat the worst of the queues.

Verne novel *From the Earth to the Moon* and gives it a contemporary twist. Whereas the original giant cannon Columbiad (of the Baltimore Gun Club) blasted riders to the Moon, now the over-sized gun barrel has been super-charged to send its vehicles much deeper into space, to discover the secrets of the universe! (Actually, the main ride is exactly the same, but the new theming is immensely convincing). You queue up through the heart of the ride itself before you reach your vehicle, which is 'loaded' into Columbiad. The dry ice flows, the (all-new) music rolls, the lights pulsate and then ... pow! You are off at gravity-defying speed to explore outer space, dodging close encounters with meteorites and other cosmic phenomena, looping the loop and corkscrewing twice past thundering comets and evading an exploding supernova into a new dimension as the unexpected climax to the 3-minute whizz. The high-tech light show alone is worth seeing and, if the description sounds disturbing, don't let it put you off. This is one of the smoothest coasters you will ride and it is a big-time thrill. It is also a FastPass ride, which is vital for peak periods as the crowds flock here from mid-morning. Souvenir photos of your ride are available at the end for €14–22. Restrictions: 1.32m (4ft 3in) TTTTT.

Les Mystères du Nautilus: As you exit Space Mountain, you encounter another *Disneyland Resort Paris* original, a clever walk-through version of Captain Nemo's famous submarine. The realism as you go down 'underground' on a circular steel staircase is all encompassing, bringing you into the Nautilus itself and a self-guided tour of this amazing Verne creation. Take your time to peer into all the nooks and crannies and admire the intricate detail, and sit for a moment at one of the big, circular portholes. Is that a giant squid moving in, too close…? You'll have to check it out for yourself! Children under 7 must be accompanied by an adult (11:30am–5:30pm only). AAA.

Orbitron – Machines Volantes: Next door is this similarly eye-catching ride, which is really only a jazzed-up version of the Dumbo ride, spinning and climbing in regulation fashion as the front-seat 'pilot' takes the controls. The clever circulation of the accompanying 'planets' really makes this ride, however, giving it the look of something more intricate, and it is another one which is fun just to watch. TTT (TTTTT for under 8s).

Star Tours: Behind Space Mountain is the impressive futuristic façade of Disney's wonderful collaboration with *Star Wars* director George Lucas. The queuing area alone is something of a masterpiece, as you are drawn into the make-believe world of squabbling 'droids C-3PO and R-2D2 as they prepare your Star Speeder for the light-speed trip to Endor. This is a faithful transplant of the ride in *Disneyland California* and *Disney-MGM Studios* in Orlando, with the one exception that the commentary provided by your robot pilot is in French. The ride itself, though, is a 24-carat thrill, as the realistic Speeders load and lift off for outer space, where all manner of mishaps lead you into a series of adventures. This was the bee's knees when it made its debut in Anaheim

in 1987 and it is still a magical experience for Disney newcomers (although those familiar with the ride from elsewhere may feel it is a little ho-hum by now). Star Tours is also another FastPass ride, which is handy because you could spend a good 45 minutes queuing at peak periods. There is no height restriction, but those with bad backs or necks might want to give it a miss, and it is probably too intense for under 4s. TTTT.

> **BRIT TIP:** Head for Discoveryland first and you can ride either Space Mountain or Star Tours without much of a queue and then pick up a FastPass for the other. The new Space Mountain: Mission 2 draws the heaviest crowds throughout the main part of the day.

6

The exit to Star Tours used to bring you into an amusing area of interactive games, L'Astroport Services Interstellaires, but sadly these have been scrapped in favour of some fairly standard (and rather dismal by comparison) video arcade fare, which you need to negotiate on your way out. Behind Star Tours is the **Discoveryland Railroad Station**, but this is a good one to miss at busy times as it is second only to the Main Street station for drawing long, slow-moving queues.

Honey, I Shrunk the Audience: Right next door to Star Tours, this 3-D film show is also a major Disney trademark attraction. Pioneered in all their American parks, it provides yet another variation on Theme Park thrills. Here, continuing where the two hit films left off, you enter a wacky science world of the

Imagination Institute (run by the highly amusing Eric Idle), where they are about to honour the inventions of a certain professor Wayne Szalinski.

> BRIT TIP: To prove Disney also thinks on a small scale as well as the large, check out the audio-animatronic pigeons (!) attached to the Hypérion airship at the entrance to Café Hypérion.

An entertaining 8-minute pre-show sets the scene for the main part of your adventure in the awards 'theatre' and then the real fun begins once you don your 3-D glasses. The inevitable on-stage mishaps are accompanied by a sequence of special effects throughout the theatre that often have the audience in hysterics (although under-5s may find it plain scary) and which it would be a shame to spoil by revealing, so just sit back and get ready to be surprised... very surprised (and beware the sneezing dog!). This is also a show that requires a full English dialogue to follow the story, and headphones are provided for non-French speakers. AAAAA (plus TTT).

© Disney

Orbitron

Autopia: Another attraction which you need to visit early on unless you want a long wait. Rather old-fashioned, this mock Grand Prix track – a 'futuristic Formula 1 circuit' – is purely for kids and sits a little awkwardly among the more sci-fi laden offerings. It is often closed for maintenance (and at off-peak times) and is notoriously slow to load, hence queues can touch an hour or more and move *very* slowly. And, unless you are under 8, you are not likely to get much of a thrill from these tame cars that run on well-defined tracks, even if they provide the illusion of driving.

Star Tours

© Disney

© Disney

Space Mountain: Mission 2

Children under 1.32m (4ft 3in) need to be accompanied by an adult but you are not really missing much if you bypass this one. T (TTT for under 8s). Rumour mill: there are suggestions Autopia will be scrapped altogether in the next few years, to be replaced by a more dynamic indoor ride.

Buzz Lightyear's Laser Blast: Due to open in 2006 (around Easter), this wonderful interactive family ride should appeal to all ages and be a highly worthwhile Discoveryland addition. Riders are 'recruited' into Buzz Lightyear's Space Ranger galaxy defence force and kids in particular will not want to miss this chance to join the great *Toy Story*

character in his battle against the evil Emperor Zurg. You ride into action against Zurg's villainous robot army – and shoot them with laser cannons! You can spin your car from side to side and score points as you would in an arcade game, which ensures everyone tries it again to improve their score. Watch out for a gift shop and ride photo opportunity as you exit. TTT (TTTTT for under 8s; FP).

Legend Of The Lion King: Sharing the impressive Café Hypérion building is the Videopolis showstage for the park's newest live entertainment offering. *Legend Of The Lion King* is a showcase of the

6

BRIT TIP: The Buzz Lightyear robot targets have different values, with anything moving worth a higher score. Watch out for the large robot as you enter the first room. Turn your vehicle around and aim for the target on his hand – it's worth 10,000 points!

Legend Of The Lion King

© Disney

animated film classic, with all the characters making an appearance in a mixture of clever puppetry and real-actor interaction. All the best-known songs get an airing in a celebration of the Lion King story, with Timon as the MC and his warthog sidekick Pumba adding some laughs. The 30-minute show is performed up to five times a day, alternately in French and English, and is extremely popular, so you need to plan carefully for this.

> BRIT TIP: If you miss out on a ticket for the Lion King show, grab a snack at Café Hypérion and go upstairs to where many of the tables have a view of the Videopolis stage.

Free tickets are distributed for the (limited) theatre seating twice a day at a kiosk outside the Videopolis entrance doors, and you usually need to queue up to half an hour before the published distribution time, then make sure you ask for the English performance. To our mind, this is a slightly cock-eyed system, but it is a high-quality show and worth the extra hassle for tickets. AAAA.
As a final word on the attractions, the inevitable video games also make an appearance in the shape of

> BRIT TIP: Between shows, the Videopolis theatre screens classic Disney cartoons, so, if you need a rest in air-conditioned comfort or shelter from the rain, or if your kids just can't face another queue, head into Café Hypérion for a drink or a snack.

Arcades Alpha and **Beta** on either side of the lower entrance to Videopolis. Older children and young teens who need a break from the family shackles for a while can head to either of these (or the arcade inside the exit to Star Tours) and shoot up a T-Rex or play football or air hockey. Be warned the games are not cheap – one token costs €2 and there is a one-token minimum per game. TT.
When it comes to eating, the aforementioned **Café Hypérion** is worth investigating even if you don't visit the counter-service diner, which serves very average cheeseburgers, chicken burgers and chicken nuggets. **Pizza Planet** (easy to miss, but it's just to the right of Honey, I Shrunk the Audience) is a disappointing offering if you expect something out of the *Toy Story* film. The interior is very plain and the pizza served here is not unlike cardboard. *Toy Story* characters do appear from time to time, though.

> BRIT TIP: Pizza Planet can be useful if you have under 5s in need of a break. It has a soft-play climb-and-slide area which allows them to let off some steam while you have a drink!

The Rocket Café at the back of Space Mountain offers an additional few snacks and drinks which you can consume in relative peace and quiet at the tables outside Pizza Planet. There are also two main gift stores, the elaborate **Constellations** (the usual range of souvenirs but with a ceiling twinkling with a 'universe' of stars) and **Star Traders** (for all your *Star Wars* related merchandise, other space toys and sports gear).

Parades and tours

If that is the full detail on each of the five 'lands', you have several other sources of great entertainment along the way. Chief among these is the daily parade (or parades if you are here in high season or a special event like Halloween or Christmas). The **Wonderful World of Disney Parade** is the main event here, except for the festive period from mid-November to early January when it is replaced by the **Christmas Parade** (described in Chapter 2). If you have never seen a Disney parade, this is a genuine must-see experience. Yes, the queues at many attractions do tend to shorten during the daily parade, but it is a shame to miss something as creative and dynamic as this just to take in another ride. Each parade starts in the Discovery Arcade corner of Town Square and continues up Main Street USA to the Central Plaza, where it turns right in front of the Royal Castle Stage and moves into Fantasyland before finally exiting next to 'it's a small world'.

BRIT TIP: Be aware people start staking out some of the best spots to view the various parades – along Main Street USA and around the Central Plaza – up to an hour in advance at peak times. And there can be a bit of push-and-shove as late-comers try to squeeze in.

Children are truly captivated by the scale and elaboration of the huge floats, as well as the chance to see a multitude of their favourite characters at fairly close quarters. The music is memorable, the dancing amazingly energetic (especially given the heat in summer) and the splendour of floats such as Steamboat Willie (in black and white), the Disney Princesses, Mary Poppins and the Little Mermaid is totally enchanting. The 12 floats chart the heritage of classic Walt Disney films, and the whole spectacle takes a good 25–30 minutes to pass by. You will take a LOT of photos – if you don't end up being side-tracked by watching children's faces around you. AAAAA.

BRIT TIP: For the main daily parades, the route through Fantasyland is less crowded than elsewhere, while the corner of the Town Square in front of City Hall is also a good place to wait as it is often overlooked and offers some shade when it's hot.

The **Disney's Fantillusion parade**, which has replaced the old Main Street Electrical Parade, adds to the picture for the high summer and winter season evenings (usually around 10.30pm), and is equally stunning. It features an eye-popping cavalcade of Disney favourites in a high-tech setting of glittering lights and dazzling floats. The parade comes in three parts and unfolds with an almost balletic grace, first as Mickey himself brings the Gift of Light, then a darker section as the Disney villains threaten to take over (with some spectacular special effects as Jafar transforms into a serpent, Maleficent becomes the wicked dragon and the winged Chernabog commands fire) and finally a joyful conclusion as the glittering heroes and heroines, princes and princesses get together with Minnie to save the day. It features a fabulous

© Disney

Fantillusion

soundtrack by Bruce Healy and a seemingly endless fairytale pageant of shimmering, twinkling lights, and the overall effect is so thrilling, even

Wonderful World of Disney Parade

© Disney

by Disney standards, it is worth keeping the kids up to see it. The whole parade stops at various points for a few well-rehearsed routines from the costumed dancers, and it can take a good 30 minutes to pass by. But, whatever you do, don't miss this one! AAAAA+.

The **Halloween Parade** adds to the daily fun throughout October (check your park map for timings) and is another visual riot of creepy-costumed capers, song and dance, with various characters joining the extravaganza. Here, the Disney Villains have usurped the stage for a darker (but still fun) cavalcade of ghosts, goblins and witches, with some wonderfully inventive, skeleton-inspired touches. Watch out for the new Pink Witches and Pumpkin Men squabbling along the way! AAAA.

It is worth taking a mental step back from all the clever artistry of the floats to appreciate the non-stop energy and quality of the many dancers in the parades, who keep up their efforts for every second of every performance, day in and day out. It takes immense dedication, but they also have a lot of fun and get a

© Disney

Buzz Lightyear's Laser Blast

BRIT TIP: The best place from which to watch the nightly fireworks is in front of the Castle or at the end of Main Street USA. The show is choreographed with, and symmetrically around, the *château* and the visual effect is stunning.

real kick out of the reaction they get from their audience – especially the kids. So don't hesitate to smile and wave back, as they certainly deserve all the encouragement and appreciation you can muster.

In high season (summer and Christmas), there is also the nightly finale of the **Wishes** fireworks extravaganza, which brings down the curtain each evening. The Wishes show was pioneered at the *Magic Kingdom Park* in *Walt Disney World*, and adapted for the different configuration of the *Disneyland Park*. There are fewer large-scale explosions and the vast majority of fireworks are low-level, but there is an amazing range of lighting and laser effects on the Castle, and the whole show has a charm that sets it apart from the big-scale American equivalent. It is magnificently choreographed with well-known Disney soundtracks and features distinct bursts of films from *The*

6

Phantom Manor

The Disneyland Park with children

Here is a rough guide to the rides that appeal to different age groups. Obviously, children vary enormously in their likes and dislikes but, as a general rule, you can be fairly sure the following will have most appeal to the ages concerned (also taking into account the height restrictions):

Under 5s

Disneyland Railroad, Main Street Vehicles, Thunder Mesa Riverboats, Pocahontas Indian Village, Critter Corral, La Plage des Pirates (Pirates' Beach) play area, La Cabane des Robinsons, The Tarzan Encounter (although check the volume isn't too loud for young ears), Winnie the Pooh and Friends, Blanche-Neige et les Sept Nains (Snow White), Pinocchio's Fantastic Journey, Le Carrousel de Lancelot, Peter Pan's Flight, Dumbo, 'it's a small world', Le Pays des Contes de Fées, Casey Jr, Alice's Curious Labyrinth, Buzz Lightyear's Laser Blast, Orbitron (not recommended for babies), Autopia, Les Mystères du Nautilus, Legend Of The Lion King, Wonderful World of Disney Parade.

6–8s

All the above, plus Phantom Manor (with parental discretion), Fort Comstock, Rustler Roundup Shootin' Gallery, Big Thunder Mountain, Adventure Isle, Pirates of the Caribbean, Le Passage Enchanté d'Aladdin, La Tanière du Dragon, Mad Hatter's Tea Cups, Star Tours, Honey, I Shrunk the Audience.

9–12s

Phantom Manor, Fort Comstock, Rustler Roundup Shootin' Gallery, Big Thunder Mountain, The Tarzan Encounter, Pirates of the Caribbean, Adventure Isle, Indiana Jones and the Temple of Peril, Peter Pan's Flight, Mad Hatter's Tea Cups, Alice's Curious Labyrinth, Arcades Alpha and Beta, Buzz Lightyear's Laser Blast, Orbitron, Space Mountain: Mission 2, Les Mystères du Nautilus, Honey, I Shrunk the Audience, Star Tours.

Over 12s

Phantom Manor, Big Thunder Mountain, Rustler Roundup Shootin' Gallery, The Tarzan Encounter, Pirates of the Caribbean, Adventure Isle, Indiana Jones and the Temple of Peril, Mad Hatter's Tea Cups, Arcades Alpha and Beta, Buzz Lightyear's Laser Blast, Orbitron, Space Mountain: Mission 2, Honey, I Shrunk the Audience, Star Tours.

Little Mermaid, *Aladdin* and *Fantasia*, with additional narration by Jiminy Cricket and the Blue Fairy. It is the perfect way to conclude any Disney visit, as the company's expertise with pyrotechnic shows is legendary and well merited. Few people have the vision and capability to present fireworks in such a thrilling and well-balanced way, and the effect of seeing the many starbursts over the Sleeping Beauty Castle is breathtaking. Be warned, however, the sound and scale of the fireworks can scare young children.

Want to learn more about the *Disneyland Park*? Sign up for a **Guided Tour** at City Hall early in the day (subject to availability; maximum 25 people) and you can

BRIT TIP: For some genuine Disney shopping bargains, check out the Plaza West Boutique, just to the right of the *Disneyland Hotel* as you exit. They stock a range of previous season's merchandise at greatly reduced prices.

take a walking tour in the company of a highly knowledgeable Cast Member who will show you what makes the Theme Park tick. At €15 for adults and free for under 12s, the tours last almost 2 hours and will give you a novel insight into the creation of this magnificent entertainment venue.

And that, folks, is *Disneyland Park* in all its detailed splendour. Hopefully, after a day here (even when crowds are at their heaviest), you will agree with us in judging this to be a work of art in the business of having fun. Take time to acquaint yourself with all that's here in advance and you should be well prepared to get the most out of this immensely diverse range of attractions. As we advise for visiting any Disney park, try to take some

time along the way to slow down and appreciate all the fine, intricate detail that's involved in the park.

There is just so much packed into this Theme Park in particular, it would be a shame if you went home without seeing the history of Dapper Dan's barber shop, the nostalgia of the two arcades and the whimsy of restaurants like Pizzeria Bella Notte and the Blue Lagoon. It is a wonderfully complete and immersive environment that really does transport you a million miles away from everyday life, so make sure you get the most out of it.

BRIT TIP: Unless you are particularly speedy in leaving the Theme Park at closing time, you might be better off taking the 15–20-minute walk back to the big hotels such as *Disney's Hotel Santa Fe, Disney's Cheyenne Hotel* and *Disney's Newport Bay Club*, as the crowds at the shuttle bus stop can mean another lengthy wait.

6

But we can't stop here. There is a whole new park to explore yet. It's on to the *Walt Disney Studios Park*…!

Walt Disney Studios Park
(or, Lights, Cameras, Action!)

If you consider the *Disneyland Park* represents the very essence of Disney magic and imagination, where does that leave the new *Walt Disney Studios Park*? That's a good question if you expect more of the same and it is a moot point as to which you should visit first as a newcomer.

Perhaps the best answer is to treat this new, smaller development as a completely different entity to its bigger brother, something that complements the first park but doesn't attempt to copy its formula of non-stop rides and fun. There are far fewer attractions, but what there are tend to be much bigger in scope and offer a vastly different experience. Put simply, if the *Disneyland Park* is the Theme Park of rides, then the *Walt Disney Studios Park* is the Theme Park of shows.

There is also a major difference in the geography and topography between the two, as well as the newer park being just half the size (although with scope to double in size by 2011). It consists of just four main areas and there are no great distinguishing features once you have passed through the entrance complex known as the Front Lot. It is also an easy park to negotiate, and getting from one area to another for the various shows is a lot less problematical than it can be at the older park. You can walk from one end to the other in little more than 5 minutes and it positively invites you to step outside for lunch in *Disney Village* as it's all so simple.

Key to Walt Disney Studios Park Map

Front Lot
1 Walt Disney Studios Store
2 Studio Photo
3 Disney Studio 1
4 Les Légendes d'Hollywood
5 Restaurant en Coulisse

Animation Courtyard
6 Art of Disney Animation
7 Animagique
8 Mickey's Trailer
9 Flying Carpets Over Agrabah
10 The Disney Animation Gallery
11 Toon Studios (Easter 2007)

Production Courtyard
12 Cinémagique
13 The Studio Tram Tour
14 Catastrophe Canyon
15 Walt Disney Television Studios Tour
16 Rendez-Vous des Stars Restaurant
17 La Terrasse
18 Production Courtyard Stage
19 Tower of Terror (2008)

The Backlot
20 Armageddon: Special Effects
21 Rock 'n' Roller Coaster starring Aerosmith
22 Moteurs…Action! Stunt Show Spectacular
23 Le Café des Cascadeurs
24 Backlot Express Restaurant
25 Rock Around The Shop

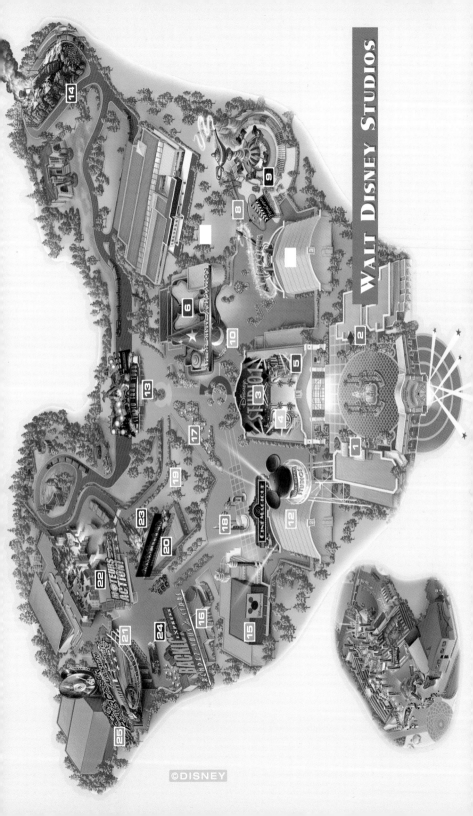

WALT DISNEY STUDIOS

©DISNEY

The Walt Disney Studios Park at a glance

See full-colour map on page 149.

Location	Off Exit 14 of the A4 autoroute, proceed to the clearly signed car park; or turn right out of the Marne-la-Vallée RER and TGV station; or through the *Disney Village* if staying at a resort hotel
Size	25 hectares (62 acres) in four areas
Hours	10am–6pm winter and spring off-peak weekdays, 9am–6pm weekends; 9am–6pm all summer
Admission	**Under 3** free; **3–11** €34 (1-Day Passport), €43, €77, €92 (1, 2 and 3-Day Park Hopper), **adults** (12+) €42 (1-Day Passport), €51, €93, €113 (1, 2 and 3-Day Park Hopper); **Annual Passports** (per person): Fantasy €119, Dream €159. *NB: All prices subject to increase from Easter 2006 (see www.disneylandparis.com)*
Parking	€8
Pushchairs	€6.50 (Pushchair shop to left of Studio Photo, on right hand side of entrance courtyard)
Wheelchairs	€6.50 (Pushchair shop)
Top Attractions	Rock 'n' Roller Coaster starring Aerosmith, Moteurs…Action! Stunt Show Spectacular, Studio Tram Tour, Cinémagique, Toon Studios (from 2007)
Don't Miss	Disney Cinema Parade, West Street Story Orchestra, Streetmosphere performers, Push, The Talking Trashcan

Hidden Costs	**Meals**	Burger, chips and coke €7.85; burger, chips and brownie €9.95; 3-course meal €21 (Rendez-Vous des Stars)
	Kids' meal	€6 (at all cafes and snack bars; €10.90 at Rendez-Vous des Stars)
	T-shirts	€9.90–21
	Souvenirs	€1.90–500
	Sundries	Superimposed photo with characters €16.50

Another notable difference is in the sound of the two parks. In the *Disneyland Park*, the accompanying music only provides a background to all the fun and rides. In the *Walt Disney Studios Park*, the music is right up front, setting the scene and providing a soundtrack almost everywhere you go, most notably in the Backlot area. This dramatic musical accompaniment underscores the film-orientated nature of the Theme Park and adds an extra layer to the overall theming.

Get with the theme

At the time of writing, there remain just the nine out-and-out main attractions, plus a daily parade, on which to concentrate. Of course, being Disney, there are always delightful extras along the way and, in the *Walt Disney Studios Park*, you

What the future holds

The *Walt Disney Studios Park* opened in 2002 with just nine principal attractions and an overall size not much bigger than Frontierland in the *Disneyland Park*. This was clearly not the recipe for long-term success but there were plans afoot to develop the park further and make it more rounded. These had to be postponed when the company's financial worries resurfaced in 2003 and it is only now, for 2006 and beyond, that we can see the real future of this park.

Visitors to the Studios will notice quite a few of Disney's 'Pardon Our Dust' signs and hoardings, which indicate new development while the growing edifice of the **Tower of Terror** right in the middle is the ideal signpost for the future, due to open in 2008 (although there is speculation it might be open in time for Halloween 2007). Meanwhile, visitors to Animation Courtyard should see a very different picture as **Toon Studios** gets ready to open in 2007. There is sure to be more associated development with these two large-scale projects, while former CEO André Lacroix indicated the Tower of Terror will NOT be the end of the upgrade. Speaking in January 2005, he said, 'We'll be concentrating heavily on the new park by creating these new attractions, but that won't be all.' The Studios park will keep growing and, in 6 years' time, it will be twice its current size.'

It also follows that as the park adds new attractions, the crowds will increase, which will affect the traffic patterns. So, stay tuned to our website www.askdaisy.net/disneylandparis and we will be able to provide you with all the latest news.

7

have Streetmosphere, a series of mini street theatres, musical acts and comedians, adding to the fun factor.

The depth and elaboration of the theming, both architecturally and in the landscaping, is not on the same scale as the *Disneyland Park* either, although some say that the Studios environment is too realistic for its own good, lacking imagination, but as one Cast Member explained, 'Well, our theme is a movie studio. What do you expect a movie studio to look like, apart from a collection of big, fairly bland buildings?' Of course, there is more to it than that, but it is a pertinent point.

The whole idea is to surround you with the magic of the movies and, to that end, the collection of large studio soundstages which house most of the attractions can look horribly functional by comparison with the neighbouring park.

However, Disney's Imagineers are adding extra embellishments all the time, and the internal effects are rarely short of spectacular (just wait until you walk into the Rock 'n' Roller Coaster for the first time!).

The one possible concern for parents with younger children is there isn't as much for them to do here as next door. There is only one main kiddie ride and one show that's purposefully for them (until the Toon Studios opens), while several attractions are definitely not for young eyes and ears (too loud or too scary). The daily parade, however, is a genuine source of family fun, and the Streetmosphere acts add to it all. Certainly, there was enough here to keep Simon's two boys well entertained for most of the day (see *What We Did Last Summer*, on page 154). You will also find it easier to meet the Disney characters here as there are several regular set-piece meet-and-greets, plus frequent appearances throughout the park.

Staying dry

The other clever element of the *Walt Disney Studios Park* is that nearly all of the attractions are under cover, which is vital in winter and quite welcome in the hotter months, too. With the exception of the Flying Carpets Over Agrabah, they provide a much longer and more involving experience. Several of the shows last half an hour or more which means you can spend a longer time doing fewer things than in the

> BRIT TIP: As with the *Disneyland Park*, you can take advantage of the Disney **Shopping Service** for purchases you make at the *Walt Disney Studios*. Instead of having to carry them around, they can be sent to *Disney Village* for you to pick up at the Disney Store from 6pm.

Disneyland Park (and less time spent queuing) but there should still be enough to keep you occupied for a full day (with the option to move

Susan at Walt Disney Studios

Simon and friends

between parks with the multi-day Park Hopper tickets – see page 106).

Another difference between the Theme Parks is the eating opportunities. While the *Disneyland Park* has a comprehensive mix of restaurants, cafes and snack bars, the *Walt Disney Studios Park* is limited to just four counter-service options, plus a series of snack wagons. With *Disney Village* just 5 minutes' walk from the front gates, it is easy to argue that you have plenty of choice (plus a chance to escape the hubbub), but we look forward to seeing what the Toon Studios development will include, as at least one full-service restaurant is needed to provide a bit of breadth to the studio style (anyone who has eaten in the Sci Fi Dine-In Theater or the 50s Prime Time Diner at *Disney-MGM Studios* in Orlando will know what we mean!). However, there are also fewer shopping opportunities in this park and you don't feel quite so much a target for the big sell.

© Disney

Walt Disney Studios at Christmas

Right on queue

What about the queues? This was a prime concern at the big preview event in March 2002 as, while the attractions themselves were all unfailingly enjoyable, we could foresee some fairly long waits in places. Summer 2002 was certainly busy enough and seemed to provide a good test of all aspects of the Theme Park's crowd management. With very few exceptions, the attractions coped well with everything that was thrown at them, with only the Studio Tram Tour

collecting some formidably long queues. Queuing for the big Stunt Show Spectacular could also be an ordeal unless you were there half an hour early, as the line snakes out into the main concourse of the Backlot area from midday to mid-afternoon, but it is a huge arena and most people usually get in.

Reviewing things in summer 2005, Disney had actually withdrawn the handful of FastPass turnstiles as there simply weren't the crowds needed to make them worthwhile. Even Rock 'n' Roller Coaster was only a 5-minute wait in mid-afternoon, while any queues were noticeable only for a couple of hours from around midday onwards.

The daily Disney Cinema Parade has been pushed back from its 3.30 outing to 4.45pm in a bid to keep people in the park for longer (there is usually a mass exodus after the parade). But that still means you have the best part of an hour left to do some of the rides with no queues, or take in the final show of something like Cinémagique, whether you hang on until the end or come back into the park at about 5pm. At that time, you should be able to enjoy rides such as Rock 'n' Roller Coaster and the Flying Carpets almost unhindered (Simon's

7

Streetmosphere

© Disney

What we did last summer

Until Simon took his two boys – then aged 6 and 4 – to *Walt Disney Studios Park*, he was of the opinion there was a lot less to do here for young children than at the *Disneyland Park*, where kids usually keep going for as long as you let them! Their experience was an eye opener as they spent nearly a full day at the park, and both boys were keen to go back the next day to see the amazing Stunt Show again.

Admittedly, they didn't arrive until almost 11am, but it was then a fairly non-stop experience until the 6pm closing, at which time they called a halt for dinner back in the *Disneyland Park*. There was only a minimal wait between attractions, too.

The regular availability of the characters in the Animation Courtyard area was another plus, as the opportunity to grab autographs and pose for photos with their Disney favourites actually proved a stronger lure than some of the rides. In addition, the Streetmosphere acts had them rooted to the spot with Simon's eldest boy often the first to stop and watch when one appeared! The visual fun and imagination of the Disney Studio 1 area in the Front Lot was also a big hit.

We have since put the repeat factor to the test and found it remains an all-day experience, with the Stunt Show providing almost never-ending fascination, along with the Studio Tram Tour, Animagique and Cinémagique. Just walking up to the gates of the new park should provide quite a thrill, as the epic icon in front of you makes it clear what's in store – film adventure and lots of fun in the inimitable Mickey style. The 33m (108ft) high water tower edifice (based on the same structure at Disney's home studios in Burbank, California), topped by a large pair of mouse ears (we kid you not), is called… wait for it… the Earful Tower (!), and sets out the visual style in no uncertain terms, as well as providing a handy marker for much of the way around the park. The construction of the 60m (200ft) Tower of Terror in the next couple of years will certainly change this perspective.

record is five goes on Rock 'n' Roller in the final hour!).

Okay, without any further preamble, let us introduce you to – the *Walt Disney Studios Park*…

If you approach from the main car park, the Studios will be straight ahead of you as you come through the moving walkways. From *Disney Village*, bear left past the Gaumont Cinemas and, from the bus or train station, continue straight on, passing *Disney Village* on your left. The park is subdivided into four main areas, although there is no great visual distinction between them, and your adventure starts as soon as you walk through the imposing gates.

Talking tactics

Unlike the *Disneyland Park*, this is not somewhere you need to be right at opening time (although you will be able to get many of the attractions done in the first 2 hours if you do). With much of the entertainment geared around the big show times such as the Stunt Show and Cinémagique, you can arrive in more leisurely style and head first for the attraction which most appeals to you, aware that you can usually get into most of them with only minimal queuing (although, as we found recently, you will find the summer crowds not inconsiderable from around midday).

BRIT TIP: Although the shows have good capacities, it is still advisable to arrive 10–15 minutes early to benefit from being the first to be seated.

Probably your best plan is to start by going to the Studio Tram Tour, where waiting times can occasionally build up to half an hour or more. If you then take in Armageddon and Rock 'n' Roller Coaster, you will have three of the biggest crowd-pullers under your belt early on. Alternatively, if you have younger children, they will certainly want to ride the Flying Carpets Over Agrabah and this is another ride where slow-moving queues can sometimes build up. So make this your first port of call before heading for something like Animagique or the Art of Disney Animation. When the new Toon Studios is open, the Animation Courtyard will certainly be the busiest area, so this will be an essential first stop.

Front Lot

Once through the turnstiles, you come into a lovely Spanish-style courtyard, that marks the entrance to the first main area, the Front Lot. This is the 'office' part of the Theme Park and houses the more functional elements such as pushchair and wheelchair hire, lost property, lost children centre, baby care centre, first aid station, cash dispenser and currency exchange. You will also find the **Studio Services** here, for any queries you may have about the park (like when and where to find the characters and which Streetmosphere acts will be performing). Visitors with disabilities can also pick up a *Guide for Guests with Special Needs* if they haven't done so already and the Blue

Card which allows access to all attractions (see pages 28–9).

This area is an extremely elegant piece of design, with the central Sorcerer Mickey fountain, flanked by palm trees, providing a great photo opportunity. The left-hand side of the courtyard is taken up by the **Walt Disney Studios Store**, the Theme Park's biggest shop, while on the right is **Studio Photo**, for all your photographic requirements (although it is better to bring your own). In the early morning, you can meet several **Disney characters** here (usually Goofy, Pluto, Minnie and Chip 'n' Dale), and it is worth pausing to enjoy the classic 1930s-style architecture as the Theme Park transports you into the world of movies, Hollywood style.

BRIT TIP: The Front Lot courtyard, **Place des Frères Lumières**, makes a good place to visit in early afternoon if the park is busy. Grab a drink or snack inside Disney Studio 1 and head out to enjoy the relaxing surroundings.

7

You really get the full effect, though, as you walk through the doors of **Disney Studio 1** (remember to pick up a Park Map as you enter), which is almost an attraction in its own right, even if it is in many ways just a covered version of Main Street USA in the *Disneyland Park*. It is 70m (230ft) long, 35m (115ft) wide and 20m (66ft) high, making it the second-largest 'soundstage' in Europe (okay, it isn't actually a working facility, but the impression is pretty good). The overall effect is as if you have walked into the middle of a Hollywood film shoot, with the paraphernalia of movie-making all around.

BRIT TIP: Visit the Studio Photo in the Front Lot courtyard and you can get your films processed in 2 hours. It's not cheap, but it is a great way to ensure those happy snaps have come out (if not, you can go back and retake them!).

Inside Studio 1

The film 'sets' are all unfinished and provide almost a kaleidoscopic montage of scenery in each direction, with a series of facades and hoardings, which change the perspective in a multitude of ways with the aid of some brilliant lighting effects. Down the left side is **Les Légendes d'Hollywood** store, while the right flank is given over to the **Restaurant en Coulisse**.

BRIT TIP: Restaurant en Coulisse gets pretty busy from midday to 2pm but is ideal between 3 and 4pm for a late lunch or early tea.

The shop is cleverly disguised behind no less than six different facades, giving the impression of a whole movie 'street' modelled on various Hollywood stores – both real and imagined – from the 1920s to 1960s. Designs that stand out include Last Chance Gas (a mock Route 66 petrol station), The Alexandria Theater (a classic Los Angeles 'movie palace') and The Gossip Column (a news and magazine stand) and, of course, you can buy a whole range of film-related souvenirs as well as the usual Disney souvenirs. Also here is **Shutterbugs**, a fun photo studio that can put YOU in the Disney picture with various well-known characters.

BRIT TIP: One of our favourite 'Hidden Gems' in the Studios park is playing with the lighting effects inside Studio 1. Look for the two big lighting consoles, one in front of Club Swankadero (marked 'Illuminazione Produzione'), which changes the lighting on the Hollywood & Vine façade, and the other inside the Liki Tiki, which lights the jungle roof, animates the Coca-Cola bottle and starts a thunderstorm!

Disneyland Resort guests

© Disney

Backlot Express Restaurant

On the other side, the restaurant is a combination of another six imaginary 'sets', with the counter-service diner concealed behind such legendary establishments as Schwab's Pharmacy (a classic 1940s' American drugstore), The Brown Derby (the famous Hollywood restaurant in the shape of a bowler hat), Club Swankadero (an imaginary nightclub), The Gunga Den (a well-known bar) and the Liki Tiki (a wonderful South Seas, thatched tropical-themed bar).

> **BRIT TIP:** The Studio 1 area has a handy Restaurant Reservations kiosk, where you can book meals for later in the day at the full-service restaurants in *Disney Village* and the *Disneyland Park*.

Here, the fare is French continental for breakfast and standard burger style the rest of the day, with pizza, lasagne and salads as your alternatives. The Menu Mickey (a double bacon burger with chips, brownie and a soft drink) is €9.95, while a Menu Pluto (double chicken-grill burger, chips, Sveltesse – fromage blanc – and soda) is €11.

There are actually 670 seats for dining here, so it absorbs a lot of people, and the upstairs terracing – 'Carmen's Veranda' (ouch!) – also provides a great view over the whole of Studio 1, as well as the best seats in the house for listening to the West Street Story Orchestra.

Linger in Disney Studio 1 for a while and you are likely to meet Streetmosphere performers **Ciné Folies**, a group of improvisational artists who are 'filming' various comedy movie shoots that inevitably involve much chaos, a lot of fun – and members of their audience. Studio 1 is also home to the excellent musical entertainment of the **West Street Story Orchestra**, who provide some big-band style for various well-known movie scores.

The Art of Disney Animation

© Disney

7

Waiting for opening

If you arrive half an hour before the official opening time, you will still be admitted through the main turnstiles of the *Walt Disney Studios*. This brings you into the courtyard in the Front Lot, where you are likely to meet Goofy or Pluto as they welcome you to the park. Children can stop for a photo and an autograph, and you can then pass into Disney Studio 1 and either have a bite to eat or browse the shops. Finally, at the appointed opening hour (either 9 or 10am), the crowd starts to gather at the doors at the far end and, with a final countdown, the Cast Members open all the doors simultaneously and let in the eager throng.

If you are looking for the thrills first, turn left and head straight for the Backlot area and Rock 'n' Roller Coaster, or go straight ahead and pick up the Studio Tram Tour. If you have young children, you will want to turn right and go into Animation Courtyard for the Flying Carpets Over Agrabah and the Art of Disney Animation. The Walt Disney Television Studios (in Production Courtyard) often do not open until an hour after the rest of the park.

Good Morning parade

A popular extra feature of the summer morning programme in 2004 and 2005 (and possibly in 2006 as well, although Disney rarely reveals whether the live entertainment schedule will stay the same from one year to the next) is a fun little welcome parade at 9.45. The **Good Morning Walt Disney Studios!** features a gathering of various Disney characters in a number of whimsical vehicles. The mini-parade emerges from between Animagique and the Flying Carpets and moves through Animation Courtyard to the Production Courtyard in front of Cinémagique. It then stops for the characters to get out and come and meet park guests for an impromptu photo session (so have those autograph books ready as soon as you see those cars!). Autumn 2005 also saw a scaled-down version of this at 10.30 each morning in the Front Lot, just entitled **The Red Carpet** with Minnie, Chip 'n' Dale, Donald and Daisy Duck and the Cine Folies.

Animation Courtyard

Turn right as you exit the doors of Disney Studio 1 and you are

BRIT TIP: Check the Information Board as you enter Animation Courtyard to find out the waiting times at the attractions and which queues to avoid.

immediately in the area of the park which caters most for the younger ones, Animation Courtyard. As well as more chances to meet, photograph and get autographs from the Disney characters, you have the one genuine kiddie ride here and the most enchanting of the shows.

The Art of Disney Animation: The first big set-piece attraction, located under the giant Sorcerer's Apprentice hat, this is a four-part adventure into the history, creation and magic of animated film. The first section concentrates on the history and is the least interesting for younger children. It is basically a pre-show area, with a series of exhibits around the room, showing how animation developed from its most basic into the art form which Walt Disney helped to pioneer. The highlight, amid several hands-on opportunities (like a Zoetrope and a

BRIT TIP: Check out the carpet in the post-show area of the Art of Disney Animation. Can you pick out in the pattern a certain set of Mouse ears…?!

Magic Lantern), is one of only two surviving multi-plane cameras, a tool developed by Walt Disney himself in the 1930s.

As the doors close behind you, a large video screen comes to life and Walt pays tribute to the European pioneers of animation, along with former Walt Disney Company chairman Roy Disney (Walt's nephew). Annoyingly for us, it is all dubbed in French (you would have thought one of the showings would be kept in English) with English subtitles, but it sets the stage for the 225-seat Disney Classics Theatre next. The doors underneath the screen then open and you pass into the mini-cinema for 8 minutes of highlights from the Disney classics that are sure to keep everyone in a happy frame of mind.

Stage three is another theatre-like auditorium, set up like an animator's office, where a part live show and part film brings Mushu from Mulan to life and explains how this dragon-character came into being (with a highly amusing voice-over from Eddie Murphy). The interaction between the live 'artist' and Mushu is wonderfully scripted and funny and, although the on-stage part is in French, there are headphones to provide a full translation (watch out for the finale as the Murphy-dragon imagines himself as The Mushu of Notre Dame!).

You exit the theatre into a final room of six 'animation stations', which give you the chance to try your hand at drawing, colouring or providing a voice or sound effects for various characters. It is great fun for children of 6 upwards, and the Animation Academy with a real artist is presented in both French and English. In all, it is a fascinating and thoroughly enjoyable look at the artistry of feature animation and the queues move steadily here, so you are rarely waiting long. AAAA.

Animagique: Opposite the Sorcerer's Apprentice hat, this is a unique live show featuring the innovative Czech art of 'Black Light' stagecraft and Japanese 'Bunraku' puppet manipulation. If that sounds a bit dry, prepare yourself for 25 minutes of pure Disney fun in the company of Mickey, Donald Duck and the cast of *Dumbo*, *Pinocchio*, *Jungle Book* and *The Lion King*.

BRIT TIP: Try to arrive a few minutes early for the Animagique show as the 1,100-seat theatre comes to life with a series of clever sound effects that ring and echo in delightful style around the auditorium before it begins.

7

The story (partly in French and Donald Duck-ese!) sees Donald stuck for inspiration at the drawing board. Ignoring Mickey's warnings, he opens the Disney vault and unwittingly lets loose a host of animated characters who run riot on stage, with a big song-and-dance finale that will have you humming the catchy theme tune as you leave. Some excellent effects surprise you along the way (which we won't reveal) but be prepared for some extra fun, especially if you are in the first dozen or so rows. The startlingly high-tech show (involving digitally synchronised lighting, audio and machinery effects, in addition to all the puppeteering) is presented 6–7 times a day and show times are posted both outside and on the park maps. AAAA.

> BRIT TIP: If you have children, try to sit in the central section of the theatre, no more than 10–12 rows back and you will enjoy one of the best special effects of the Animagique show.

As you exit Animagique, children will probably want to head straight for **Mickey's Trailer** on the other side of the concourse. This you will probably have to queue for, and the 'star' does need a break from time to time, so it can take a while. But it is a well-organised line (unlike a few of the scrimmages that can develop around the characters in some places) and children are usually quite well-behaved when they can see the famous Mouse at the end! Watch out, too, for the 'stars' of the latest Disney films, in front of the Art of Animation, which in 2005 included *The Incredibles* and *Chicken Little*.

Flying Carpets Over Agrabah: At the innermost end of Animation Courtyard is the main children's ride, which is another variation on the Dumbo/Orbitron attractions of

Flying Carpets over Agrabah

the *Disneyland Park*. This has been transported with a slightly different theme from the ride in Orlando's *Magic Kingdom Park*.

> BRIT TIP: Don't head for the Flying Carpets ride just after the daily Disney Cinema Parade, as the parade finishes in Animation Courtyard and a large part of the crowd following it ends up in the Carpets queue.

Here you line up (in a loosely themed area like a film 'green room', where actors prepare for their next scene) to take part in a 'casting' for a role in a movie, with the Genie (from the 1992 Disney film *Aladdin*) as the director (in French and English). Once aboard your four-person 'flying carpet', there are controls in the front seats to make it go up and down and in the rear seats to add a bit of tilt 'n' turn. In all honesty it is a fairly tame ride, but children under 10 always seem to get

Animagique show

Studio Tram Tour

a thrill from it. However, the queues can build here through the middle of the day, so it is best to visit early on or wait until the last hour of the day. From 2007, this attraction will also be incorporated into the Toon Studios area. TT (TTTT for under 10s).

Toon Studios: The next big development at the *Walt Disney Studios* (opening Easter 2007) is this mini-land tucked between the Art of Disney Animation and the Flying Carpets, and extending some way back into new park territory. It is designed to be a mixture of indoor and outdoor attractions, with a series of large-scale, multi-coloured facades that draw you into a working film studio – populated purely by

Toons. More importantly, it will house two all-new rides, plenty of character interaction and a restaurant (although the latter may take a bit longer). For rides, expect **Crush's Turtle Twister** to be a novel dipping coaster through a mock undersea world, full of inventive lighting and special effects, with part of the ride outdoors before diving back inside again. It should appeal to most of the family, although it may be a bit too dynamic for under 6s. (TTTT – expected). Then a proposed **Cars** ride is designed to be completely family-friendly, with a variation on the bumper cars theme given a clever twist to fit in with the latest film from the Pixar Animation Studios. (TTT – expected).

For a snack in this area, the **Studio Catering Co** has two outlets, themed like truck trailers, offering hot dogs, burgers, fish and chips, club sandwiches, popcorn, ice cream, doughnuts, muffins and cookies, as well as drinks. There is only one shopping opportunity, but it is an excellent one, **The Disney Animation Gallery** at the exit of the Art of Disney Animation (inside the giant Sorcerer's Apprentice hat). This offers a rather upmarket range of souvenirs and some serious collectables – figurines, statues, books and genuine Disney film cels – for those who have a fascination for the true art of Disney.

7

Christmas character meet 'n' greet at Production Courtyard

Production Courtyard

Retracing your steps past Studio 1 (or turning left out of Studio 1's doors) brings you right into Production Courtyard. This is the middle section of the Theme Park which offers three contrasting main attractions.

Cinémagique: One of the park's undoubted highlights and a real *tour de force* of imagination, this half-hour film show, exclusive to *Disneyland Resort Paris*, starts out superficially as a tribute to the history of both European and American cinema, but soon takes a dramatic turn for the unexpected. It ends up as a hilarious series of scenes featuring comedian Martin Short as a hapless 'time traveller' through a whole range of cinematic genres linked together by a wonderful love-interest storyline.

The show includes numerous funny scene shifts (the 'cowboy shoot-out' scenario is truly inspired) and a couple of eye-popping special effects which we won't reveal but which add hugely to the fun (hint: an umbrella might be a good idea!). French actress Julie Delpy is the co-star of the show and the whole thing takes place inside a beautiful 1,100-seat theatre with an art deco theme that harks back to the classic movie palaces of 1930s' Hollywood.

BRIT TIP: Waiting in the holding pens for Cinémagique is fairly dull, but the large capacity of the theatre ensures everyone usually gets in, while you can often wait until the last minute and still find a seat. There are up to eight shows a day in high season, and it is perfectly possible to see this twice in one day.

It probably won't hold the attention of younger children (say, under 4s) for the full 30 minutes, but there is enough amusing on-screen action to keep most entertained and adults will enjoy the clever interweaving of scenes, with Short popping up in all manner of unlikely well-known film scenarios. AAAAA.

BRIT TIP: Disney does change the live Streetmosphere shows at regular intervals, so look out for something new in 2006. One possibility is the return of one of our favourite acts – the inspired percussive mayhem of Rhythmo Technico.

Just outside the Cinémagique theatre, the Production Courtyard Stage is home to more live entertainment. In summer 2005 it was the lively **Lilo & Stitch Catch The Wave Party** featuring Minnie, Goofy and Pluto as well as the mischievous alien and his owner. The 25-minute production features a variety of song and dance numbers. We saw Lilo & Stitch celebrating the Hawaiian family tradition of 'Ohana (guests were invited to dance the hula!). AAA. You may also catch another street entertainment show here, but **Starring Cruella De Vil**, which was new in 2005, is not one of Disney's better ideas. The rather tortuous 20-minute show includes audience participation and those taking part are definitely luckier than those who have to watch the end product. The story is feeble and the actors not much better. A.

Studio Tram Tour: The biggest attraction of the area (and arguably of the whole park), this large-scale, 15-minute ride experience has been adapted from the *Disney-MGM Studios Park* in Orlando and enhanced with several brand new elements. Cleverly arranged with an English-French soundtrack, this is a tour of mind-boggling proportions.

The tram takes you on a behind-the-scenes movie studio tour, learning some more tricks of the film world trade, such as location sets, props, costumes and special effects. Each tram has a video screen with a full commentary (the English version supplied by a wonderfully laconic Jeremy Irons) that points out the key areas along the way. You pass a whole array of film props and scenery (notably the imposing Waterfall City facade from the *Dinotopia* mini-series) before entering the tour highlight, **Catastrophe Canyon**.

BRIT TIP: Young children may be scared by all the dramatic special effects in the Studio Tram Tour. Explain to them what's going to happen and reassure them that it is all quite safe and just another film trick. The left-hand side of the tram may also get a little wet.

Here, you are supposed to get a dry-run version of a hugely elaborate special effects situation but the 'director' mistakes the tram for his film 'extras' and starts the action sequence with you in the middle! Before you know it, the tram has been subjected to earthquake, fire and flood, and the culmination, when 265,000 litres (58,300 gallons) of water are dumped on the flaming set, is quite breathtaking.

Having 'survived' the canyon, you continue on past some more film props (look out for some planes from *Pearl Harbor*) and the costume studio, before passing the **Star Cars** garage exhibit of well-known movie vehicles (like Cruella de Vil's car from *101 Dalmatians*, the Humvee from *The Rock* and the sports car from *Runaway Bride*). Finally, you enter the smoking ruins of London, circa 2022 (or at least a remarkable film set facsimile). Here, for anyone familiar with the summer 2002 blockbuster film *Reign of Fire*, you get a close encounter with one of its 'stars'. Well, not actually one of the dragons, but a fairly 'hot' close-up of its fiery breath, which blasts out twice on the right side of the tram. The shock effect, the noise of the fire and the feel of the heat will definitely scare young children (and some adults!), so think carefully before taking your youngster on this tour. However, the encounter is over pretty quickly and the rest of the set is something to marvel at. Avoid this just after a Stunt Show has finished in the Backlot area, as many of that 3,000-strong crowd head straight here (and there's not much to see while waiting). AAA/TTTT.

Walt Disney Television Studios: The final attraction in Production Courtyard is this rather tame walk-through of the actual Walt Disney Television Studios. The French version of the Disney Channel is filmed here, and you do get a good look inside the studios, but that is as exciting as it gets and will not interest young children for long (it has already been given two revamps).

There is a multi-lingual welcome presentation and then you enter the Transmission Control Room, where a human presenter interacts with various Disney characters to explain how the TV studios work (children may find the English sub-titles hard to follow). You then move into a viewing room that affords a look into the real working part of the studio but, unless there is a

© Disney

Television Production Tour

programme being filmed, it is not that enthralling.

The tour is rescued by the final section, which provides a whole array of interactive Disney games, puzzles – and the brilliant CyberSpace Mountain. Taken from the now-defunct Chicago DisneyQuest, this is a coaster simulator in a massive box, with all the twisting, turning fun of the real thing. You choose and design your track first and then head up to the 'pods' to check out how it works. Huge fun for kids (especially the grown-up ones!). AA/TTTT.

When it comes to grabbing a bite to eat, the Production Courtyard has the best of the Theme Park's dining in the shape of the **Rendez-Vous**

des Stars Restaurant, a cafeteria-type diner in full art deco style. The speciality is a meat carvery but the range of food is extremely broad, from baked salmon to penne pasta Bolognese, roast chicken, vegetable lasagne and a variety of salads (main courses €8.50–13.80; set menu €22, children's menu €10.90). Inside on the walls is a fine array of authentic Hollywood photographs and film memorabilia, including one of the 26 Oscars won by Walt during his long movie career.

> BRIT TIP: For that extra special occasion, you can order a birthday cake at the Rendez-Vous des Stars at the beginning of your meal. It costs €22 and serves 4–8. But be warned: don't come here when the Stunt Show has just finished and 3,000 people are in the vicinity!

Alternatively, **La Terrasse** is a covered area in the middle of the Production Courtyard, with a 264-seating capacity for the six **Studio Catering Co** outlets sprinkled

Halloween make-up workshop

© Disney

© Disney

Moteurs...Action!

around here. Nearby, look for the **Finding Nemo photo spot** with a giant shark!

The Backlot

The Backlot area is past the Rendez-Vous des Stars and features the most action-packed offerings in the park, with three highly contrasting top-drawer thrill elements.

Armageddon: Special Effects: This unique, wonderfully elaborate show that puts YOU at the heart of the action (although it's not one for young children) is the first of the thrills. You enter into a pre-show area, full of models, exhibits and diagrams from the blockbuster film, starring Bruce Willis (there are two studios for this purpose, 7A and 7B, and the array of models, etc, does vary), where a Cast Member greets you and acts as the show's 'director'.

> BRIT TIP: The props on display in the pre-show area of Armageddon: Special Effects include the spacesuit worn by actor Ben Affleck in the film.

With the help of your director and a video that explains the eye-popping scenario of the film, your role as 'extras' in a special effects scene is explained in amusing detail (in English and French). The screen is then turned over to a tribute to Frenchman Georges Méliès, who is credited with inventing film special effects. It shows how the movie world has taken his ideas and developed them with astonishing creativity in the last 100 years.

The video continues with the explosive arrival of Michael Clarke Duncan, another of the *Armageddon* stars, who explains how the film's technical wizardry was carried out. You are then invited to come and see for real how it is done and walk through, under 'directorial' guidance, into an amazing mock-up of the movie's Russian space station – just as it comes under threat from a meteor shower! The ensuing chaos, as the station almost literally blows up all around you, is brilliantly scripted and the array of effects incredibly realistic, with smoke, sparks, bursting pipes, buckling doors and a huge central fireball that adds some very real heat to the proceedings.

In our opinion, the sights and sounds (it is pretty loud) are much too intense for under 7s, but there are no real warnings of this outside. However, the space station itself is a work of art and the hectic action is

Rock 'n' Roller Coaster

© Disney

> BRIT TIP: It is a good idea for an adult to experience an attraction first to check on its suitability, if you are worried that certain elements of it might be too scary for your children.

suitably breathtaking. They could do with adding a bit of interest to the extremely plain waiting area outside, though. TTTT.

Rock 'n' Roller Coaster starring Aerosmith: This next attraction is a real blast of a ride that rockets you from 0–100kph (62mph) in just 2.8 seconds! It is a slightly revised version of the ride of the same name at Orlando's *Disney-MGM Studios Park* in *Walt Disney World*, making it a different experience.

> BRIT TIP: Listen out for Aerosmith lead singer, Steve Tyler, completing a clever 'sound-check' as you board the Rock 'n' Roller Coaster – it all adds considerably to the fun.

Here, you enter the rock 'n' roll world of the American supergroup Aerosmith, as they discuss the creation of this unique rockin' ride, described as a 'revolutionary musical experience' produced by Tour De Force Records.

As the record company's VIP guests, Aerosmith invite you to enter the 'research and development' area to try it out at first hand and you pass into the launch area, complete with 'sound engineers' and computer models of the ride systems, which feature 'Soundtracker' cars. These are fitted with five state-of-the-art speakers per seat so you literally 'ride the music'. Once you are firmly

harnessed into your seat, the countdown begins and you blast off into a topsy-turvy 'rock video' that features two loops and a corkscrew as well as some eye-popping lighting effects on the way round. There are five different music tracks that accompany the ride, hence there are five variations on the ride experience. Aerosmith have even re-recorded a couple of their tracks, so see if you can notice the new lyrics (hint: the 'adapted' songs are *Love In An Elevator* and *What Kind of Love Are You On?*). Waiting time can top half an hour at peak periods but there is rarely much of a queue for the first couple of hours or from late afternoon.

It is not recommended for anyone with back or neck problems or for pregnant women. Restriction: 1.2m (3ft 9in). TTTTT.

> BRIT TIP: The queue for the Rock 'n' Roller Coaster drops off during a performance of the Stunt Show next door but it should be avoided just after the show finishes as many people make a beeline for it.

Moteurs...Action! Stunt Show Spectacular: Next door to the Rock 'n' Roller Coaster, this is one of Disney's most remarkable shows. Full of genuine high-risk stunts and hugely skilful car and motorbike action, it will have you shaking your head in amazement for quite a while afterwards.

Seating starts a good 20 minutes before one of the three or four shows a day, and there is some amusing pre-show chat (in English and French) and freestyle show-boating by one of the bike riders to keep people amused before the

BRIT TIP: People start queuing for the Stunt Show a good half an hour before a performance at peak times and the middle shows of the day are always absolutely full. It is better to head for the first one, or stay until the last to minimise your wait.

serious stuff starts. Various audience members are recruited to help in one of the scenes and a roving cameraman picks out people from the crowd to highlight on the big video screen in the centre of the 'square'. The huge set is based on a typical Mediterranean village and is magnificently crafted to have an 'aged' appearance.

Once the preliminaries are completed, you are treated to a 45-minute extravaganza of daredevil stunts, with a Car Ballet sequence, a Motorbike Chase and a Grand Finale that features some surprise pyrotechnics to complete a truly awesome presentation (keep your eyes on the windows below the video screen at the end). Each scene – featuring a secret agent 'goody' and various black-car baddies – is set up and fully explained by a movie 'director' (and the need for bilingual commentary is handled skilfully).

BRIT TIP: Be aware there is some (loud) mock gunfire during the Stunt Show, which can upset young children, while the motorbike scene includes a rider catching fire, which can be quite frightening for them.

The results of each 'shoot' are then played back on the video screen to show how each effect was created and how it is all spliced together to create the desired end product.

All the cars were specially created for the show by Vauxhall and there are some extra tricks (including an amusing appearance by Herbie from *The Love Bug* film) in between the main scenes. The whole thing was designed by Frenchman Rémy Julienne, the doyen of cinematic car stunt sequences, who has worked on James Bond films *Goldeneye* and *Licence to Kill* and other epics like *The Rock, Ronin, Gone in 60 Seconds* and *Enemy of the State*.

It all adds up to a breathtaking show, and kids are sure to want to come back to this, which is another good reason to see it early in the day. There is nothing like it in any other theme park in the world (apart from the copycat version which opened in *Disney-MGM Studios Park* in Orlando in 2005), and the fact that so much of it involves genuine, live co-ordination makes it a truly thrilling experience.

However, the exit is quite a scrum as 3,000 people have to leave through two fairly narrow thoroughfares and it can take 10–15 minutes to get clear of the auditorium, so if you can sit towards the front either on the right or left of the grandstand, you will be out quicker. TTTTT.

When you need to stop for something to eat in the Backlot, **Le Café des Cascadeurs** is an imaginative little diner (themed like an art deco studio cafe for the stuntmen and women) around the corner from Armageddon, serving a fairly simple selection of salads, sandwiches, hot dogs and crisps, but the train carriage setting is good fun. **The Backlot Express Restaurant** is a counter-service cafe with another highly themed interior – like a studio's art department, full of

7

The Walt Disney Studios Park with children

Here is a rough guide to the attractions in this park, which are most likely to appeal to the different age groups (taking into account any height restrictions):

Under 5s
The Art of Disney Animation, Animagique, Flying Carpets Over Agrabah, Meet Mickey, Studio Tram Tour (with parental discretion), Moteurs...Action! Stunt Show Spectacular (also with parental discretion), Disney Cinema Parade, Lilo & Stitch Catch The Wave Party, Push, The Talking Trashcan

6–8s
All the above, plus Disney Studio 1, Cinémagique, Armageddon (with parental discretion), Streetmosphere

9–12s
All the above, plus Rock 'n' Roller Coaster starring Aerosmith

Over 12s
Disney Studio 1, Art of Disney Animation, Animagique, Studio Tram Tour, Cinémagique, Armageddon, Rock 'n' Roller Coaster starring Aerosmith, Moteurs...Action!, Streetmosphere

---

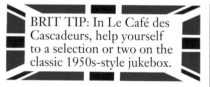

BRIT TIP: In Le Café des Cascadeurs, help yourself to a selection or two on the classic 1950s-style jukebox.

props, tools, light fittings, furniture and other film accoutrements – that makes dining fun. The food is fairly ordinary – toasted sandwiches, pizza, baguettes, bagels and salads – with the standard Menu Mickey at €9.95 and the kids' menu at €6.80 but it holds up to 500 inside, plus there is some outdoor seating in the summer. Look out for the big model suspended from the ceiling – the motor speeder from *Star Wars VI: Return of the Jedi*.

The only shop around here is **Rock Around The Shop**, at the exit to the Rock 'n' Roller Coaster, offering a range of Aerosmith and rock-related goods, plus the chance to buy a photo of yourself on the ride (€12 and €19).

Here comes the parade

In best Disney park fashion, no visit is complete without the daily procession and here it is, the **Disney Cinema Parade**, at either 1.45pm or 4.45pm according to the season. Starting between the Backlot Express Restaurant and the Rock 'n' Roller Coaster and winding down into Animation Courtyard, it is a positive extravaganza of kids' favourites, from *Mary Poppins* to *Toy Story* and *Pinocchio*. The series of elaborate floats – starting with Tinker Bell, then Minnie and ending with Mickey Mouse – also include *The Lion King*, *Peter Pan* and *101 Dalmatians*, and a host of characters on foot, while a handful of guests are also chosen to ride aboard with Mickey. The whole thing takes about 25 minutes to pass as it stops at regular intervals for the cast to interact with onlookers (especially children) along the route, backed by

West Street Story Orchestra

another wonderfully infectious theme song. It is also an easy parade to catch and watch in relative comfort as it doesn't usually draw the huge crowds of the *Disneyland Park*. Wait in the Production Courtyard area and you should get a great view. AAAA.

Streetmosphere: The park's additional fun is provided by various alternating performing acts who patrol the Theme Park and pop up here and there to give impromptu shows that have a central theme but include some improvisation, too. **Road Movies**, in the Backlot, is a good example, with a film crew turning up – but minus the extras: audience members are recruited and a good degree of (carefully scripted) chaos ensues. Special acts perform at Halloween and Christmas (including an *a capella* carol group), which vary from day to day, so you never know who's going to appear.

Push, The Talking Trashcan: New in late 2005 was this remarkable interactive 'performing rubbish bin', which moves, rattles and even talks to visitors! Look out for Push mainly in the Back Lot (along with its heavily disguised remote control operator).

For those keen to learn more about the park, there is a 1-hour **Guided Tour** (€10 for adults, children 11 and under free), which gives an in-depth view of the history and architecture. Book at Studio Services (see page 155) when you first arrive (subject to availability).

As with the *Disneyland Park*, the *Walt Disney Studios Park* looks even better in early evening, when all the clever (and hidden) lighting effects come into play. There is definitely room for improvement, and the 2007 enhancements will not come too soon. But the high quality of the attractions here (Cinémagique and Moteurs…Action! are true works of art) still provides a rich and rewarding experience. You will also leave with an improved knowledge of the movie business and a heightened respect for those who work in it.

The essence of a theme park is that it envelops you with its sense of design and purpose and this, we feel, the *Walt Disney Studios Park* does, ensuring you believe you have truly had a movie-world adventure.

Right, that should be your fill of the Theme Parks for now. But the fun doesn't stop here. Oh no! There is still plenty to do and see when we visit the *Disney Village*, Val d'Europe and more. It's time to go beyond the Theme Parks…

7

Armageddon: Special Effects

8 Beyond the Theme Parks

(or, Let's Shop Till We Drop, and Other Fun Pursuits)

Having led you, quite literally, up the theme park path, it is now time we took you beyond those confines and explored some more of what makes this resort – and this whole area of the Ile de France region – so enticing.

To backtrack slightly and put things in context, the Île de France is the central region of France, the 'island' around which lie the other great regions of Normandy, Picardie, Champagne-Ardennes and Burgundy. The Ile itself is made up of eight *'départements'*, namely **Yvelines, Essonne, Seine-et-Marne** and **Val d'Oise** (which form a large outer ring) and then **Hauts-de-Seine** (immediately to the west of the city), **Seine-St-Denis** (to the northeast), **Val-de-Marne** (to the southeast) and Paris itself. The *département* of Val-de-Marne should not be confused with Marne-la-Vallée, where *Disneyland Resort Paris* is situated, in the *département* of Seine-et-Marne.

Prior to 1989, when construction began, there was little here apart from sugar beet fields, but the development since has been swift and dramatic. There is, in fact, no real town or village of Marne-la-Vallée, it is a made-up name given to the RER/TGV station here, which acts as the terminus for the RER's Line A. The nearest sizeable village is Chessy, hence the RER station is properly known as Marne-la-Vallée Chessy. However, to all intents and purposes, Marne-la-Vallée IS the site of *Disneyland Resort Paris*, hence this is how the majority refer to it.

Marne-la-Vallée is also (highly confusingly) a sub-district of the Seine-et-Marne *département* closer to Paris (between the towns of Noisy-le-Grand and Lognes). When driving, therefore, you should always aim for 'Les Parcs Disneyland'.

More to see and do

When it comes to the associated attractions 'beyond the Theme Parks', there are five distinct topics to cover. First and most obvious is all the fun, fine shopping and dining of **Disney Village**. Second, Disney has also developed its own sporting connections – at **Disneyland Golf**, plus the novel challenge of **Davy Crockett's Adventure** nearby. Next, the neighbouring development of **Val d'Europe** offers another scintillating array of great shops and restaurants, including the Auchan supermarket and the outlet shopping village of **La Vallée**. Finally, the highly family-friendly **Sea Life** aquarium centre is situated inside the Val d'Europe shopping centre and is another excellent reason to go beyond the Theme Parks. Sadly, Disney's in-resort collaboration with the **Manchester United Soccer School** was only a short-lived one; starting in spring 2004, it lasted until November 2005 before it was closed down, with no sign of whether it might be revived one day in a different format.

Disney Village

1 Planet Hollywood
2 Annette's Diner
3 King Ludwig's Castle
4 Sports Bar
5 New York Style Sandwiches
6 Billy Bob's Country Western Saloon
7 The Steakhouse
8 Rainforest Café
9 Café Mickey
10 McDonald's
11 The Disney Store
12 Buffalo Trading Co
13 The Disney Gallery
14 Disney Fashion
15 Hollywood Pictures
16 World of Toys
17 Gaumont Cinema
18 Buffalo Bill's Wild West Show
19 Hurricanes
20 Marina Del Ray/ Panoramagique
21 IMAX Cinema/ NEX Fantasy Leisure Zone

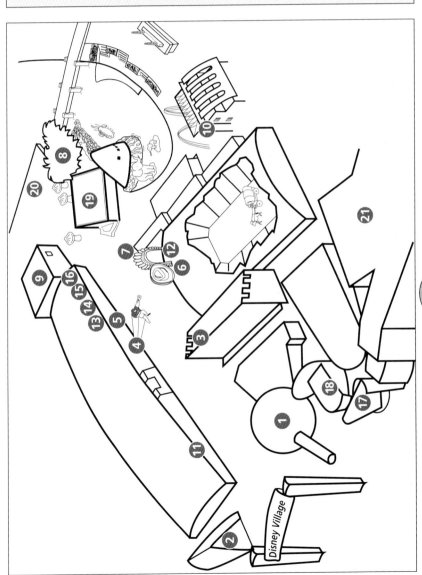

8

The golfing opportunity is obviously primarily for devotees of the sport but the other four should all be on your must-see list if you are here for 4 days or more (or if you are on a repeat visit). The new **Panoramagique** balloon flights over *Disney Village* are quite breathtaking and especially worthy of note here.

As this is primarily a new-town area (the great Disney trail-blazing has given rise to a flurry of modern suburban development all around), there are not many other out-and-out tourist attractions here, but it does make a great base from which to explore Paris and some of the more genuinely historic points of interest in the region (notably the towns of Provins and Meaux, see Chapter 9).

Between the Parks

Disney Village

Starting at the top, it is almost impossible to miss this hugely colourful and imaginative entertainment centre situated between Disney's hotels and the Theme Parks. This impressive complex was designed by American architect Frank Gehry, who was also responsible for the Guggenheim museum in Bilbao, Spain, and it features a host of complex, almost abstract ideas designed to link the village to the railway station.

If you come straight in by car or train, you just might not notice *Disney Village* on your left as you scamper headlong for the *Disneyland Park*, but otherwise it is fairly obvious. From one end (nearest the Theme Parks), it is dominated by a massive gateway topped by a huge red banner with 'Disney Village' emblazoned across it. From the hotels end, you enter via the Lake Disney entrance, with a spread of restaurants – Café Mickey, Rainforest Café and McDonald's – before you.

Disney Village

© Disney

Rainforest Café

In a way, it is easy to see the Village as just one big merchandising opportunity. There are a dozen different ways to spend money here – from the shops to video games – and even some of the restaurants have their own gift store. But, ultimately, this has the hallmark of the Imagineers once again (even if the Rainforest Café, Planet Hollywood and McDonald's all have their own internationally recognisable stamp).

It has a wonderful outdoor cafe style, especially in the evening and the brilliant lighting is well worth stopping to see (although this was being dramatically redesigned in late 2005). Famously, Cast Members tell of the family who were into their second day in the resort when they stopped a shop manager to ask where all the rides were – they hadn't yet made it out of *Disney Village*!

The main Central Stage provides periodical live entertainment (weather permitting), and there are other stalls, vendors and street performers from time to time, which all help to create a carnival atmosphere (as well as set-piece seasonal events, such as St Patrick's Day, the Festival Latina in June and the Christmas festivities). When you add in the entertainment possibilities of Buffalo Bill's dinner show, the cinema complex, the live music of Billy Bob's and the late-night disco, Hurricanes, you have a serious array of choice. The one thing, perhaps surprisingly, they don't have here is a good coffee bar.

What's there

Roughly speaking, you can divide the offerings of *Disney Village* into the **Restaurants and bars**, the **Shops** and the **Entertainment**. But, to get maximum enjoyment, you need to be aware of a couple of things. Firstly, the restaurants normally start to fill up from 6–7pm.

8

Acrobatics on Central Stage

© Disney

The Rumour Mill

The basic form of *Disney Village* has changed little since the early days of the resort, with King Ludwig's (2003) the only substantial addition in recent years. However, if the rumour mill is to be believed, there is a LOT of new development in store.

The main thrust of the suggestions is that, with the closing of the old open-air car park and the provision of a multi-storey version, a new area of the Village will be developed at the lower end, creating a whole new 'street' behind the existing one. Certainly, there is plenty of room for expansion, from the new IMAX cinema (behind the main Gaumont multiplex) all the way back to the old car park area (behind McDonald's on the lake side of the Village).

The most likely of the proposed scenarios is for this new area to consist of the **ESPN Sports Club** (like that in The Boardwalk Resort in *Walt Disney World in Florida*), the **NEX Fantasy Leisure Zone** (a new gaming, billiard table and 10-pin bowling complex underneath the IMAX cinema), a themed **Chinese restaurant**, a giant **World of Disney** store and a brand new nightclub (which may mean a change of character for the existing Hurricanes). The arrival of the ESPN Club would mean a change for the current Sports Bar, with an **Italian restaurant** being a possible replacement there.

The likely timescale of all this dramatic development is from 2006–2010, with a new **RER station** entrance also included in the design.

In high summer, when the Theme Parks are open until late, the peak period for the restaurants and shops is more likely to be 9pm. Unless you've made a booking (and only four of the restaurants actually accept bookings), you are likely to find queues of up to half an hour for places such as The Steakhouse, Planet Hollywood and even Annette's Diner.

The other factor is the weather. On a fine evening, it will be easier to get a table while, if it is wet, everywhere fills up extremely quickly, so you need to anticipate the rain to avoid being left out in it!

BRIT TIP: The restaurants at the Theme Parks end of *Disney Village* fill up the quickest, with Planet Hollywood being the most popular venue.

It is also worth pointing out that the Village is relatively quiet during the day, so it is the ideal spot for a more relaxed lunch away from the parks and some leisurely afternoon shopping. You have free pick of all the restaurants (apart from Billy Bob's, where the buffet is available evenings only) and it is particularly convenient if you are in the *Walt Disney Studios Park*, where there is no table-service dining. If you just need a quick snack, there are plenty of fast-food carts dotted throughout the Village.

Restaurants and bars

Planet Hollywood: Taking *Disney Village* from the Theme Parks end, as soon as you come through the gateway you face the immediately recognisable two-storey edifice of this popular international chain. Planet Hollywood is a huge draw from early evening until late and reservations can be made in early evening only, which takes care of most of the queues. But, if there is a line, there is a great bar area and some snazzy bar staff to make the wait more fun. An unhurried lunch is also available from 11.30am–3pm during the day. If the queue can be seen outside, you'll be waiting a good 30-minutes for a table.

> BRIT TIP: When the *Disneyland Park* is open until 11pm, head to Planet Hollywood for dinner at about 6pm and you should have your pick of their best tables.

The huge variety of movie models, costumes, portraits and other memorabilia in this 500-seat restaurant is subdivided into differently themed areas, each with its own video screen that shows well-known film clips, music videos and (worth looking out for) special trailers for forthcoming movies. The memorabilia, which will certainly get film buffs wandering around to study it, varies from James Cagney to Wesley Snipes, Arnold Schwarzenegger and Sylvester Stallone. The upstairs section includes a sci-fi dining area and an adventure area, as well as the lively bar, while downstairs there is a *Raiders of the Lost Ark* type section and the Zebra Room (for obvious, stripy reasons). In the inevitable gift store, also downstairs, you will probably find the Planet Hollywood merchandise a bit cheaper here than in London.

Curiously, different nationalities seem to eat at different times of the day. The Brits tend to eat earlier, hence there will be a UK predominance in the restaurants from 5–7pm, while the Spanish are almost invariably the last ones out!

Usefully, they offer a Cinema Special meal, a set, 1-course dinner with a drink and cinema ticket (€19), which they can usually turn around quickly if you are in a hurry. There is a set lunch (€12) and all-day set 3-course menu (€23). The menu has also been adapted for the more European mix of customer, so several dishes have been tweaked (Spinach Dip replaces the more usual nachos, and their lasagne is a house speciality). Several regional specialities have been added (such as the typically French Croque Monsieur, a ham and cheese toastie).

The full range offers salads (€14–14.50), sandwiches and burgers (€14–14.75), steak, chicken, ribs, salmon, grilled lamb and fajitas (€18.50–22.50), pasta dishes (€14–15), while desserts include chocolate brownie, banana frosted cheesecake, strawberry shortcake, ice cream and an excellent white chocolate bread pudding. And, of all the Planet Hollywood restaurants we have visited, the food here is consistently the best, which we ascribe to that extra bit of French flair. They also freshen the menu from time to time and have some tempting cocktails, including an exclusive Summer Specials menu. TVs in the bar show all the major sports events and the latest football results are usually available.

If you haven't been to a Planet Hollywood before, you will probably be wowed by their lively entertainment mix (even their soundtrack is carefully balanced so you can talk at the table without having to shout), so you should make a beeline for this one. If you

8

> BRIT TIP: Save money at Planet Hollywood if you visit the cinema by showing your cinema ticket stub for a €5 discount.

© Disney

McDonald's at Disney Village

are already familiar with their style, head here anyway and try their LA Lasagna (a layered pasta that is rolled, cut in half, deep fried and then smothered in their tomato sauce), which will make your taste buds quiver with delight and your waistline shudder!

We will admit to being slightly biased in our liking for the brash cinema-style motif that is Planet Hollywood, but we reckon it is one of the most fun dining experiences in the whole resort – and it stays open until the last person leaves!

Annette's Diner: Opposite PH stands this classic 1950s' rock 'n' roll-style restaurant. Straight out of *Grease* and *Happy Days*, the bright, vivid decor provides a suitably fun, family atmosphere, with waiters and waitresses who dance on the bar top

Annette's Diner

© Disney

at various moments. The large icons are all typical Americana from this period, and the menu is equally in keeping with the theme, with a typical line-up of burgers, hot dogs, chilli, fajitas, salads and sandwiches. On two (rather noisy!) levels, the mezzanine floor offers the best views of the restaurant, which also features a classic Cadillac and Corvette photo opportunity at the entrance.

The kids meal (for under 11s) is €10.75, while the burgers range from €8.50–15.50. The desserts are possibly their best feature, with a range of ice creams, sundaes and shakes to appeal strongly to those with a sweet tooth. When the queues get long (as they often do), there is a handy take-away window at the side of the restaurant. Annette's is open 11.30am–11pm Sunday to Thursday, and 11.30am–midnight (Friday and Saturday).

BRIT TIP: To book any of the restaurants in *Disney Village* call 01 60 45 60 45 or make a reservation through the concierge at your hotel.

© Disney

Inside King Ludwig's Castle

The menu is designed to appeal to international tastes, with starters (€4.50–15) such as Weisswurst (sausages with mustard), traditional Leberkase (a Bavarian meatloaf, with potato salad) and Goulash soup, and main courses (€14–25) such as Wiener Schnitzel, Beer-Braised Pork with mashed potato and split peas, and Royal Sauerkraut (smoked pork loin, bacon, sausage and potato on a dome of sauerkraut), while desserts (€5.50–8) include Black Forest Gateau, various strudels and the delicious Kaiserschmarrn (pieces of thick pancake mixed with a fruit marmalade and custard sauce). There are also more straightforward salads and pastas, plus a simple kids' menu (€12), but the feature dishes are all quite delicious.

This can all be washed down with a good choice of beer and schnapps and they even have their own version of the Oktoberfest beer festival on Friday and Saturday evenings and Sunday lunchtimes (mid-September to 5 October), with a set menu at €26 (including a 1-litre beer) and Bavarian bands. A magnificent design inside and out, the Castle has a more fantasy-

8

King Ludwig's Castle: Continuing along the main Disney Village thoroughfare brings you next to this hugely elaborate establishment, which opened in June 2003. Inspired by Neuschwanstein Castle in Bavaria (built by 'mad' King Ludwig II), King Ludwig's has been designed primarily for German visitors but will, we think, appeal widely to anyone who enjoys good beer, Bavarian food and castles in general. With 297 seats (a substantial increase on the Rock 'n' Roll America bar/diner which it replaced) on two floors, the interior of the restaurant is redolent with castle theming, including wooden panelling, flags and ornate carvings.

King Ludwig's Castle

© Disney

orientated and whimsical touch rather than the usual more formal approach. The set lunch menu is €18–23, and their gift shop sells branded merchandise – glass, porcelain and the inevitable swords – under the mark of Prince Luipold of Bavaria (a direct descendant of King Ludwig II and the owner of the Kaltenberg brewery).

Sports Bar: A regular haunt for many Brits, this is the nearest the village gets to a proper pub and stands diagonally opposite the Castle. With an outdoor terrace, indoor seating and a cinema-style video screen at one end (plus a dozen TV screens sprinkled through the bar), this is the place to come for a British-style beer, a quick snack and, more importantly, the footy on telly at weekends and midweek! They show a great variety of European action and keep all the latest scores and tables on big blackboards behind the bar.

> BRIT TIP: For smokers, the Sports Bar has a tobacco kiosk at the front that is open 10.45am– midnight daily.

Popular with Disney Cast Members, the Sports Bar can be a lively place most evenings, but especially at weekends when the locals come out to play. The draught beers are Kronenbourg 1664, Budweiser, Beamish (stout and ale) and Carlsberg, while there is a good choice of bottled beers, including Foster's, Heineken, Corona, Guinness, Beck's, Stella Artois, Kriska and Hoegaarden.

Open 11.30am–1am (until 2am on Friday and Saturday), hot dogs, baguettes, pizza, nachos, chicken nuggets, chicken wings, chips and crisps are also available (until 11pm).

It is usually packed for the big European football games and does get very smoky, so it is not an ideal atmosphere for children, although they are welcome.

New York Style Sandwiches: Immediately next door to the Sports Bar (and sharing the same outdoor terrace), this rather nondescript deli-style, diner/take-away offers baguettes, hot and cold sandwiches, chicken wings and nuggets, salads, ice cream, fish and chips, hot dogs, crisps and drinks. The set children's menu (choice of cheese sandwich, hot-dog or chicken nuggets and chips, plus a yoghurt and a drink) costs €8, while main menu items run from €4–9. The deli is open from 9am–midnight every day (8am–midnight Saturdays).

Billy Bob's Country & Western Saloon: Just down from King Ludwig's Castle, you come to this wonderful mock cowboy saloon, with a large bar and a stage for live music every evening (with occasional guest performers in addition to the excellent house band, Big Joe and the Space Cowboys). The three-storey Grand Opry-style building (copied from an original in Austin, Texas) is superbly designed inside (anyone who has been in the old Cheyenne Saloon in Orlando will know the idea), with tiered balconies all providing a good view of the stage. You can learn to line dance here or just sit back with a drink and enjoy the Space Cowboys, who are genuine American exponents of the Country & Western genre (even if

> BRIT TIP: If the other restaurants are heaving in the evening, try Billy Bob's Buffet. Not many people actually notice it and it is usually possible to get a table without much of a wait.

it's not your usual cup of tea, their live style is worth checking out).

Bar snacks include chicken wings, spare ribs and nachos, or try out the excellent **Billy Bob's Buffet**, which is at the top of the bar at the back (go up the stairs to your left and keep going!). The buffet is available from 6–10.30pm, and it offers a great value meal (€27 for adults and €12 for kids) featuring salads, roast pork and beef, fajitas, chilli con carne, fresh salmon and vegetables, chicken wings, spare ribs, cheese tray and a huge choice of desserts. Billy Bob's can be booked in advance through your hotel concierge.

Billy Bob's is open from 4pm–1am Sunday to Thursday and 4pm–2am Friday and Saturday, with snacks served from 6–10.30pm. Early evening usually sees a kids' dance session when the saloon is given over to a more youthful, energetic vibe ideal for the 8–14 brigade. To book before you go, call 00 33 1 60 45 70 79 from the UK.

The Steakhouse: Right next door, this offers the real fine-dining opportunity in *Disney Village*, in fact, only the California Grill in the *Disneyland Hotel* and Hunter's Grill in *Disney's Sequoia Lodge* can rival this for quality. It is a spectacular venue, with a Chicago-style warehouse interior in three sections, the main warehouse, the smart bar and the conservatory-like annexe. It is all decorated in 1930s' Americana, with lots of dark woods, rich upholstery, wood panelling and elaborate candelabra lighting effects. The bar area is straight out of the TV programme *Cheers*, but it is also extremely elegant for such a large restaurant and provides a great backdrop for a special occasion meal (although it is also popular with families early in the evening and you will find a lot of children here).

The mouth-watering menu is pretty broad-based, too, although the obvious speciality is steak (fillet, entrecôte, rump steak, sirloin and steak tartare) along with spare ribs, a special mixed sausage kebab, a couple of excellent fish dishes (try the pan-fried bass fillet), duck, a chicken curry and a vegetarian main course. The à la carte prices are not too outrageous (the steaks are €15–28, while the starters are €5.50–18), and there is a set menu for €28 which offers a choice of four starters, main courses and desserts.

For children, the Scrooge McDuck Menu (€13) is also a cut above the usual kiddie fare (although they can still get the ubiquitous chicken nuggets). Reservations are highly recommended at most times and the restaurant is open daily midday–11pm (midday–midnight on Friday and Saturday). This is also the place to come for a superb **Sunday Brunch** with Disney characters, midday–3pm. It's a tad pricey at €32/adult and €12/child, but it does make a memorable meal and is rarely crowded, so the kids have plenty of time with the characters. Call 00 33 1 60 45 70 45 from the UK to book.

Rainforest Café: This unmistakable, international chain restaurant, providing a larger-than-life jungle adventure and whose decor owes a lot to the artistry of the Imagineers, is next up on the grand Village restaurant tour. Here you will find tropical aquaria, waterfalls, streams and a host of (animatronic) animals to accompany your meal, all in a realistic rainforest setting punctuated by thunderstorms and rainfall. You don't just go to eat here you go 'on expedition' and it is as much the decor as the food that creates the experience.

In truth, the food is fairly regular diner fare given a bit of a twist and a few fancy names (Rasta Pasta is penne pasta with chicken, broccoli, peppers and spinach tossed in a

8

cream sauce, while Mojo Bones is BBQ ribs with coleslaw and chips), but the portions are huge and usually work out good value for money. Salads, pasta, burgers and grills (try the Swordfish Grill or Siva's Curry – chicken and shrimp with pineapple in a mild, creamy curry sauce) range from €15–25, while the starters are €5.50–8.50. Cocktails and desserts are both specialities, and the Monsoon Chocolate Cake is worth coming in for on its own (along with the delicious Banana Cheesecake and Bambas Pancake).

Children in particular love the rainforest style and pick up on the many environmental messages, while the kids' menu (€14.50) is one of the best. The Café doesn't accept reservations, so you just have to turn up and wait, but there is a huge gift shop to inspect before you eat and plenty of audio-animatronics to keep the kids happy (the big 'alligator' outside seems to provide an almost endless source of amusement).

The Rainforest Café is open 11.30am–midnight every day, with the gift shop open from 9.30am.

© Disney

Café Mickey

Café Mickey: New in spring 2002 (replacing the Los Angeles Bar & Grill), Café Mickey is another really fun and lively venue which stages character meals throughout the day. Once again, the decor is both bright without being garish and amusing without being obvious. TV screens showing classic Disney cartoons help to keep children happy if the food doesn't (and the food is way above average), but it is more likely to be the excellent character visits that make their day.

Sports Bar

© Disney

Disney Village at night

A big breakfast buffet runs 8–10.30am (with separate seatings at 8 and 9.30am), while lunch is available noon–5pm and dinner 5–11pm (Sunday to Friday) or 5pm–midnight (Saturday). The dinner menu is basically just an extended version of the lunch one.

> BRIT TIP: Tigger, Pluto and Co appear in front of Café Mickey (weather permitting) in early evening to strut their funky cartoon stuff and amuse the younger crowd.

Perhaps here you can most see the European influence at work, providing a wide-ranging choice and a highly thoughtful and appetising selection (from pizza and pasta standards to seafood, vegetarian dishes and even a curry), way above usual diner fare. Try the Fantasia Mushrooms starter, then progress to Captain Hook's Double Mixed Grill or Genie's Agrabah Curry, followed by a wonderfully tempting array of desserts (of which Baloo's Vacherin – mango and coconut ice cream and meringue pie – is quite dreamy!). The 3-course set meal is €34 for adults and the upstairs dining area also has a magnificent view over Lake Disney from the terrace.

Children (under 12) get their own menu (€15) and a special Mickey surprise at the end. The characters circulate fairly constantly to keep everyone happy and the smart decor ensures adult sensibilities are not forgotten either. Booking is highly advisable, though (with the possible exception of lunchtime). In France, you can call 01 60 45 71 14.

8

Wild West antics in Disney Village

BRIT TIP: If *Disney Village* is too crowded for your tastes or you can't get a table for dinner, try going to *Disney's Hotel New York* (see page 74) for their Parkside Diner, where you can usually get a table at any time, or the upmarket Hunter's Grill at *Disney's Sequoia Lodge* (see pages 77–8). Both have great bars, too.

McDonald's: Completing the impressive spread of restaurants throughout the Village is the inevitable McDonald's, albeit quite a smart, almost high-tech version of the ubiquitous American burger chain. Open from 8am–midnight (8am–1am on Friday and Saturday), it is a major draw in the evenings as it is obviously one of the cheaper options, but it also has a high capacity with an outdoor terrace, providing a pleasant place to sit in the right weather. The original architecture is based on Italian theatre and the split-level arrangement also offers a games area for the kids.

Hand-carts: Finally, if you're after a late-night snack, there are various hand-carts throughout the village where you can grab a hot dog, popcorn, crêpes, ice cream or toffee apples, to send you on your way.

Shopping

Okay, if that sums up your eating opportunities in the village, the retail therapy offerings aren't quite so wide ranging, as you will find some of the merchandise recurring in different shops. However, there is still a wonderfully imaginative array of gift stores and it is worth wandering through the likes of The Disney Store and the Rainforest Café shop just to have a look at the splendid decor.

The Disney Store: This is first on your left when you enter *Disney Village* from the Theme Parks end. It's the biggest in the resort, selling the full selection of character and souvenir wares, from books and cuddly toys, to videos, watches and jewellery plus an extensive clothing selection and, nearer the festive season, an array of Christmas decorations, too. Kids will love browsing in here (if they can be prevented from trying to buy everything in sight) and above them are a load of amazing things to watch, a series of large-scale moving models and mobiles – including Mickey Mouse flying a spaceship.

Planet Hollywood: This gift store is almost opposite, for restaurant souvenirs and other movie memorabilia. You can also check out the movie and TV star hand prints on the wall outside.

King Ludwig's Castle: Next door, this fun restaurant also has a specialist shop, with various Bavarian souvenirs as well as a selection of toys and the all-important swords and shields for kids!

Buffalo Trading Co: Continuing down the right of the main thoroughfare brings you to the Buffalo Trading Co, which offers a wide variety of Disney-branded merchandise, all with a Wild West theme (plus some smart Western gear, like overcoats, leather jackets and waistcoats). You may be hard pressed to extricate your offspring without buying them some kind of cowboy paraphernalia. This becomes the Halloween store during September and October, with some suitably spooky special effects and lighting.

Disney Gallery: This is opposite the Buffalo Trading Co, offering a more upmarket selection of gift items for cinema and art fans. Disney collectors will want to make a beeline here to check out the range of limited series of lithographs and original animated film cels. There are some great books (here's where you can get a copy of Didier Ghez's superb book *Disneyland – From Sketch to Reality*) and photographs, and it also has the latest collections of china figurines and snow globes, plus novelties like a Mickey telephone (every home should have one!).

Disney Fashion, Hollywood Pictures and World of Toys: Immediately next door, you enter one of three interconnected shops (handy in the rain) and, while you will probably have seen some of the merchandise already, there is more novel stuff, too. Disney Fashion (formerly the fun Team Mickey) is a rather ordinary clothing store (everything from hats to shoes), Hollywood Pictures offers an array of film-themed clothing, photo albums and gifts (and the inevitable cuddly toys) and World of Toys is almost a reprise of The Disney Store, with yet more kids' playthings (beware the pirate paraphernalia and swords!), Disney costumes and a big sweet counter.

Rainforest Café: Finally, inside the main entrance to this cafe lurks an animal-themed gift shop just waiting to ensnare the unwary with another line-up of soft toys, games, clothing and environmentally aware souvenirs. Their audio-animatronics make it fun for children too, and should keep youngsters amused while the grown-ups browse.

Other shops: Essential services are provided by a **bureau de change** next to The Disney Store, while there is also a big **tourist information office** just outside the *Disney Village* gates in front of the train station. There used to be a **post office** in the Village but that is now just inside the RER station, facing the tourist office. A **first aid station** can be found in the middle of the Village, next to the Sports Bar, through the (unmarked) doors in the back left corner.

Village entertainment

If all that isn't enough to keep you occupied, then Disney has a third array of opportunities to entertain and amuse. Foremost of these is **Buffalo Bill's show**, plus **Hurricanes** nightclub, but there is also live music and other street performer-type entertainment throughout the Village (weather permitting, once again). When you consider the big seasonal events, like Christmas, Chinese New Year, St Patrick's Day and the Festival Latina, which are all either based or have a significant presence here, this can be an exceptionally lively scene at times.

One of the most eye-catching features of the Theme Parks end of the Village, however, is the fully modern 15-screen **Gaumont Cinema** complex, which is largely a French-language operation, and the neighbouring **IMAX Cinema**. However, Monday night is Original Language night (usually at 7.45 and 10.30pm) and there is always one major current-release film shown in English without the drawback of French sub-titles or dubbing.

The IMAX can offer both the signature giant-screen films and 3-D movies, as well as DMR productions – digitally re-mastered versions of normal-screen films (like the Matrix series) which can be shown in clear, sharp pictures on the IMAX screen. The plush interior was designed by French design guru Christian Lacroix and features some of the most comfortable cinema seats

8

anywhere, plus the kind of sound system to make audio fans salivate. Unfortunately, all presentations are in French, although they were due to be fitting headphones for other languages in late 2005. They will need to be particularly good, however, to be able to compete with the cinema's own powerful surround-sound system.

Underneath the IMAX is the new **NEX Fantasy Leisure Zone**, a mix of games arcade, billiards/pool hall and 10-pin bowling alley, complete with the latest video games, ride simulators and high-tech bowling lanes.

Imax and Gaumont cinemas

Buffalo Bill's Wild West Show

Next door to the Gaumont – and arguably the most prominent feature of the village – is **Buffalo Bill's Wild West Show**, a near 2-hour sit-down dinner spectacular that relives

> BRIT TIP: Buffalo Bill's is not advisable for anyone who suffers from asthma or other respiratory complaints as the animals kick up a fair bit of dust in the indoor arena.

the myths and legends of America's cowboy country. The huge indoor arena, some eye-catching stunts and the full Western style ensure this is a hit with all the family (but especially children in the 4–12 age range).

The food is unremarkable, but there is always plenty of it – chilli con carne, chicken, ribs, sausage, corn on the cob and potatoes, plus apple cobbler, ice cream and either tea or coffee – and there is a separate children's platter (roast leg of chicken, sausage, corn on the cob, potatoes and chocolate mousse, plus a soft drink or mineral water), which always seems to go down well. There is also a constant supply of

Buffalo Bill's Wild West Show

either beer or Coca-Cola (with the meal only – you pay for your drinks in the pre-show 'saloon' area) as part of the entrance price. Everyone gets a straw cowboy hat to wear, and you sit in one of four colour-coded sections corresponding to the different cowboys in the show, who go through a series of games and competitions to decide the 'numero uno' for the evening.

> **BRIT TIP:** In summer, watch out for Wild Bill's cavalcade in the *Disney Village* at 6pm as a prelude to the first show of the day.

You need to be in best audience participation and hat-waving mood as you cheer and clap for your cowboy and hiss and boo the others, and it all adds up to good, fun, raucous stuff. Annie Oakley, the 'Queen of the Winchester', puts in an appearance and literally shoots the lights out (there are some magnificent horse-riding tricks and skills, too), and much of the narration is carried out in English as the 60 performers are nearly all American. A Native American element also features and, at one point, the curtain at one end of the auditorium rises to reveal a majestic rocky outcrop, which complements the superb lighting and sound

> **BRIT TIP:** A vegetarian or pork-free menu is available upon request at Buffalo Bill's, and you can also order wine or champagne (at additional cost).

effects. There are wagon trains and cattle drives, cavalry charges and rodeo games, along with a big finale with the inevitable stagecoach – and it is all performed with great gusto and zest by the large cast.

The degree of authenticity is also remarkable, with the Native Americans from a variety of tribes (including Blackfeet, Sioux and Cherokees), the buffalo from Canada and longhorn cattle from Texas, while the horses are all original Pintos and Appaloosas (for the Native Americans) or quarterhorses (for the cowboys). It is staged twice a night – at 6.30 and 9.30pm. Guests can arrive up to 45 minutes early and enjoy the saloon bar atmosphere and live music, and, while it is on the expensive side at €53 for adults and €33 for children (3–11), it provides an excellent mix of entertainment, spectacle and fun.

You can book your tickets in advance by calling (from the UK) 00 33 1 60 45 71 00, but it is usually possible to book when you arrive, either at your hotel or at the ticket office in *Disney Village*.

8

Fireworks over Lake Disney for Bonfire Night

Hurricanes

If the Wild West is not your scene, then the dance club **Hurricanes** may be (especially if you can arrange child-minding or baby-sitting for the evening through your hotel concierge). Here, upstairs and to one side of the Rainforest Café, the late-night crowd can really expend some energy as Hurricanes only gets going at 11pm and keeps bopping until 4am every morning. The weekdays are usually quieter (especially out of season), but Fridays and Saturdays can be extremely lively when the locals flood in. The dance floor is large, the sound system excellent and, if the bar service is a little slow when busy, that is only a minor quibble.

Hurricanes offers free entry for all Disney hotel guests (with hotel ID) and Annual Passport holders, otherwise it costs €12/person. The evening line-up varies from week to week, but there are regular themed nights, like Revival Night, White Evening and 1980s Night.

Of course, you can also check out the live music (and dance) at **Billy Bob's Country & Western Saloon** (see page 178) with two or three sessions a night (highly recommended if Big Joe and The Space Cowboys are playing), or the soccer on the big TV screens in the **Sports Bar** (see page 178).

Central Stage

In the heart of *Disney Village*, the **Central Stage** is another outlet for live entertainment of various kinds, from music to circus acts, hula-hoop contests to quizzes. When the stage is not in use, a live DJ keeps the music going in this area, creating a party atmosphere through much of the early evening. The majority of the big set-piece events take place here (notably at Christmas and during the Festival Latina), while the big video screen adds another fun element. Regular free concerts from up and coming bands (usually around 8.30pm) are also staged here.

> **BRIT TIP:** The Village's main toilets are located between the Sports Bar and The Disney Store. However, their cleanliness often leaves something to be desired, so a dash across the plaza to The Steakhouse is usually a better alternative.

Fun, games – and Panoramagique

Disney Village is sprinkled with various types of fun games (all of which require a few extra euros), such as mechanical bull riding and Ring the Bell (the typical fairground attraction). There are also – strictly for kids – three variations on the remote-control driving games, with boats and trucks. The more energetic might also like to try their hand (and feet) on the bungee trampolines at either end of the Village, plus a new rock-climbing wall, which adds another – extra cost – element to the entertainment line-up.

Then, from the **Marina Del Rey** on Lake Disney, you can hire pedaloes, junior jet-skis (VERY slow moving) and *bateaux electrique* (not much faster!) from 1.30pm every day until early evening (again, weather permitting). They cost from €6–12 for 20 minutes and you need to wear a life jacket at all times but, on a summer evening, it is a great way to while away some Disney time. Or you can stick to dry land and hire **Surrey bikes** (or Rosalies, as they call them here), which make a very gentle and fun pedal around the whole of Lake Disney. Two-seater bikes cost €8 for 20 minutes, 4-seaters are €12.

At peak times and for seasonal events, the Village comes alive with a series of **street performers** such as jugglers, stilt-walkers and diabolo throwers, which all helps to enhance the carnival nature and intent of this long entertainment thoroughfare. It is definitely a lively, and occasionally even raucous, affair (not a big hit with seniors usually), although the atmosphere is decidedly different in the cold and/or wet.

The newest facility here is easily the most dramatic. **Panoramagique** is a magnificent tethered balloon that takes flight over Lake Disney up to eight times an hour, soaring to 100m (328ft) over the Village with a truly superb view in all directions. The flights last around 6 minutes and can carry up to 30 passengers a time. It is the largest balloon of its kind in the world, taking off and landing from its own purpose-built platform on the water, and is styled in best Jules Verne Victorian fashion. It can fly in most weathers (although you wouldn't want to go up when visibility isn't good) but winds of more than 35kph (22mph) will see the balloon grounded for a while. It costs €12 for adults and €6 for children (3–11) and, on a clear day, it is possible to see all the way to Paris and the Eiffel Tower.

However, the real fascination is getting a true perspective on *Disneyland Resort Paris* itself, seeing how all the elements fit together, including the hotels of Val de France, getting a bird's eye view of the parks and looking at all the areas of future development. It is truly amazing just how much you can take in and its smooth take-off, ascent and landing – plus the huge size of the cage-like metal basket – mean you feel totally safe. We would certainly rate it a must-do attraction for the resort. However, it is

> BRIT TIP: Susan – not the happiest of people with heights – found she could ride Panoramagique quite comfortably as long as she looked out to the sides and not down the middle at the balloon's cable system!

probably not the ride for you if you have a fear of heights or suffer from vertigo at all.

If you are staying at a Disney hotel or even if you are at a hotel nearby, you are very conveniently placed for *Disney Village*, and the new multi-storey Vinci Car Park, which brings you out by the new IMAX cinema. Once on site, everything is within a short walking distance and it is so easy just to wander around, sample a variety of different establishments, and then wend your way 'home' again in this safe, well-organised and thoroughly entertaining environment.

Of course, for those without a car or a Disney hotel booking, the usefulness of the **RER station** is paramount. Here, you can enjoy the convenience of a public transport system that runs on schedule 99 times out of 100 and keeps working until a little after midnight each day, ensuring you can get back to the great number of hotels linked to the Line A (and within walking distance of the stations along the way). It may

8

> BRIT TIP: The new Vinci car park, which costs €2/hour, is free to Disney hotel guests. Just take your ticket and show your hotel ID to the office on the ground floor when you are ready to leave.

not be America (for those who think in such terms), but it is still efficient, user-friendly and good value. Miss out on a night in *Disney Village* at your peril!

Disneyland Golf

Golf aficionados will certainly be keen to indulge in their favourite sport at the **Disneyland Golf Course** in the neighbouring village of Magny-le-Hongre, which is barely 10 minutes' drive from the resort itself. Although quite a modern set-up, it has all the characteristics of something a lot more mature and its three nine-hole courses should provide a good test for all standards of golfer, as well as offering what amounts to three different 18-hole rounds. All three courses start and finish right in front of the clubhouse so they can easily be combined.

Open year-round, 7 days a week, the facilities are second to none in the Paris area (there is another good course at nearby Bussy-St-Georges, but the variety and challenge at *Disneyland Golf* are far superior). A driving range and practice green (complete with a well-known Mouse head silhouette!) are situated to either side of the clubhouse, which has an extremely pleasant bar and

© Disney

Enjoying a round of golf

restaurant, and an outdoor terrace where you can enjoy the best of that summer weather.

From the striking circular restaurant building, the view over the green of what is, effectively, the 18th hole, the driving range and the practice green is superb and highly conducive to a satisfying lunch. There is also a well-equipped pro shop that hires electric and manual carts, full sets of clubs and golf shoes, as well as offering the usual range of equipment and clothing to buy. A TV lounge, changing rooms and showers complete the clubhouse set-up, and there is a large car park.

Disneyland Golf

© Disney

© Disney

Davy Crockett's Adventure

Green fees start at €27 for a winter weekday 18-hole round and go up to €56 for a summer round on a weekend or bank holiday. For a nine-hole round, prices are €23–39, with reduced rates for under 18s. Club hire is €5 per club or €24 for a full tailor-made set, while hand-carts are €5 and electric ones €25 for an 18-hole round. A bucket of 30 balls for the driving range costs €3.50, five buckets is €12 and 11 buckets €26. Tuition is available from one of the two fully qualified instructors from €23 for a half-hour lesson to €70 for an accompanied round. For more details about playing there, visit www.disneylandparis.com and click on the Golf section.

Davy Crockett's Adventure

Thrill-seekers with a love for the natural will surely enjoy this unique forest adventure next to *Disney's Davy Crockett Ranch*. The **Davy Crockett Adventure** comprises five trails with more than 80 activities in five levels of difficulty, from green – the easiest, accessible to children at

least 1.10m (3ft 7in) tall – to black, for real daredevils. The activities are linked by platforms and ropes that blend in with the environment.

Each course features suspended stations (Tyrolean traverses, monkey bridges and swings) linked by platforms and cables, and adventurers move from tree to tree using special harnesses, tethers, karabiners and pulleys. The course includes creeper-swinging, suspended bridges, wobbly tree trunks and monkey bridges, as well as a dizzying 200m (656ft) suspended footbridge and their trademark 16m (52ft) Tarzan leap.

Davy Crockett's Adventure covers 5 hectares (12 acres) of the Grains national forest full of 100-year-old oak trees. The entrance is just to the right of *Disney's Davy Crockett Ranch* (see pages 81–4), just after the reception (off Exit 13 of the A4). Access, parking and reception are all located at the Ranch (and you will have to drive here as no transport is laid on). There is a 30-minute initiation on the equipment and safety rules, but then participants are on their own to tackle the course progressively, under the close watch

8

Val d'Europe

of the course supervisors. It should provide around 3 hours of physical challenges in the great outdoors and costs €25 for those over 1.40m (4ft 7in) tall and €15 for those shorter. It is open from midday Monday to Friday (last departure 3pm) and 10.30am at the weekend (last departure at 3.30pm). However, you MUST book in advance, either on 0825 150 280 (in France) or online at www.aventure-aventure.com.

Val d'Europe

It is finally time to leave the immediate environs of *Disneyland Resort Paris* behind and venture a little further afield (although not very far!). If you are staying at *Disney's Newport Bay Club* (or you peer over the back walls of the *Walt Disney Studios Park*), you will be able to see, across the fields in front of the hotel, the huge, sprawling structure (still surrounded by cranes and other building construction) that is the **Val d'Europe** shopping, leisure and business complex. Opened in October 2000, it has an RER station and has given rise to a mini-city development. Covering some 24.5 hectares (60 acres), it is basically a glorified (but highly attractive) mall, with two additional

> **BRIT TIP:** Need petrol? The Shell service station in the Val d'Europe car park is rated the cheapest in the Ile de France, so it is the ideal place to fill up for the journey home. However, you CANNOT use the ground-level petrol pumps (they accept only French credit cards), so you must use the services in the underground car park.

elements in the central part (the Sea Life Centre and a big health and fitness centre called Moving) plus the associated development of La Vallée outlet shopping village (in an outdoor 'street' at one end).

> **BRIT TIP:** If you are finding it too expensive to feed your brood at *Disney Village*, head for Val d'Europe where prices are much lower and you can stock up on snacks, etc, at the Auchan hypermarket.

For anyone who enjoys retail therapy, this should definitely be high on their list of priorities. The two-level mall itself has a huge number of high-quality shops (around 130), many of which are internationally recognisable (Levi's, Naf Naf, Gap, Zara, Benetton, Swatch, Swarovski and H&M) or uniquely French and wonderfully chic. Choose from the likes of L'Occitane en Provence (candles, perfumes and cosmetics, made with plants and flowers from southern France), Yves Rocher (make-up and beauty products with the accent on health), Carnet de Vol (men's fashion and sportswear), Carré Blanc (household items such as towels and carpets, all with that essential French style), Origins (well-being oils, scents and candles), Maisons du Monde (some fabulous interior decor items from around the world), Petit Bateau (the must-have women's T-shirts), Armand Thierry (men's and women's fashions), Le Tanneur (leather handbags, luggage and wallets) and – women take note – Orcanta lingerie. There are seven shoe shops (check out Tanco and San Marina for the latest fashions), nine jewellery outlets, five children's clothing shops (with Sergent Major offering a whole range from 1 month to 14 years) and two sports stores. There is even a high-quality Paris souvenir shop, Articles de Paris, where you can get that essential mini Eiffel Tower!

Services

The clean, airy, uncluttered confines of the mall, some wonderful architecture (inspired by the great Parisian styles of the late 19th century) and the user-friendly way of doing things all add up to a true 21st-century shopping experience, enhanced by an array of tempting cafes and rest areas (around 250 armchairs are dotted throughout the mall). If you avoid the weekend, you will also find it free of crowds and easy to negotiate – no queues here! There are five 'welcome points' (including two in the huge car park) to assist with finding what you need, along with baby-care centres for nursing mothers where hostesses can even provide jars of baby food. Four free play areas are available for children, with a variety of slides and climbs (excellent for 3–8s). Other services include valet parking, shoe repairs, photo printing, hairdressers (two) and opticians (three).

Hypermarket

Also here, and on both levels, is the **Auchan hypermarket**. If you have brought the car, this is where you can fill up with essentials such as wine, beer, spirits and a host of other items. The lower level features all the food (a huge choice in serious quantities!) while the upper (ground floor) level stocks a massive range of domestic goods, clothes, books, CDs, toys and even furniture. The two levels are linked by a sloping moving walkway, which means you can take your trolley around the whole store with ease.

BRIT TIP: If you regularly take the car to Calais to stock up at the many hypermarkets, Val d'Europe offers a much more civilised and user-friendly way to do that much-needed shopping.

The Auchan chain is well known all over France and offers considerable savings on comparable goods in the UK, so it is worth having a good look round. The whole store covers some 21,000sq metres (more than 5 acres!) and is open 8.30am–10pm, independent of the rest of the mall. Look up more on www.auchan.fr.

Les Terrasses

The Val d'Europe RER station is only 5 minutes from Marne-la-Vallée, and the mall is only a couple of minutes' walk from the station (turn right as you exit and it is straight in front of you). Walk right through the mall and you come to the main cafe area, **Les Terrasses**, a monumental conservatory-style annexe, with luxurious vegetation filling the iron-and-glass construction. Here, your choice of dining options is both wide and mouth-watering, from a fine tea-house and crêperie (just called Paul) to a proper Italian pizzeria, a fine seafood restaurant (the boat-themed La Criée), an elegant Chinese (Le Dragon d'Europe, with set menus at €10, €13, €15 and €22, plus a kids' menu at €9), a wonderfully fresh and inviting cafeteria, the eclectic Hippopotamus (beef, lamb – and ostrich!), and the inevitable McDonald's (although even that has a much smarter appearance than usual). You will also find live

8

Sea Life Centre

Sea Life Centre

On the lower level of Les Terrasses (down the escalators) is the Moving health and leisure centre and the excellent **Sea Life Centre**. If you have children aged between 2 and 12, this interactive aquarium (belonging to the UK-based Merlin Entertainments Group, which has six similar Sea Life Centres in Britain and another 23 in Europe and beyond) will keep them amused for a good couple of hours, and provides a welcome diversion from all the hectic theme-parking.

Many hotels offer a free daily shuttle to Val d'Europe, so you can usually come straight here, or you can just get a bus to the Marne-la-Vallée RER station and take the 5-minute train ride. Seasonal special offers for Sea Life – such as 'free child entry with every full-paying adult' – are worth looking out for.

Sea Life Centre walkway

entertainment, with shows for the children and music in the evenings for an older audience.

The shopping part of the mall is open 10am–9pm from Monday to Saturday (closed Sunday) but Les Terrasses is open 9am–10pm every day. Visit www.valdeurope.fr (then click on English version and 'Vos magasins') for more information.

> BRIT TIP: For an excellent cup of tea and the chance to sample some exquisite crêpes, give yourself a break at Paul and just sit and admire the wonderful architecture of Les Terrasses.

La Vallée

Opened in April 2001, this 'aquatic park' offers a marine journey through 50 contrasting displays, exhibits and shows that trace an underwater journey from the source of the Seine river out into the Atlantic and on to the Caribbean. From tiny shrimps to menacing sharks and moray eels, from small tanks to the gigantic main aquarium holding 600,000 litres (132,000 gallons) of water, there is plenty to amuse, entertain and educate young minds.

The journey starts with a theatre experience (in French but with English sub-titles), which offers a strong environmental message about sea life conservation. The 5-minute film introduces you to the aquarium and all it portrays, including the hands-on stuff for the kids. Children can also pick up a scratch card at the entrance, which invites them to visit the 10 question panels throughout the centre and choose the right answer on their card. Get more than eight correct and they win a prize! All the explanations are bilingual and staff can also give talks and answer questions in English.

Each fish tank and aquarium is presented in a different way, and the highlights are the walk-through underwater tunnel (a 360-degree experience, with sharks, rays and other fish swimming all around you), the Lost City of Atlantis exhibit, the Stingray Pool (where children can actually touch one of these fascinating creatures if they are patient and gentle), a film presentation on the Atlantic Ocean (and how deep-sea exploration developed), and the Coral Reef tank.

> **BRIT TIP:** The Sea Life Centre is a good alternative when the weather turns cold and wet. It is also worthwhile when the temperatures go sky high, as it is air-conditioned and blissfully cool on hot days.

The whole interactive theming, with different walkways, passageways and alcoves, invites you to explore every nook and cranny – and learn quite a bit along the way. Talks and demonstrations with the sharks, stingrays and touch-pool are given at regular intervals, while various feeding times add still further to the experience. At the end, there is a handy little seating area, with vending machines, where parents can grab a drink and sit while they unleash their offspring in the play

La Vallée

BRIT TIP: You can come and go as you please once you have bought your Sea Life Centre admission. That means you can go shopping and come back later in the day if there is a particular show or demonstration you want to see. The Sea Life Centre is also fully accessible for the disabled.

area, which has a ball pool, climbing structure, nets and slides – a very thoughtful addition.

They have a new feature every two years and, in 2005 it was 'Octopus – the secret experiment', an amusing presentation by 'Professor Argonaut' into the fascinating world of the octopus. Sea Life is open 10am–5.30pm every day and costs €12 for adults, €9.50 for senior citizens and €9 for children 3–11 (under 3s free; children under 14 must be with an adult). For more details, call 00 33 1 60 42 33 66 (from the UK) or visit their excellent website, www.sealife.fr.

La Vallée

Now, step through the doors of Les Terrasses and you enter **La Vallée**, right outside the Val d'Europe complex, and one which will appeal most to dedicated shoppers, for this is an outlet shopping village – meaning major bargains on big-name brands. All prices are guaranteed to be reduced by at least 33% on High Street stores and you can save much more in many instances.

The 70-plus shops vary from homeware, luggage, shoes and accessories to high fashion, but most are clothing stores, with the accent on designer names and famous labels. Luxury goods feature

strongly, too, but, at prices like these, they are more akin to regular High Street offerings. There is a **Starbucks** coffee shop and a (much better, to our mind) French cafe called **Bert's** when you need a drink or a bite to eat.

BRIT TIP: Unlike Val D'Europe, which closes on Sundays, La Vallée is open 7 days a week.

The village design, with its winding streets, encourages you to stroll the length of the complex, and all the shops are unfailingly inviting, with courteous staff seeming light years away from the usual High Street surliness and disdain. There is a useful **Welcome Centre** to get you started, a well-designed children's play area and clean, well-maintained toilets and baby-changing facilities. Start by visiting the Welcome Centre for the latest news and store promotions, and you can also use their pushchairs and umbrellas, if necessary.

For decoration and homeware you have the choice of Bodum, Villeroy & Boch (a famous glass and china store), Anne de Solène (household linens), Lagostina (top-quality Italian kitchenware) and Lalique (one of the leading French brands), while the Samsonite store, the French Lancel and Lamarthe and the Italian Furla and Mandarina Duck offer a wide range of luggage, handbags and accessories.

For outlet children's wear, you have Donaldson, Tartine et Chocolat and Miniman (all famous French brands) and Bebebo (the Italian version). Teenagers can choose from well-known names such as Miss Sixty/Energie, Murphy & Nye and Cerruti Jeans. If you are hunting for designer shoes, check out Charles Jourdan, Robert

Clergerie, Heschung, Maud Frizon (all French), Fornarina (Italian), Camper (Spanish) or Manfield-Bowen (international).

Women's high fashion is represented by Anne Fontaine, Arayal, Batiste, Blanc Bleu, Façonnable, Kenzo, Gerard Darel, Cachemire Crème, Celine, MaxMara, Versace, Christian Lacroix, Givenchy, Furla, Zadig & Voltaire, Nitya and Ventilo, plus the Lingerie Shop, Calvin Klein and Chantelle for lingerie, while the men can choose from Café Coton, Porsche design, Charles Tyrwhitt, Gianfranco Ferre, Mexx, Feraud Homme, Kenzo and the Spanish casualwear brand Gerry.

International brands positively abound, and you will find tempting outlet stores for all of the following: Longchamp, Diesel, Polo Ralph Lauren, Salvatore Ferragamo, RiverWoods, Barbour, Molton Brown and Tommy Hilfiger, plus other well-known names such as

---

BRIT TIP: Stop at Bert's for a truly delicious lunch. Bert's specialises in a health-conscious range of salads, sandwiches and quiches, plus some delicious pastries, fresh fruit yoghurt and muffins.

Reebok, Puma, Timberland, Dunhill and Burberry. And there is plenty more besides.

For serious shoppers, it is a veritable Aladdin's cave of desirable items, and all with some major mark-downs which make you wonder why we ever bother paying the usual High Street rip-off prices (you can tell we enjoy shopping here!). There is so much packed in, you can't fail to come away with a major bargain or three.

La Vallée is open 362 days a year (closed on Christmas Day, New Year's Day and 1 May) 10am–8pm Monday to Saturday (to 7pm 1 October to 30 April) and 11am–7pm Sunday. A useful daily shuttle bus service operates from the Disney and Val de France hotels. Check with your hotel concierge for details and visit www.lavalleevillage.com.

And that sums up all the various alternative fun and entertainment on offer away from the Theme Parks. A meal in Les Terrasses is highly recommended at any time, while the general opportunity to travel easily thanks to the great convenience of the RER line (and the good road system) comes as a major bonus for those who like to explore a little.

But let's not stop here. There is much more to be seen in the city itself – and beyond – so we'll conclude with a closer look at the main attractions of Paris and the Ile de France…

8

The Attractions of Paris
(or, Getting an Eiffel of the City)

Okay, we will admit to a certain bias here but Paris is a wonderful city and we reckon you'd be crazy to spend several days just 32km (20 miles) away and not consider paying a visit. Even with children to keep amused, there is a huge amount of family-friendly fare on offer, while the Eiffel Tower itself remains one of the greatest sources of child fascination and wonderment in the world.

Given that it is so easy to get into the city centre from Marne-la-Vallée on the RER (and even easier from some of the off-site hotels in the vicinity of Line A), visiting some of the great monuments, parks and museums of Paris is a natural adjunct to all the Theme Park frolics. Public transport around the city is plentiful and reliable, and is far and away the best, cheapest and most hassle-free way to see the sights (driving – and the eternal bugbear of parking – is not recommended, even if you are comfortable with using your own car in France).

> BRIT TIP: Arguably the best ticket in town is the *Paris Visite*, a travel card enabling you to use all the public transport services. The all-day, go-anywhere pass covers the RER, Métro and bus systems, and a 1-day pass costs around £14 (see pages 198–9).

It takes just 35–40 minutes to go from Marne-la-Vallée into the city centre, which means you can have almost a full day in one of the Disney parks and then head off for

Place de la Concorde

A view across the city

an evening in Montmartre, the Latin Quarter or just a stroll along the Champs Elysées. Paris is chock-full of evening entertainment of all kinds, from humble bars to fabulous restaurants and full-blown dinner cabarets like the Moulin Rouge and (a much better prospect, we believe) the **Lido de Paris**. For couples, it is hard to imagine a better city and a more tempting array of possibilities, especially for a meal out.

It is not our intention here to give a detailed description of all Paris has to offer but we can't let the opportunity pass without providing a brief look at what makes the city so special, highlighting the real must-see and must-do opportunities – and also point out those the whole family will enjoy.

The city is fairly easy to get to grips with and you should be able to get a decent perspective in just a day or two (and the organised bus tours are a great way to start here – see page 199), even if the heavy traffic sometimes makes it seem like one of the most chaotic places on earth.

Introducing the city

Paris is laid out like an architect's dream in 20 districts or *arrondissements* all running out in a spiral from the first at the centre (and all locations in the city are referenced according to their *arrondissement*, hence the Louvre is in the first, the Arc de Triomphe in the eighth, etc).

The architectural core of the city dates back to Baron Haussman in the 19th century, whose urban development programme from 1852–70 essentially created the

9

The Louvre

outline plan we see today, with its grand boulevards, wide streets and geometrically elegant squares. It is city design on an epic scale (although constrained within relatively modest confines – the whole of Paris covers just 106sq km/ 41sq miles – less than *Walt Disney World Resort in Florida*), punctuated at key points by great monuments such as the Arc de Triomphe (Napoleon's 'Triumphal Arch' commissioned in 1806 and finally finished long after his death in 1836), the Place de la Concorde (dating back to 1755), the monumental Ecole Militaire (the army school and museum of the 18th century) and the Louvre (arguably the greatest art gallery in the world and home to the *Venus de Milo* and the *Mona Lisa*), the oldest part dating back to the 12th century.

> BRIT TIP: You can pick up a *Paris Visite* card at the Eurostar ticket offices in Waterloo and Ashford.

Paris is also effectively split in two by the River Seine, the **Left Bank**, or southern half and the **Right Bank** or northern sector of the city. The most famous landmark though, is 'only' 117 years old and the brainchild of Gustave Eiffel. Built for the International Exposition of 1889, La Tour Eiffel offers three stages up its 324m (1,063ft) height, with a view from the topmost of up to 80km (50 miles). More modern developments have seen the construction of the *périphérique* ring road (1973), the modernist Pompidou Centre (1977) and the Louvre Pyramid (1989).

Getting around

Thanks to the comprehensive public transport, a truly integrated system

involving the trains (RER, or Réseau Express Régional), underground (the Métro) and buses, getting to the sights is a doddle. Sign-posting is usually clear, the modern buses each have a route map and a board indicating each stop and reliability is outstanding.

The Métro system will get you to every tourist site in the city with only the minimum of walking and it runs until around 1am every day, while the last RER service back from central Paris to Marne-la-Vallée is around midnight (check www.ratp.fr for public transport details – in English as well as French).

The **Paris Visite** card is almost an essential adjunct to sight-seeing, and can be purchased at any Métro ticket office, RER and SNCF railway station, bus terminal counter, both main airports and all of the Paris tourist offices.

The card provides unlimited travel on the whole Paris public transport system, including the SNCF (suburban) trains and the Montmartre funicular. The system is divided into eight regional zones, and *Disneyland Resort Paris* is situated in zone 5. An adult 1-day *Paris Visite* card is €21 for zones 1–5, a 2-day card would be €33 and a 3-day card €45 (€10, €16 and €22 for 4–11s; under 4s free).

> BRIT TIP: The *Paris Visite* card offers 10% off a set menu at one of the four à la carte restaurants in the *Disneyland Park*, so, if you're definitely heading out to the city for some sight-seeing, it pays to buy the card before you go to the Theme Park.

The card also comes with an array of discount deals and special offers with a host of tourism partners in the city, including the Cité des Sciences (the excellent Museum of Science), Canauxrama river cruises, France Miniature and Le Paradis Latin cabaret show.

Do it all with Disney

With all these possibilities virtually on the doorstep, it stands to reason Disney would see a way to give guests even more value and purpose to staying on-site. So they have teamed up with **Cityrama bus tours**, offering a daily sight-seeing excursion into and around the city on one of their big, modern double-decker coaches.

They run daily at 9.45am from *Disney's Hotel New York* and have proved immensely popular, so it is advisable to book early – with your tour operator in advance or at the hotel concierge desk when you check in. The tour returns about 6pm, so you still have some park time left at the end of the day. The Cityrama buses are very comfortable and well equipped, with air-conditioning, toilets, drinks service and an audio commentary on multi-lingual headphones.

The basic route takes you into the heart of the city to start with, and provides a well-narrated overview of the geography, architecture, art, history and culture. The history is graphically illustrated with sites like **La Bastille** (one of the city's oldest districts, now transformed into a more upmarket and happening area, with nightclubs, restaurants, piano bars and cafes) and **Le Marais** district, a mini city in its own right, full of original little streets, markets and several substantial mansions, now occupied by some chic art galleries, cafes, health food shops and piano bars.

> BRIT TIP: The key word to look for in shop window displays is 'Soldes'. This means 'Sales' for all keen bargain hunters!

At the heart of Paris is the **Ile de la Cité**, the original settlement site, which dates back to the third century BC. The tour continues through the **Quartier Latin** (Latin Quarter), the famous Left Bank district that has been the centre of the city's university life for more than 700 years, and offers a cheaper selection of cafes and shops for more student-like budgets. You then pass the magnificent **Palais du Luxembourg**, with its 20-hectare (50-acre) gardens, and travel along **Rue Bonaparte**, Paris' version of Bond Street for exclusive shopping.

The Louvre

Across the **Pont Neuf**, one of the 12 main bridges which link the two halves of the city, you drive past the **Louvre**, the massive repository of just about every example of artwork known to mankind. Its principal claims to fame are the exhibits of the *Venus de Milo*, *Mona Lisa* and Van Gogh's *Sunflowers*, but you can easily spend a day or more investigating the wealth of art on display. It is divided into seven departments – Oriental Antiquities (including Islamic Art); Egyptian Antiquities; Greek, Etruscan and Roman Antiquities; and, for the modern period, Paintings, Sculptures, Art items, Prints and Drawings. Open 9am–6pm daily (with late opening on Wednesdays to 9.45pm), entry is €8.50 (or €6 from 6pm–9:45pm). For more details visit www.louvre.fr.

Continuing your coach tour, you head back along the Left Bank and through the St Germain area,

9

The Louvre Museum

passing the **Musée d'Orsay**, another of the great repositories of French artwork. A conversion of the Orsay Railway Station inaugurated in 1900, it houses an art gallery of the finest

> BRIT TIP: Many Paris museums are free on the first Sunday of the month (although queues will be longer then). The museums owned by the Ville de Paris (except the Catacombs) are free every Sunday from 10am–1pm, visit www.paris info.com/museum_monum ents/ for details.

Pont Alexandre III

order, from 1848–1914. Open from 10am–6pm Tuesday to Saturday, 9am–6pm Sunday (with late opening until 9.45pm on Thursdays; open 21 June to 18 September from 9am), entry is €7.50 (€5.50 on Sundays; €5.50 for 18–25s; under 18s free; free to all on first Sunday of each month). It is closed on Mondays. Visit www.musee-orsay.fr.

Champs Elysées

A drive around the vast octagonal expanse of the **Place de la Concorde** then reveals some more of Baron Haussmann's outstanding design, especially as you continue along the **Champs Elysées** and into the **Place Charles de Gaulle** (aka Etoile), at the centre of which stands Napoleon's magnificent **Arc de Triomphe**.

> BRIT TIP: If you are going into central Paris on public transport the main Métro stops to look out for are Concorde, Charles de Gaulle–Etoile, Trocadéro, Palais Royal–Musée du Louvre and Cité.

© Leonardo.com

Arc de Triomphe

Along Avenue Kleber you can marvel at some more monumental architecture, especially as you enter **Place du Trocadéro et du 11 Novembre**, where a statue of the First World War military leader Marshall Foch stands in front of a grand vista representing three centuries of architecture. The view here across the Seine to the Eiffel Tower is breathtaking and on a par with the great landmarks of the world such as the Sydney Opera House, the Acropolis and the Statue of Liberty.

The **Hôtel des Invalides** is another significant 17th-century landmark and its Musée de l'Armée showcases some 2,000 years of military history, from Antiquity to the end of the Second World War, in an opulent setting. The Dôme within contains the tomb of Napoleon Bonaparte and is open from 10am–5pm from October to March, and 10am–6pm April to September, €7.50 for adults,18s and under free.

River trips

After all this coach-bound sight-seeing, it is time to step on to a different mode of transport (all part of the Cityrama tour) and view the city from the River Seine on the **Bateaux Parisiens**.

Here, either under a glass roof or out on deck soaking up the sun, the English commentary (on a hand-held audio device) continues to cover just about every angle of the city, ensuring you get a well-rounded experience and an in-depth view of the history and accomplishments of Paris and its people (or just a fabulous view if you choose to put your feet up and watch the vistas as you sail by).

9

Notre Dame

Les Bateaux Mouches

Paris is famous for its river tours along the Seine, providing both a great view of many well-known monuments as well as a relaxing and highly enjoyable form of transport. The collective name for the half a dozen or so companies which run these tourist boats is Les Bateaux Mouches, and they ply their trade along the central section from the Eiffel Tower to the Ile de la Cité and back, with plenty of history during the day and a generous helping of romance in the evening, when you can choose just an alternative view of Paris by night or a more elaborate dinner cruise.

In low season (October to March) they run every hour from 10am–10pm (some half-hour departures; no departure at 1.30pm) and every hour 10am–11pm in high season (April to September; no departure at 1.30pm). They cost around €9.50 for adults and €4.50 for under 12s (under 3s free). A dinner cruise (8–11pm) costs from €92–135, but needs to be booked in advance. There is also a special Children's Cruise (in French only) for an hour every Saturday, Sunday and bank holidays, and during French school holidays every day at 1.45 and 3.45pm. It costs €9.50 per person, or €8 per person for a large family. Call 00 33 1 44 11 33 44 (from the UK) or visit www.bateauxparisiens.com.

Notre Dame

Your boat drops you off back in the Ile de la Cité for lunch – and an opportunity to visit the stunning cathedral of **Notre Dame** (open 7.45am–6.45pm daily). This masterpiece of Gothic architecture

> BRIT TIP: There are two handy, quiet restaurants on the Quai de Montebello, on the south bank of the river flanking Notre Dame. Stroll to the rear of the cathedral, turn right across the bridge and the crowds quickly disappear.

was built between 1163 and 1345, and is free to enter to sample the awe-inspiring serenity of its vast interior. There are some serious queues here at most times of the day (you'll be used to that at Disney!), but they move steadily. There is a small fee to visit the belfry and you may have to wait 30 minutes or so for your turn. You have a good 90-minute break here, so it is up to you to divide your time between the cathedral and lunch.

Up the Eiffel Tower

You get back on the boat at the Ile de la Cité pier and continue your hour's cruise, finally returning to the marina at the Port de la Bourdonnais in front of the **Eiffel Tower**. Your city tour then finishes off in style with an organised visit to the tower itself. Your tour guide will lead you up the steps and across the Quai Branly to one of the lifts and a trip to the first floor (the second and third floors are extra, but you usually

> BRIT TIP: At peak times in summer (midday to around 5pm), the Eiffel Tower often stops selling tickets for the top deck, and the second floor becomes very crowded too.

have plenty of time if you wish to go the extra distance yourself). This 324m (1,063ft), 10,100-tonne steel edifice is a breathtaking sight close up, and the trip up by lift or stairs is a rewarding one, both for the view and the story of the tower told along the way.

The perspective on the city is quite startling (especially from the glass-sided lifts between the first and second floors!) and totally unequalled. There is even a high-quality restaurant on the second floor – the Jules Verne – which you can book separately; but if the price tag here (in excess of €100) puts you off, try the first floor Altitude 95, with its decor reminiscent of a 1930s' airship (book from the UK on 00 33 1 45 55 20 04 for Altitude 95 and 00 33 1 45 55 61 44 for Jules Verne).

The Eiffel Tower has three lifts (at the north, east and west legs) and three staircases (south, east and west) and ticket office queues reach up to an hour in high summer. However, if you are travelling independently, arrive early and you will enjoy this amazing attraction at its very best, while the evening sees it in truly sparkling mode, with a magical lighting presentation. From dusk until 2am (1am in winter), the Tower's 20,000 special light bulbs (requiring 40km of electrical cord and 120kw of power) come to life in a glittering display each hour on the hour for 10 minutes. Once you have been up this modern marvel, you can

BRIT TIP: The Eiffel Tower draws some sizeable crowds during the day attracting the inevitable vendors (selling bottled water and trinkets) who are a constant nuisance. Take extra care with your belongings.

then walk the gardens of Le Champ de Mars for the full ground-level perspective.

At the north leg you can check out the memorial to Gustave Eiffel, while ticket-holders have access to the clever lift machinery which he designed under the east and west pillars. A Bureau de Change can be found in the concourse under the Tower, plus a Paris Tourist Office (not to be confused with the ticket office) and souvenir shops (as well as those on the Tower itself), plus a cafeteria-style snack bar.

For those coming independently, the nearest RER station is Champ de Mars–Tour Eiffel (on Line C; from Marne-la-Vallée, change at Châtelet Les Halles, go one stop south on Line B, then it's four stops west on C), while you can also use the Métro at Ecole Militaire or Trocadéro. The Eiffel Tower is open every day, 9.30am–11pm for the lift and 9.30am–6.30pm for the stairs (1 January to 10 June, and 29 August to 31 December); and 9am–midnight (11June to 28 August). To take the lift to the first floor costs €4.10 for adults and €2.30 for under 12s (under 3s free); to the second floor is €7.50 and €4.10; and to the top is €10.70 and €5.90; the stairs (up to the second floor) are a single rate of €3.80 (25 and older, €3 under 25s). For more info, visit www.tour-eiffel.fr.

All in all, the Cityrama day tour provides a pretty comprehensive beginner's guide to the great city of Paris and the perfect way to get a thumbnail appreciation of all the main sites in the space of a few hours. For Disney resort guests, it costs €63 for adults and €33 for children 3–11 (lunch not included).

Paris By Night

If that is the story by day, Cityrama's **Illuminations** tour (from 1 October to 3 April), also organised by Disney,

9

is basically the city by night. Paris fully deserves its alternative title of 'The City of Light', and the tour portrays this to the full. The English commentary, via individual earphones, is especially adapted to the ambiance of Paris by night, bringing its history to life with a series of amusing stories, accompanied by background music and French songs that celebrate the city. The Cityrama coach departs every Tuesday, Thursday, Friday and Saturday at 9pm from the front of *Disney's Hotel New York*, and returns to each Disney Hotel at around midnight (depending on traffic). It costs €44 for adults and €13 for children (the tours are sometimes not available on a few dates in June, July and October).

And there's more

Of course, the bus tours are only a snapshot (albeit a fairly wide angle one) of the city and there is plenty more in store for the keen sight-seer. A great number of attractions are geared for families, which are worth highlighting here.

The Eiffel Tower

Montmartre: One of the must-sees of Paris, this district was a separate village up until the 19th century and became the intellectuals' and artists' quarter. Its two main focal points are the **Place du Tertre** (peaceful and serene during the day, humming with activity in the evening) and the breathtaking church of the **Sacre Coeur** (Métro Anvers), set on a hill with fabulous views of the city.

Bateau Mouche

Pompidou Centre

Entry to the church is free, but to visit the Dome and the Crypt costs €5. You can also enjoy the highly child-friendly funicular ride up to the Sacre Coeur (included in the *Paris Visite* card, see page 198).

Pompidou Centre: (Métro Hôtel de Ville) This will appeal to all lovers of modern art as it has one of the world's finest collections of modern and contemporary art, from 1905 to the present, featuring Miró, Giacometti, Dubuffet, Picasso, Matisse, Léger, Chagall, Warhol and much more. The ultra-modern design of the building is not to everyone's taste, but it is a fitting showcase for its contents. Open every day (except Tuesday) from 11am–10pm, it costs €10 for adults and is free for under 18s (www.centrepompidou.fr).

Parc de la Villette: Perhaps right at the forefront of the great new family opportunities is the futuristic complex of this science park. Set in the 19th arrondissement in the north-east corner of the city (just inside the *périphérique*, Métro Porte de la Villette), it provides a comprehensive, 52-hectare (128-acre) panorama of science and technology in an extremely entertaining, hands-on fashion. It includes the science museum itself (**Cité des Sciences et de l'Industrie**), with a wealth of exhibitions, shows, models, lectures and interactive games, in addition to the Planetarium, the Mediterranean aquarium, Louis Lumière cinema (films in 3-D), and multimedia library.

In the park, there is also the Argonaute – a real submarine – La Géode, a giant sci-fi IMAX cinema with a 1,000sq m (10,764sq ft) hemispherical screen and Cinaxe, a

Montmartre

BRIT TIP: At the Parc de la Villette children (3–12) will enjoy a junior version of the science village at La Cité des Enfants which has an adventure playground, Electricity (5–12s) and Techno Cité (11 and up) and lots of hands-on experiments.

large-scale simulator ride. Open from 10am–6pm Tuesday to Saturday (10am–7pm on Sunday), it costs €7.50 for a Cité Pass (€5.50 under 25s, under 7s free), €5 for the Cité des Enfants, €8.75 adult and €6.75 under 25s for La Géode, €3 for the Planetarium, €3 for the Argonaute and €5.50 for Cinaxe. The Aquarium is free. For more info, call 00 33 1 40 05 80 00 from the UK, or visit www.cite-sciences.fr.

Bois de Boulogne: Out in west Paris (Métro Porte Maillot) this 846-hectare (2,090-acre) park is ideal family territory, providing a multitude of walks and pleasant spots. Special attractions for children include the 24-lane **Bowling de Paris** and the **Musée en Herbe** in the **Jardin d'Acclimatation**, a dedicated children's museum set in an imaginative play garden with a

BRIT TIP: In the Bois de Boulogne, bikes can be hired opposite the main entrance of the Jardin d'Acclimatation daily mid-October to mid-April and Wednesdays, weekends and public holidays mid-October to mid-April. There are 35km (22 miles) of cycle routes to explore.

carousel, train ride, hall of mirrors, go-karts and mini-menagerie (€2.70 for entry to the gardens with extra tickets for rides and attractions – a book of 15 tickets costs €30; 25 tickets cost €45). It is open from 10am–7pm daily, 10am–6pm October to May. In fine weather, people flock to the banks of the two lakes, where you can go rowing or just watch the model yachts at play.

Shakespeare plays are put on in the Jardin Shakespeare at the **Théâtre de Verdure**, by the Pré Catalan park in the centre of the Bois de Boulogne woods.

Parc Zoologique de Paris: (Métro Porte Dorée) For animal lovers (and most kids!), this excellent zoo is another ideal place for children to visit, extending over 15 hectares (37 acres) in the middle of the Bois de Vincennes in the south-east corner of the city. It houses some 1,200 species – from lions, elephants and giraffes to the little microcebe from Madagascar – in a series of naturalistic settings (no tiny cages here). Open 9am–6pm in summer, 9am–5pm in winter, €8 for adults and €5 for children (4–16).

Aquaboulevard: Paris can even offer the more up-to-date children's fun of an indoor water park out on the southerly outskirts (by the Balard Métro station). The wonderful tropical theming is divided into three sections – The West Indies (especially for young 'uns), Réunion Island and Polynesia – with a whole series of giant slides, wave machines, water cannons and waterfalls set around a large central lagoon.

Year-round warm weather is guaranteed and there is even an outdoor beach when the summer is in full swing. Open 9am–11pm (Monday to Thursday), 9am–midnight (Friday), 8am–midnight (Saturday) and 8am–11pm (Sunday), €20 for adults and €10 for under 12s.

Parisian gardens: When it comes to the more small-scale delights, take a stroll in the thoroughly British **Champs Elysées gardens** (Métro Champs Elysées-Clémenceau), where you might discover a puppet show (hourly on Wednesday afternoons and weekends), or the **Jardin des Tuileries**, adjacent to the Louvre (Métro Concorde), with its child-friendly pony rides, trampolines and fun fair in July and August. Both are open year-round (except for public holidays) free of charge.

Versailles: The final must-see Paris attraction is a trip to the magnificent château at Versailles (actually a 30-minute ride on the RER line C to the south-west of the city centre). Another of the world's most famous heritage monuments, it was commissioned by The Sun King, Louis XIV, in 1668.

> BRIT TIP: The immediate environs of the Château de Versailles are also worth exploring, with a series of narrow streets and quaint shops – plus several mouthwatering crêperies!

The buildings trace the architectural styles of the 17th and 18th centuries and include the Royal Apartments, the Hall of Mirrors, the Chapel, the Royal Opera and the Museum of the History of France. The park, designed by André Le Nôtre, is tastefully adorned with statues, flower beds, ponds and fountains, with several further buildings, the Grand and Petit Trianon, the Temple de l'Amour and the tiny hamlet of Queen Marie-Antoinette.

The Château is open 9am–6.30pm (May to September) and 9.30am–5.30pm (October to April). Admission is arranged into different categories: state apartments €7.50 (under 18s free); audiotour of King's Chamber €4.50 (under 10s free); guided visits with audiophones €5 (1 hour), €7 (90 minutes) and €9 (2 hours) for adults, (€4, €5.50 and €7 for 10–18s); Le Grand and Petit Trianon €6.60 (under 18s free); park and gardens €3; coach museum €2 (under 18s free). Happily, there is also now a full 1-day pass which covers the entire domain of Versailles, including the audiotours. In high season (end of March to end of October) it costs €20 for adults and €6 for 10–17s; in low season (November to March) €15.50 and €4. For more info, call 00 33 1 30 83 78 00 or visit www.chateauversailles.fr.

A recent addition to the line-up here is the Palace's **Academy of Equestrian Arts**, a specialised teaching college open to the public year-round (it was recommissioned in 2003) that puts on daily performances of horsemanship. The three different shows are the 1-hour dressage of *Les Matinales des Ecuyers* (€8 for adults, €3 for 5–18s; at 10 and 11am Thursday to Sunday), which also includes a guided tour of the stables; the 75-minute *La Reprise Musicale*, which illustrates the work of the apprentice riders with musical accompaniment, and a visit to the stables (€16 for adults, €8 for 5–18s; weekends at 2.30pm); and *La Reprise Musicale Nocturne*, an amazing 75-minute night-time show (€20 for adults, €10 for 5–18s; on special dates). For more info, call 00 33 1 39 02 62 72 or visit www.acadequestre.fr.

Lido de Paris

Having geared the majority of the chapter towards family activities and sight-seeing, here's one that is definitely for adults only and is highly recommended as one of the most entertaining – and surprising – shows in the city. The Lido de Paris is one of several internationally renowned cabarets but is, in our

Château de Versailles

view, easily the most sophisticated and eye-catching.

It is also extremely popular with both couples and singles right across the age spectrum (although the majority tend to be couples in the 45–55 age group). It is a touch risqué, with topless dancers at various points, but it is all extremely tasteful and highly glamorous. You can opt for the dinner-dance and the full 90-minute show or just the dazzling show itself.

For dinner, there is a choice of three separate menus, all of which have been designed by top French chef Philippe Lacroix and which include a half bottle of champagne.

Moulin Rouge

Within the three options (Soirée Plaisir, Soirée Bonheur and Soirée Champs-Elysées respectively €140, €170 and €200), there is a choice of three starters, main courses and dessert, and even the Soirée Plaisir menu is barely less than spectacular, meaning the Champs-Elysées lives up to the very highest standards of cuisine (the starters include duck foie gras or lobster salad with pearl barley and pistachio oil, while the main courses offer filet mignon, rack of lamb, fillet of beef or sea bass). The meal takes a leisurely 2 hours to serve and clear away, and there is dancing to a large orchestra throughout.

One of the two alternating large-scale shows – *C'est Magique!* and *Bonheur* – then follows for the next hour-and-a-half, with a remarkable

BRIT TIP: The Lido dinner show is totally fabulous but beware the drinks' prices – a half bottle of champagne will set you back around €45.

Tuileries Gardens

mix of spectacularly choreographed dancing, live music, ice-skating, acrobatics and magic, all cleverly interwoven into themed sections. The staging is quite breathtaking at times, with some truly stunning special effects, and the high quality and originality of the acrobats and magician lend an air of grand pageantry to the whole extravaganza (and if the acrobats don't leave you

with your jaw on the floor, you need to check your pulse!). The majestic finale, when the whole stage seems to unfold before your eyes, provides a fitting conclusion to what can only be described as superb entertainment.

Admittedly, it is not a cheap option (the show on its own is €100),

BRIT TIP: Getting to the Lido from *Disneyland Resort Paris* couldn't be easier. You simply take the RER from Marne-la-Vallée to Charles de Gaulle–Étoile Station (about 45 minutes), then change to the Métro for one stop to George V, and the Lido is right outside the station. If you go for the first show, you exit just after 11.30pm and there is an RER service back to Marne-la-Vallée from Charles de Gaulle–Étoile at 12.02am.

Lido de Paris

9

but we feel it is terrific value for money and you are unlikely to be disappointed. There are two shows a night, the first at 9.30pm preceded by the 2-hour dinner-dance, and the second (a show only) at 11.30pm. For more information, call 00 33 1 40 76 56 10 (from the UK), or visit www.lido.fr. There is also a handful of Sunday lunch show matinees at 1pm, plus a special children's show several times a month, with an array of aerial ballet, giant fountains, ice-skating and song and dance to positively mesmerise youngsters.

Paris information

Of course, there are dozens of museums, churches, monuments, gardens, memorials and parks, not to mention the shops, restaurants and nightclubs and other modern city paraphernalia that make Paris such a deliciously heady brew. For all the essential information, contact:

Maison de la France: 178 Piccadilly, London W1J 9AL; France Information Line: 09068 244123 (60p per minute), email: info.uk@franceguide.com or visit www.franceguide.com.

Ile de France Tourist Office: Tel 00 33 1 44 50 19 98 (from the UK), or www.pidf.com.

Paris Tourist Office: Tel 08 92 68 31 12 (in France), or log on to www.parisinfo.com.

BRIT TIP: The *Carte Musées-Monuments* costs just €17.99 and gives no queuing, no-limit access to 70 museums and monuments in Paris. It is on sale at Métro stations, the tourist office and FNAC shops.

Further afield

If you would prefer to escape from the hubbub for a while, the **Seine-et-Marne** region can offer some more down-to-earth but equally enchanting sources of fascination. With a car, there are some wonderful possibilities a little more than an hour's drive from the resort, and where you can get a feel for rural France untouched by the hectic rush and modernity of the city.

BRIT TIP: The Seine-et-Marne region has an excellent tourist office in Fontainebleau – tel 00 33 1 60 39 60 39 (from the UK), www.tourisme77.fr. They also have a tourist office next to the Marne-la-Vallée RER station open 9am–8.45pm every day.

Barely half an hour away from the Disney resort is the magnificent 17th century masterpiece of **Vaux-le-Vicomte**, a historic château and gardens some 24km (15 miles) to the south down the D471. In the rich land of Brie, this pinnacle of period architecture – created by some of France's greatest artists, including Le Vau, Le Brun and André Le Nôtre – was the inspiration for the Château de Versailles. Here you will

BRIT TIP: If you can visit Vaux-le-Vicomte on a Saturday from May to October or Fridays in July and August, you can enjoy the amazing Festival of Light, when some 2,000 candles are lit through the château and gardens.

discover the full splendour of Vaux-le-Vicomte, from the kitchens to the magnificently decorated reception rooms (which have featured in many films).

Your visit should include a full tour of the château (complete with audio-guide), the extensive French gardens, designed by Le Nôtre, who was also responsible for the Jardins des Tuileries in Paris, plus the Carriage Museum and the Le Nôtre exhibition in the cellars. Every second and last Saturday from April to October, you can see the eye-catching Fountain Show from 3–6pm. The château is open every day from mid-March to mid-November, 10am–6pm (closed weekdays from 1–2pm), and costs €12 for adults and €9.50 for children (6–16), or €15 and €13 for the Candlelight evenings (8pm–midnight). For more details, call 00 33 1 64 14 41 90 from the UK or visit www.vaux-le-vicomte.com.

> BRIT TIP: A perfect complement to any visit to Vaux-le-Vicomte is dinner at the L'Ecureuil gourmet restaurant, open 11.30am–6pm (11pm on Candlelight evenings).

The nearby city of **Melun** is also worth exploring. The ancient capital of the Capétiens Kings offers some interesting walks, an artistic museum and the listed building of St Aspais Church – plus its speciality, the Brie de Melun, often regarded as the ancestor of all Brie cheeses. Just outside, August 2006 marks a significant event with the re-opening (after a year's restoration) of the fortified **Château de Blandy-les-Tours**, a superb example of 16th century military architecture and a little-known gem of the Ile de France.

Bohemian **Barbizon**, 'The Painters Village', is about 70km away (44 miles) to the south (down the N104, A5B, N105 to Melun, N372 and the N37). Here, against a backdrop that an array of famous landscape painters have made utterly timeless, you can discover the Auberge Ganne, a museum-home of the 19th century and a tribute to an era of artists who influenced the world's landscape and colourist painters (closed Tuesdays – 00 33 1 60 66 22 27).

Take a slight detour to the south-east and you come to **Fontainebleau**, and its 16th-century château, home to the kings of France from the Middle Ages (closed Tuesdays). Another major architectural and artistic gem in the panoply of French monuments, its extensive gardens and the Napoleonic Museum of Military Art and History offer a fascinating glimpse into another world (http://www.musee-chateau-fontainebleau.fr).

Travel still further (about another 10km/6 miles) south-east again and you come to **Moret-sur-Loing**, a medieval city curled up between the banks of the Seine and Loing rivers. Wander the town and see why it was the inspiration for some of the Impressionist painters such as Monet, Renoir and especially Sisley.

Further south still you come to Souppes-sur-Loing and the stunning **Château Landon**, perched on a rocky outcrop overlooking the verdant valleys of the Fusain. The medieval city boasts a host of memorable monuments, including the Notre Dame church, the St Severin abbey, the St Thugal tower and St Andrew priory, plus the beautiful Parc de la Tabarderie.

Closer to home

Nearer to Marne-la-Vallée (just off the A4 at Ferrières-en-Brie), you have the **Château de Ferrières**, a

Night time at Disney Village

sumptuous pastiche of Renaissance architecture, embellished with one of the most extraordinary English parks in France. The town of **Champs-sur-Marne** just to the west (on N34) boasts another stately home emblematic of the bourgeoisie in the Chateau de Champs-sur-Marne, the residence of Madame de Pompadour in 1757, with stately gardens, flower beds and ornamental lakes.

Then travel east for 20km (12 miles) on the N34 to **Coulommiers**, another medieval town whose commander's residence was built by the Knights Templar in fortress style in the 12th century. Make sure you visit the St-Anne Chapel and the round dovecote, plus the stunning Capucins Park. You can also enjoy some picturesque river trips from Coulommiers on the Grand Morin.

A short drive to the north-east is another destination full of Middle Ages character, that of the Episcopal city of **Meaux**. The impressive St-Etienne Cathedral is well worth a visit, along with the Episcopal Palace (which now houses the Bossuet Museum) and the Jardin Bossuet. On particular weekends from June to September, you can also enjoy the stunning *Meaux Grand Spectacle*

Historique, an epic event featuring 500 actors, dancers and equestrians, re-enacting the saga of the city.

In between Meaux and Coulommiers you will find the **Abbaye de Jouarre**, the region's most outstanding sacred site, with 12th-century crypts displaying some astonishing sarcophagi from the early Merovingian era. Food lovers will be interested in the Musée Briard, which traces the history of Brie's cheese-making traditions.

BRIT TIP: Don't leave Meaux until you have tried the local culinary speciality – Brie and mustard.

Provins

The jewel in the region's crown is the World Heritage Site and medieval city of **Provins**, some 60km (37 miles) down the D231 to the south-east. Pass the 12th-century ramparts and you are truly transported back to the Middle Ages, with narrow streets, half-timbered houses, monuments (and dungeons!). Here you can try various medieval crafts, such as calligraphy and stained glass, design coats of arms and watch the free-flying birds of prey.

Provins provides the perfect setting for various amazing period events (www.provins.net) organised every summer and, if you happen to be in the area during the last week of August, definitely stop by to experience some of the week-long **Carnival**, which is one of the highlights of the Seine-et-Marne region. There are also three large-scale medieval shows, including a spectacular jousting competition.

Auvers-sur-Oise

Art lovers may well be lured away to the north-west of Paris to spend a half-day or so in the utterly charming village of **Auvers-sur-Oise**, the burial place of Vincent Van Gogh. Although the great artist lived here for only 3 months before his untimely death, the stay produced some of his most startling work, and its inspiring influence is still present today (not surprisingly, as Cezanne, Pissarro, Daubigny and others also painted here). The village also hosts a grand International Musical Festival every year (late May to June), which attracts some high-quality performers.

Start by visiting the Office de Tourisme on Rue de la Sansonne to see the 15-minute audio-visual presentation on the village and Van Gogh, then wander out and drink in the wonderful scenery, the quaint farms (and the cafes!) that inspired so many great painters.

To reach Auvers-sur-Oise, take the A15 out of Paris to Exit 7 (Mery-sur-Oise), then pick up the N184 alongside the River Oise into the village (www.auvers-sur-oise.com).

Now it's up to you!

And that, folks, is that. You now have all the essential wherewithal to not only plan and prepare for your holiday in *Disneyland Resort Paris*, but also to get the most out of it when you are there. As you can see from the last two chapters, there is a lot more to a holiday here than just theme park frolics (although, if you choose to do just that, you will still have a pretty good time!).

It is a world of almost infinite charm and substance, a combination of Imagineering pixie dust and ages-old culture and allure. The Walt Disney Company wasn't that crazy when it brought its major slice of Americana to Europe and, while it was not an instantly comfortable fit, the Franco-European influences now sit comfortably and enjoyably alongside the transatlantic ones.

© Disney

Sleeping Beauty Castle by night

Most of all, however, we hope you have taken on board how much sheer artistry is involved in providing such obvious entertainment, whether it be on the rides, the shows, the restaurants or the hotels. The resort is the product of 50 years of imagination, perspiration and inspiration, with some pretty amazing architecture and engineering thrown in along the way (not to mention the vast backdrop of Paris and her environs).

After countless visits to Disney theme parks (we lost count many years ago!), we still find them absorbing, fascinating and downright fun. There is so much involved, we would hate for anyone to pay their hard-earned money and then miss out on some of the essential 'magic'.

So, we challenge you to keep this book with you at all times, read and inwardly digest the contents before you go, and then get out there and have FUN!

Bonnes vacances…

10 Your Holiday Planner

Here is a way to help you decide what you can do given 3 or 4 days in *Disneyland Resort Paris*. This planner is simply designed to give you an idea (from our own practical experience) of what a typical family might be able to achieve in the time allotted. Obviously, you are free to make up your own schedule (on the blank form at the end), but be aware of the different requirements of the Theme Parks and associated attractions. The two examples are designed around a visit in high season (the summer), and are for different modes of transport and different durations (reflecting two of the most popular packages being booked in 2005). Have fun with your planning!

Example 1: 2-night/3-day trip with Eurostar

Day and time	Schedule	Notes
Day One		
9.39am	Depart London Waterloo	
1.29pm	Arrive Marne-la-Vallée	Check bags in with *Disney Express* at station
	Have lunch in *Disney Village*	Nice and quiet in Planet Hollywood!
2.45pm	Head to Disneyland Park	Closing time 11pm
	Visit Fantasyland	
4pm	Wonderful World of Disney Parade	
5.15pm	The Tarzan Encounter	
7.15pm	Winnie the Pooh and Friends, Too	
7.45pm	Stop for dinner	Great pizza in Pizzeria Bella Notte!
9pm	Leave the park and walk back to *Disney's Hotel New York* to check in	Our bags are already here!
Day Two		
9am	Head for buffet breakfast in Parkside Diner	Bit of a late start! Book Billy Bob's Buffet for dinner tonight
10am	Off to *Walt Disney Studios Park* and start with the Studios Tram Tour	
11am	Moteurs…Action! Stunt Show	
11.45am	Get in the queue for Armageddon	
12.15pm	Cinémagique showing	Watch some of Lilo & Stitch show from queuing area
1pm	Lunch at Backlot Express	

Afternoon	Do all the attractions of Animation Courtyard	Did Animagique twice!
4.35pm	Catch the parade	
	Stop for refreshment in En Coulisse Restaurant	Listen to the West Street Story Orchestra
5pm	Watch the Stunt Show (again)	It's loud but the boys love it!
7.15pm	Have dinner at Billy Bob's	
8.15pm	Then it's on to the *Disneyland Park*	
8.45pm	See Honey I Shrunk The Audience show	
9.15pm	Star Tours and Autopia, also in Discoveryland	
10.15pm	Find a spot for the Fantillusion parade	Head back to Town Square for the best view!
10.45pm	Time to take two tired but happy boys back to the hotel	Catch the bus at the station – no crowds, as the fireworks haven't finished yet
Day Three		
9.30am	Another slow start – not up until 9.30am! Just time for breakfast	Check bags in at hotel with *Disney Express* system. We'll see them later! Book late lunch at Blue Lagoon
10.30am	Off back to the *Disneyland Park*	Get FastPass for Peter Pan
Morning	Frontierland	Do Big Thunder Mountain Railroad (with FastPass) and Phantom Manor
2.15pm	Time for lunch in our favourite restaurant	Blue Lagoon
4pm	Chance for kids to play after lunch on Adventure Isle, as many people are watching the 4pm parade	
Afternoon	Do Pirates of the Caribbean and last main rides	
5.30pm	Stop to play in Fort Comstock in Frontierland on our way out	
6pm	Head back to the station	
6.43pm	Return on Eurostar to London	
8.27pm	Arrive at Waterloo	Boys both asleep – tricky final journey home!

10

Example 2:
4-night/5-day coach trip with Leger Holidays

Day and time	Schedule	Notes
Day One		
Noon	Pick-up from home bus station at midday	
1.30pm	Arrive Dover	
2.15pm	P&O ferry to Calais	Stock up with drinks and snacks on the ferry for the 4-hour coach journey to *Disneyland Resort Paris*
4.30pm	Arrive Calais; brief stop at hypermarket	Don't forget the 1-hour time change!
Evening	Long, rather dull drive through northern France	
9.30pm	Arrive at *Disney's Hotel Santa Fe*	Check in and go straight to room
Day Two		
8am	Up for hotel breakfast	Book character lunch at Lucky Nugget Saloon at hotel front desk
9am	Off to the *Disneyland Park* for the day	Get FastPass for Peter Pan
Morning	*Disneyland Park*	
1pm	Stop for lunch at Lucky Nugget Saloon	Have fun with Chip 'n' Dale, Goofy and Pluto!
Afternoon	*Disneyland Park*	
4pm	Catch the afternoon parade	
5.15pm	Winnie the Pooh show	
6.30pm	Leave park and head for *Disney Village*	
7pm	Dinner at Planet Hollywood – only 10-minute wait for table	
8.30pm	Slow wander back to hotel via *Disney Village*	
Day Three		
9am	Slow start this morning!	Book character breakfast for tomorrow at Plaza Gardens Restaurant in the *Disneyland Park*
10am	Head for *Walt Disney Studios Park*	
11am	Catch the Animagique show	Stop to watch Lilo & Stitch Catch The Wave Party

Noon	Do the TV Studios tour then head next door to Cinémagique	Just missed midday Cinémagique – go on to Art of Animation instead
1.30pm	Stop for lunch at Restaurant En Coulisse	Live music from the West Street Story Orchestra while we eat!
2pm	Stop at concierge desk in Disney Studio 1 to book dinner at Silver Spur Steakhouse in *Disneyland Park*	
2.10pm	Queue for 20 minutes to get in to 2.30pm Moteurs...Action! Stunt Show	
3.30pm	Catch the Cinémagique	
4pm	Stop for a drink at Studio Catering Co outside after show	
4.45pm	Time for the Disney Cinema Parade	
5–6pm	Enjoy the last hour at park with no queues for Magic Carpets ride and Rock 'n' Roller Coaster	
6pm	Head next door and have dinner at Silver Spur Steakhouse	
7.30pm	Head back to Fantasyland for boys' favourite rides	
10pm	Bag a prime spot to watch evening Fantillusion parade on Main Street USA	Dad goes off to get drinks! Long queues at most of the counter-service cafes still
	Straight back to the hotel on the bus after parade	
Day Four		
8am	Manage to get everyone up and out to make breakfast booking in *Disneyland Park*	
8.45am	Stop at City Hall to book evening meal at Blue Lagoon	
9am	Off to Fantasyland!	In the first hour, we do Peter Pan, Snow White, Pinocchio (twice!) and the Carousel before the crowds arrive
11am	Leave park for RER Station	
11.15am	Catch train to Val d'Europe – 5-minute journey	
11.30am	Visit Sea Life Centre	Spend 2 hours looking round all the exhibits, and boys finish up in the soft-play area!
1.30pm	Have great lunch at pizza restaurant	
2.30pm	On to La Vallée outlet shopping village	Boys get to play in playground while Dad enjoys a coffee!

10

4pm	Quick tour of Auchan hypermarket before catching train back to Disney	
5pm	Catch Animagique show at *Walt Disney Studios Park*	
5.30pm	Quick refreshment stop at Studio Catering Co	
5.45pm	One last Flying Carpets ride before closing	
6pm	Time to leave for *Disneyland Park*	
8pm	Dinner at Blue Lagoon	Boys learn to shout '*bon appetit*' back to Pirates riders!
8.30pm	Just time for another trip to Fantasyland!	
9.30pm	Back to *Disney's Hotel Santa Fe* on shuttle bus	Pack cases for coach tomorrow
Day Five		
8am	Up early and straight off to breakfast	
10am	Coach departs for Calais hypermarket; then on to ferry	
3pm	Ferry leaves Calais	2pm UK time
4.30pm	Arrive back at home bus station	Mission accomplished!

Blank form:
Your holiday – have fun now!

Day and time	Schedule	Notes

Further Reading

Disneyland Paris – From Sketch to Reality, by Alain Littaye and Didier Ghez (Nouveau Millenaire Editions; €45; or $95 on www.amazon.com). A truly sumptuous book, in full colour and with a wealth of brilliant photography, it charts the building of the *Disneyland Park*, *Disney Village* and the hotels. It also provides a magnificent insight into the creativity of the Imagineers.

Walt Disney Imagineering – by The Imagineers (Hyperion, £21.99). Another lavish 200-page volume providing a riveting look at how Disney's creative force thinks and works, with a fascinating series of original concept illustrations from their attractions worldwide.

Disney – The First 100 Years (David Smith and Steven Clark; Hyperion £27.50). For true fans of all things Disney, this 203-page epic charts the story of Walt and all his creations, from his humble beginnings to the 100th year after his birth, looking at the annual landmarks of the man and his company.

Acknowledgements

The author wishes to acknowledge the help of the following in the production of this book:

The Walt Disney Company, Maison de la France (French Government Tourist Office, London), Eurostar, Leger Holidays, Eurotunnel, P&O Ferries, Hoverspeed, SpeedFerries, Thomas Cook Signature, Port of Dover, Air France, Ségécé (Val d'Europe), Cresta Holidays, Thomson Holidays, Lido de Paris, Aéroports de Paris, Cityrama, Paris Travel Service, Newmarket Group, Inter Continental Hotels, La Vallée Outlet Shopping Village, Planet Hollywood, Sea Life Paris, Seaview.

In person: Nicole Walsh, Claire Fine, Sarah Brody, Louise French, Nikki Palmas (Walt Disney London), Ian Benjafield (Walt Disney Paris), Natalie Goulet, Eugenio Raez (Maison de la France), Sandrine Parriaux (Tourisme Seine-et-Marne), Marco Mori (Leger Holidays), Gareth Headon, Sarah Kettering (Eurostar), Barbara Cottage, Kevin Charles (Eurotunnel), Jaynie Ness (BCT Travel Group), Rob Radmore (Thomson), Julian Stockdale (Thomas Cook Signature), Jeremy Griffin (Newmarket), Sebastien Farris (Aeroports de Paris), Sarah Chambers (Air France), Andy Brannan (Planet Hollywood), Emma Doggart (InterContinental), Carole Humphries (Hoverspeed), Nick Stevens (Norfolk Line), Natalie Hardy (P&O Ferries), Marianne Illum (SpeedFerries), Chantal Villeneuve (Sea Life), Sebastien L'Hôte (La Vallée), Fethi Abdennadher (Holiday Inn at Disneyland Resort Paris), Pierre-Marie Vasseur (Explorers Hotel), Susanne Meinhard (Mövenpick Dream Castle).
Special thanks also go to David Simpson (Seaview).

Special plaudits go to several others who have provided help, advice and fact-checking above and beyond the call of duty, including Robert Rees and Ian Benjafield; Pete Werner and the crew at the DIS (www.wdwinfo.com); and Caroline Radula-Scott for all her input and creativity. Readers' tips from: Tony Watt, John Magee, J Alyas, Karyn Don, Christopher Ashcroft, Jonathan Lewis-Jones, Jon Stele & family, Virginia Simpson and Grenville Riley, via email. On the DIS: Bonnie, Bonitatime, Renate, Ware Bears and dlpSteve.

Index